D0936547

DAPPER *Dan*
IS...

"A legend." *Ava DuVernay*

"Black fashion's greatest treasure." *BET*

"The ultimate success saga." *André Leon Talley*

"The godfather of hip-hop fashion." The Source

"America at its best." *Michaela angela Davis*

"The epitome of style and grace." *La La Anthony*

"A creative icon." *Bethann Hardison*

"The original influencer." *Ashley Graham*

DAPPER DAN

MADE IN HARLEM

A Memoir

DANIEL R. DAY

With Mikael Awake

RANDOM HOUSE NEW YORK

Copyright © 2019 by Dapper Dan of Harlem LLC

All rights reserved.

Published in the United States by Random House, an imprint and
division of Penguin Random House LLC, New York.

RANDOM HOUSE and the HOUSE colophon are registered
trademarks of Penguin Random House LLC.

The photo of the newsletter *40 Acres and a Mule* reprinted in the photo insert
is courtesy of the New York Urban League (NYUL). All other images,
unless otherwise credited, are courtesy of the author.

LIBRARY OF CONGRESS CATALOGING-IN-PUBLICATION DATA
Names: Day, Daniel R., author. | Awake, Mikael, author.
Title: Dapper Dan: made in Harlem: a memoir /
by Daniel R. Day with Mikael Awake.
Description: First edition. | New York: Random House, [2019]
Identifiers: LCCN 2018036839 | ISBN 9780525510512 (Hardback) |
ISBN 9780525510529 (ebook)
Subjects: LCSH: Day, Daniel R. | African American
fashion designers—Biography. | Harlem (New York, N.Y.)—Biography.
Classification: LCC F128.68.H3 D39 2019 | DDC 746.9/2092 [B]—dc23
LC record available at https://lccn.loc.gov/2018036839

Printed in the United States of America on acid-free paper

randomhousebooks.com

2 4 6 8 9 7 5 3 1

FIRST EDITION

Endpaper, title-page, and part-title pattern by Dana Leigh Blanchette
Book design by Dana Leigh Blanchette

To Lily and Robert Day

CONTENTS

PART II

MIDDLE PASSAGES

PART III

THE SHOP THAT NEVER CLOSED

PART IV

UNDERGROUND RUNWAY

PROLOGUE

Harlem, 1989

It was a midnight like any other at the store. The lights were on out front, the door unlocked, the grate rolled halfway up. Dapper Dan's Boutique was open. My night crew of tailors was in the back filling orders. Jackets, jumpsuits, parkas. Their sewing machines hummed into the wee hours. I was lying on my bed in the little apartment I'd built in back for myself. Most nights, you could find me there, re-reading a book of philosophy or spirituality or trying to sneak in a nap.

I had good reasons for never closing the shop and rarely leaving it. For one, a lot of my customers preferred late-night visits, for anonymity during the week or for the after-hours vibe of the weekends. I also had to keep an eye on my employees, who were backdooring my designs. It was my name on the awning out front, and in my world, your name means everything. It was my reputation, my brand, and people came from all over the city and beyond—from Philly and Chicago, Houston and Miami—because they wanted a Dapper Dan. I was the store, and the store was me.

We were open all day every damn day for nine straight years.

And yet I couldn't really complain. After three decades hustling in the streets, it was my first legitimate hustle, and business was good. Real good.

That night, I heard someone walk into the store and got myself out of bed. I closed the book, washed my face to wake up, and glanced in the mirror to make sure I looked decent. I wasn't young anymore. I had a wife. I had grown kids and babies. With a deep breath, I put on my shop persona and emerged into the light.

Standing in the store was a Puerto Rican drug dealer from the Bronx who had been in before. People called him Serge. I greeted him with a warm handshake and shoulder clap, and we made small talk. How's your night going? Where you coming from? You watch the fight yesterday? He was in a good mood, and his good mood put me in a good mood.

Before I ever made anything for a rapper or basketball player, I catered mostly to gangsters and drug dealers, guys with real money in the community, guys like Serge. When I started out, I didn't know the first thing about selling clothes, let alone making them myself. Starting a custom-clothing shop was by far the riskiest gamble of my life, and that's coming from someone who used to shoot dice with gangsters. The stock market had crashed. New York City was broke. But it had worked out somehow. My business was thriving because of the underworld. Sure, hip-hop had taken the popularity of my clothes to the next level, but early on, if it hadn't been for hustlers like Serge, I would have been out on my ass. They made the boutique what it was.

I saw the glimmer of his jewelry, I saw his clothes, I saw he was fly. I would soon see the big stack of money he was about to whip out of his pocket.

What I failed to see was the truck parked across the street with its lights off. Waiting.

"Listen," said Serge. "Got some beef uptown. I heard you got some new shit. What's good?"

Hanging on a rack behind the register were a number of custom pieces waiting to be picked up. I showed them to Serge to whet his appetite. "This is a new Fendi lambskin jacket I made for Big Daddy Kane," I said, casually dropping names as I flipped through the rack. Finally I came to the full-length parka I knew he was waiting to see. "This is the snorkel you heard about."

I rapped my knuckle against the leather and it sounded back solid. Serge ran his hand along the printed Louis Vuitton logo on the front. "This shit really bulletproof?" he asked, his eyes widening.

"Go test it on the roof right now," I said. "You got your gun?"

He shook his head in awe. I could tell he was getting excited.

"Can you make mines Gucci?" he said, placing his hand on his midsection. "With two big-ass Gs on the front."

I hadn't even thought about that. Now I was getting excited. "Yeah, yeah, I like that," I said as he pulled out his stack of cash, peeling off three thousand dollars' worth of large bills like they were Kleenex.

"I can even make you a matching hat, protect your head."

"With the Gs, too?"

"All in red and green?"

"Yeah, that's it!"

The secret to what I do is to capture what you think you look good in. But I also had a slogan: "Everything in your mind don't look good on your behind." I would build on how a customer like Serge felt about himself and how he wanted to look, and we'd work from there. When I get them right in that zone where we're both excited and hollering and giving each other five, that's when I know I've got something good. *Yeah, that's right. Yeah, man. That's it!* I love that moment. I live for that moment.

Serge slapped me five and peeled off a couple more Franklins. "For the hat."

I could tell that, underneath his hard exterior, he was buzzing with excitement as I casually went through more of my inventory, showing him what else I had. It was the late 1980s, and everybody who was anybody had an order in at my store. On the rack was a sweater waiting for a Grammy-winning singer, a jacket for a Knicks point guard, an embossed suit for a rap supergroup.

As Big Sek, my head tailor, began to take Serge's measurements, Serge launched into stories about parties and women, funerals and court cases, and I began to drift off. I was often somewhere else in those days. I saw reflections of myself in hustlers like Serge, diamonds and gold sparkling from ropes around his neck. I had been just like him, and I owed my success to risk-taking young men cut from a similar cloth. It was a terrible time to be a young person born into poverty, and I understood the desperation that could drive a guy like Serge to the lure of fast money. After heroin and cruel law enforcement turned neighborhoods like Harlem and the South Bronx into ghettos, crack and AIDS arrived to turn our lives into waking nightmares. Serge had come of age in that madness. My job was to make him feel welcome and important for the brief moment that he was in my store, collaborating on his custom clothes, and to make him look and feel good when he left.

While he lingered inside, chatting up the salesgirls, I couldn't help but feel thankful for Serge and for hustlers like him who were my first and would remain, years after I finally closed the store-front, my most loyal customers.

Until I opened my boutique, I'd spent my whole life hustling on the streets of Harlem. I'd done everything from being a shoeshine boy to a drug dealer to the guy with unbeatable dice who gambled drug dealers out of their money. When I decided to launch Dapper Dan's Boutique at the age of thirty-seven, it meant that I was finally leaving the streets and saying goodbye to the painful, unglamorous, often cursed life of a street hustler. Selling clothes was a much better way to make a living, but I was still connected to the underworld through my clients. I'd left the streets, but the streets hadn't left me. The tension between my inner life and my outer reality was overwhelming at times. I was older and thinking more about my purpose on this planet, about the sublime, about what it meant to live a good life. A few blocks away, my wife, June, would wake up later that morning to go to her job in the billing department of a hospital, completely in the dark about how I ran my store, who my clients were, or what they talked about when they were with me. The store was off-limits to her and my sisters, but I thought of my family often, and when I did, it only made me feel more alone. The time and effort it took to run Dapper Dan's Boutique was taking a heavy psychological toll.

Saying goodbye to Serge, I went back into my makeshift apartment and shut the door behind me to read. But only for a moment, because the next thing I knew, my tailor flung open the door.

"Monsieur Dap," said Big Sek. "Come out please."

There was a fear in my trusted tailor's eyes that I'd never seen before. And when I came out onto the floor, I saw the reason why. On the other side of the big plate-glass windows out front, a group of masked men had surrounded Serge on the sidewalk with their guns drawn. My salesgirls had run into the back of the store for cover.

"Call nine-one-one," I heard someone say.

I did nothing. I knew calling the police was out of the question. We had to just let whatever was gonna happen happen. Maybe it was a misunderstanding that would fizzle out in a minute. Maybe Serge had it coming, and there was nothing we could do about it now. Either way, I wasn't going to put us all in danger.

Whatever the gunmen were trying to tell Serge, he wasn't hearing it. He was shaking his head and barking back in defiance. Serge squared off against them with his fists balled, and in a flash, the men were on him, bashing him over the head with the butts of their guns, pistol-whipping him bloody. "Oh my God!" one of the girls cried out.

A soft voice inside me whispered, *You gotta do something*.

But right behind that was another, more familiar voice, a voice I trusted because it had kept me alive my whole life. It said, *Mind your business*.

We watched the masked men strip Serge of his jewelry, his expensive gold chains. That shoulda been the end of it. But it wasn't. A truck pulled up to the curb out of nowhere, and the men started forcing Serge into it. Suddenly, it became clear to us that this wasn't just a robbery. This was a kidnapping.

Big Sek stepped forward. I knew he carried a pistol on him, and now he had it drawn at his side. "We need to stop them," he said, tightening his grip on the gun and coming out from behind the counter.

I grabbed him by the arm. "Listen," I said, feeling sick. "This ain't got nothing to do with us."

Outside the store, Serge was still resisting as the kidnappers tried to push him into their waiting truck. Inside of me, there was another war going on. I knew the drug game was cursed, but I also felt responsible for this young man's life. Like me, my brothers, and so many others, he was just trying to pull himself out of poverty the best way he knew how. But my window of opportunity quickly slammed shut. The kidnappers finally managed to wrestle him into the truck, then disappeared into the night.

The image of that truck driving away still haunts me. My decision to do nothing still haunts me. I should have done something. I could have done something. I felt responsible because, even though I minded my business like anyone from the streets would, I *knew* better. I didn't do what I should have done—spiritually. I knew there was a higher code than the code of the streets. In the days that followed, the shoulda-couldas weighed on me, and I was filled with a growing sense of dread that must have been a premonition, because a week later, I'd be staring down the barrel of a gun held by someone trying to kidnap me.

PART I

—

DANNY BOY

Anyone who has ever struggled with poverty knows
how extremely expensive it is to be poor.

JAMES BALDWIN

CHAPTER 1

———

Nobody's Poor

I'm old enough to remember another Harlem. Before the heroin game overtook the numbers game, before crack overtook heroin, before a US president moved his offices uptown, and before white people started pushing strollers across 110th Street, I knew a Harlem where you didn't have to lock your front door.

I'm talking about a Harlem that was still in the midst of its Renaissance, a Harlem swinging to jazz and bebop, a Harlem beating with the warmth and life of gospel music by day and teeming—*teeming!*—with people and excitement and glamour by night. I'm talking about a Harlem where older women from the South with uncanny multitasking abilities sat outside on stoops or in windows high above the street sewing clothes, peeling vegetables, and spreading gossip, all while keeping watch over the neighborhood children, missing nothing. "Danny, go get your sister Dolores outta that street," Miss Marguerite, a neighborhood woman who knew us all by name, would snap from her window lookout.

A Harlem crowded with lounges, restaurants, music venues, ballrooms, and movie theaters. A Harlem where my friends and I would hold taxi doors for women in mink stoles and crouch at the feet of men in suits and bowlers, shining their patent-leather shoes to a sparkle. Lexington Avenue had cobblestones, and every now and then you'd see a horse and wagon clopping up the street. A Harlem of life, lights, and all kinds of humanity. Black restaurants, Irish bars, Italian social clubs, Latin dance halls. That Harlem, the Harlem of the 1950s, was the first Harlem I knew, the Harlem I inherited, the Harlem I was born into. My mother, Lily Mae Day, didn't trust doctors or hospitals, so she gave birth to me at home with my grandmother Ella getting off her sickbed to play midwife. I never met Grandma Ella cause she died only two days after I was born, so all I can do is imagine her holding me and wrapping me in a blanket: "It's a boy, Lily Mae."

"Another one?" I can hear my mother's exhausted reply. "Lawd."

It was the summer of 1944, and I was my mother's fourth boy in a row. It couldn't have been easy. When I came out the womb, everyone marveled at the size of my head: "Wow, his head as big as Moon's." Moon was my older brother James, two years old at the time, nicknamed on account of the planetary size of his head. Mine was just as big, so they nicknamed me Little Moon and started calling James Big Moon.

The official name they gave me was Daniel, but when my parents went downtown to file my birth certificate, some clerk screwed it up and put me down as "Danial." It wasn't just me, either. My mother gave birth to three more children, all girls, and we each had inaccurate information on our birth certificates. Wrong gender. Wrong surname. Misspelled mother's maiden name. They were minor human errors in the grand scheme, but they symbolized a larger feeling of neglect. It was understood, literally from birth, that the system didn't really care about keeping our information correctly, that it didn't really care about us.

Cause we were poor as hell. Poorest of Harlem's poor. Dirt poor. We lived in East Harlem in a five-story tenement building on Lexington Avenue and 129th Street. My parents had come to the city as part of the Great Migration, and they struggled and fought to survive in an overwhelming new urban reality. My father, Robert Day, worked three jobs, while my mother managed us seven kids, a thankless full-time job. My parents and their generation were new to city life. They had come from tight-knit rural communities in the South where everyone knew each other, and in the early days of black Harlem, they did their best to re-create those communities.

All the doors to the apartments in our building stayed open all day long. Aunt Mary, my mother's first cousin, lived above us and could holler out her apartment to ask my mother to borrow sugar, and my mother could holler back a reply. We never needed house keys. The front door of our building was always kept propped open by a heavy rock, and our mutt and two cats just came and went as they pleased, in and out, just like us. Each block was its own microcosm of small-town Southern life. Each neighborhood was associated with a particular region, so that you had the people who came from South Carolina living in one area, the ones from Virginia in another. I didn't meet a black person whose family was from North Carolina until I visited Brooklyn, where a lot of them had settled. That's how specific these neighborhoods were.

And not only that, if you were from a particular town in the South, say Spartanburg, South Carolina, you often came to the city specifically to live on the Spartanburg block. Every bar and church and restaurant on that block would be full of folks from your little hometown. Folks knew each other from back home. And that generated respect and a sense of safety. People bonded over their shared histories, slang, and culture. But in the years to come, as these small neighborhood communities in Harlem were bulldozed and replaced by high-rise project buildings, the city started grabbing people with no concern for where they'd come from, disconnecting folks from each other and their way of life. Neighbors didn't know each other, didn't share anything, didn't feel a sense of respect or safety among each other. Doors started getting padlocked. You ask me, I think a lot of the bigger problems in Harlem today can be traced back to the destruction of those houses and that more connected way of life.

Our building was in a neighborhood almost exclusively made up of folks who had come from South Carolina and Virginia, with maybe a sprinkling of folks from Georgia. We knew everyone in our building. It was a private tenement, real intimate, and my father worked as the superintendent. Nine of us Days lived crammed together in a small three-bedroom apartment, sharing a single bathroom. There was a restaurant run by a Greek guy named Jimmy on the ground floor where my father also worked maintenance and where we'd often get free leftover soup for dinner.

Every single morning, we'd wake up to gospel music coming from the radio, which was my mother's doing. She was deeply religious and started the day with the sounds of Joe Bostic's *Gospel Train,* the oldest and most famous gospel radio show in the country. Bostic, a pioneer in his own right, mainstreamed gospel music and introduced gospel legend Mahalia Jackson to the world in 1951. Of course, us kids didn't think too highly of him. I can appreciate gospel music now, but back then we couldn't stand it, especially the show's repeated tagline, "The train is a-coming!"

In the kitchen, we'd pull a box of Corn Flakes out the cupboard and a bottle of milk out the icebox. Everybody had iceboxes back then, no fridges yet. You'd have to actually buy ice to fill the thing and keep the food cold. We bought our ice from Del Monte, an Italian who used to ride around the neighborhood in a blue truck, calling out from the street: "Ice for the icebox! Twenty-five cents apiece!" For a quarter, he'd put a big block of ice in his bucket, lift it onto his shoulder, and carry it upstairs for you. We'd pull out the cold milk, then we'd smack the cereal box on its side two times—*whack, whack*—to make sure we got the roaches out before we started pouring it into our bowls. Then we'd eat our cereal.

For our first years of school, my mother sent me and my older brothers, Carl, Cary, and James, to a Catholic school two blocks from our house, All Saints, on Madison Avenue between 129th and 130th Streets, which is still there. They had a little sunken play yard where they'd let us out during the day. The mothers used to come and throw pennies and nickels down, and the kids would take the change and line up to buy candy. Every morning, I'd always ask my mother, "Mom, could you please come and throw me a nickel during recess?"

But she never came.

When I got older, I was grateful to my mother for sending us to a good private school in the first place; I realized that she was far too busy at home with my younger sisters, Dolores, Deborah, and Doris, to come back to school to throw me a nickel. She woulda had to load up three kids in the middle of the day just so I could get a piece of candy. But at the time, it just made me so sad. Looking back, an experience like that probably made me a good hustler. On a subconscious level, I understood that if I wanted anything, I'd have to get it myself, cause ain't nobody coming.

I was always hungry. Three times a week, Mom dragged us to church, but the real reason my siblings and I went was because they'd feed you there, or at least give you hot chocolate. All major religions have holy days that are marked by an abstinence from food. It's a gesture of putting spiritual concerns above the earthly. I think about that a lot in relation to my memories of being hungry as a child. Nothing makes you question the purpose and meaning of life like hunger. Hunger is physical, it's real. It's so universal that all of us have experienced a taste of it, but if a person has never experienced it through the daily uncertainty of poverty, it's hard to understand the way it shapes the rest of your life, especially when you realize that not everyone grew up feeling that way about food.

All my friends were just as hungry as I was. Each morning on the way to class, I would draw straws with my friends Curtis and Bill to see who'd have to steal what from the grocery store. One would steal meat, another would steal bread, while the third would provide the distraction. And at school, we would look forward to class trips, not because we were excited for a zoo or a museum, but because of the free lunch we got. They would give you a brown paper bag, curled down at the top, and inside you'd have a nice sandwich, usually peanut butter and jelly. You'd have an apple, maybe a banana, in there, too. Central Park, the Met, the botanical garden: that wasn't the highlight. The highlight was holding that nice brown paper bag and feeling its weight in our laps as the bus took us through the streets of the city. We couldn't wait until lunchtime to go into that bag.

Besides feeling hungry all the time, my feet were always hurting. Because of the poor quality of our shoes, my friends and I all had the same holes in our soles. Dirt and pebbles would come through the holes, making it painful to walk. At first, we put cardboard in our shoes to patch the holes, but cardboard didn't last very long. So later I figured out that the patch would last longer if I used linoleum, the stuff they use for floors. But linoleum isn't the most comfortable material; it's like stepping barefoot on wood. When I couldn't stand the pain anymore, I'd have to beg my mother for a new pair. "Please, Ma. My feet hurt."

But my mother, whose only income came from throwing the occasional poker party, didn't have money to get me new shoes. And my father was a maintenance man for the New York City Housing Authority, income he supplemented by working as the super of our building and at Jimmy's downstairs. With seven children, my parents always had to be working. One time, my older brother Cary overheard my cries for a new pair of shoes. "Ma, I got it," he said, turning to me. "Danny Boy, come on." Then we flew out the door. I followed him all the way to a Goodwill on 124th Street and Lexington Avenue, my feet aching the whole way. The store had the musty smell of secondhand clothes, appliances, and shoes. He led me to the racks of gently used footwear. "See anything you like?" he asked.

A pair of brown leather split-toes with a middle stitch running down the front caught my eye. "I like these right here."

"Try em on, try em on."

I slid them on. They felt real good. Didn't look bad, either.

"You like em?"

I nodded.

"Okay," said my brother. "Put your old ones on the rack." I did as my brother said and placed my busted, linoleum-patched shoes on the Goodwill rack. *Good riddance,* I thought. I was glad to be done with them. Before I could even ask how he planned to pay for my new shoes, he said, "Aight. Now let's go." It didn't matter that the shoes were cheaper than a new pair, we still didn't have money like that. So out I walked with my split-toes. They were the first pair I'd ever picked out for myself. Someone might have had them before me, but there was nothing secondhand about the way they made me feel. My feet were in heaven.

Everybody was poor. We were all on welfare. But we didn't know we were poor, because everybody we knew was struggling just like us. Didn't matter how many low-paying jobs they worked. In the tenements, I knew families who had it even worse, living fifteen or twenty to an apartment, kids barefoot in the streets. Looking back, it was like we lived in a third-world country. A lot of people who made the Great Migration weren't able to survive in the Northern cities. Many were surprised to find the same racism they'd experienced down south, only different. Instead of cross burnings and lynchings, they found employers who wouldn't hire, landlords who wouldn't rent, banks who wouldn't loan. Many returned to the South in defeat.

That meant families like mine were survivors. We may have been poor, but we weren't miserable. The opposite: we had so much fun. On weekends, my siblings and I would strip down to our underwear and jump into the Harlem River, splashing around without a care in the world. And at night, someone would always be hosting a rent party or a poker party, a tradition dating back a generation to the height of the Harlem Renaissance, where a family would invite folks from the neighborhood over for dancing, music, and cards, selling moonshine and fried porgy, potato salad and chitlins out their kitchen, money they'd use towards that month's rent and expenses. My father was a regular at poker parties in the neighborhood, and some of them would last all weekend long. He'd leave on Friday night, and we wouldn't see him until Sunday, which didn't make my mother happy. Sometimes, my parents would host a poker party and we'd get to watch the adults have a good time in our own apartment all night long.

I'll never forget one particular party in our apartment, when some of the grown folks were trying to get my older brother, who couldn't have been more than eight years old, to dance.

"Show us the moves, James! We know you can dance!"

My family was a dancing family. Every last one of us kids loved to dance. If you lived in Harlem, you knew how to dance. It was in the air. Many evenings, my mother would have to walk down to the corner candy shop, which had a jukebox, carrying a switch to get my sister Dolores to stop dancing with her friends and come home. I still love to dance. We were all good at it, too, especially James. James taught us all the older jazz dances, the camel walk, the Lindy Hop. I'd bring in the trendier new Latin moves. But James wasn't in the mood that night. He kept on refusing. Then someone had the bright idea to loosen him up with a shot of Seagram's 7.

"He only a kid!"

"He can handle it. Can't you?"

James took the shot, and as soon as that whiskey hit my brother's belly, his feet started moving uncontrollably. He was a dance machine! He was dancing for days. Before you knew it, the grown folks were throwing money at him like he was a street performer, cheering him on.

We were poor, but we had love. And the fun we had was real fun, because it was all built on love.

I've known a lot of tough men in my life. I've talked to guys who wound up serving long sentences in prison. I've known killers and hustlers. Hard, broken men. Men whose lives were ruined by the streets, by violence, or cut short by the underground drug game and the drug war. And all my old friends from the neighborhood, the toughest and roughest and most fearsome street guys, we try to figure out what meant the most to us, what mattered. Was it the gold chains? Was it the cars? Was it the women? Something else kicks in when you're faced with the prospect of your own life laid out before you. A belief system takes hold that you don't discover you have or even need until there's a real crisis—like prison or the death of a loved one.

That's when all these tough guys finally realize, it was the little moments that mattered most. It was the joy they felt swimming in the river, dancing with their sisters at the party, footraces in the park. It was those moments of love and freedom from fear that are the most valuable. Not the gold, not the cars, not even the clothes.

But most never discover that until it's too late.

CHAPTER 2

Like a Raisin in the Sun

On Sunday mornings at eleven o'clock, everybody emptied out into the street, the whole neighborhood heading to their preferred churches. We had four or five storefront churches on our block, twenty congregants maximum in each, all twenty usually related to each other. I remember coming out on the stoop with my mother and my siblings on our own way to church and seeing how beautiful that looked: the good people of Harlem walking around in their finest clothes, while the bad people of Harlem would be creeping back home from a long night at the bars and after-hours spots. Seventh Avenue on Sunday morning, nicknamed the Stroll, was the greatest runway in the world.

The church my mother dragged us to was a Holy Ghost Baptist church, the kind where people would scream and holler and catch the Spirit. My uncle, Reverend Hudson, was a minister there. Our whole congregation was maybe thirty-five people, and nineteen of them was related to us through my mother, cousins, and second cousins. The Holy Ghost would take turns hitting them—it was something. To say people were God-fearing was an understatement. It was a living presence. The Holy Ghost lived in the houses when we was growing up, thanks mostly to the women.

The men who ran the churches were a different story, and I started to question organized religion when I observed their behavior. I can't think of one pastor in the neighborhood who didn't drink and wasn't a womanizer. I saw one pastor of a storefront church on our block who also worked as a barber having sex in his barbershop late one night with a young woman who wasn't his wife. I had suspicions that our own pastor was trying to have an affair with our mother. I recognized the con of organized religion early on. They preached one way but lived another. Later, when I started learning about the history of world religions, I got interested in why people need these stories of afterlife and resurrection. What made a certain myth more popular than others? And how can oppressed peoples draw power from these fictions? I'm very careful with beliefs. When beliefs get codified into dogma, that's where problems arise. It don't matter what belief it is. I've come to believe that religion is like a wall. If you're leaning on the wall and it falls, then you fall, too. It's better to be your own wall, to build your own spiritual and religious understanding. That's been my approach to religion at least.

As a kid, though, I had a firm belief in heaven, hell, and the Bible. Whenever someone did something wrong in our house, my mother would say, "Get the Bible." And, boy, if you did it, your ass would be shaking. Because we knew, if you lie on that Bible, you goin to hell.

One night, my brother James, the troublemaker of the family but also my mother's favorite, ate something he shouldn't have out the Frigidaire, and when my mother went to question him about it, he claimed that he hadn't done it. "Get the Bible," my mother said, sensing a lie. I said to myself, *Uh-oh. Boy, James gone get it tonight.* I knew he wasn't gonna lie on the Bible. Which meant he was gone get his ass whipped for lying to our mother. My mother held out her Bible, and James placed his hand atop it. "I swear to God, Ma," he said. "I ain't eat that food out the Frigidaire."

I ain't say nothing out loud, but in my head, I was devastated. *Oh, no. Oh, God! James is going to hell.* Later that night, after our mother had gone to bed, James must have seen how upset I was and told me a secret to calm me down. "Danny Boy," he said, "you know what I did? I had my fingers crossed behind my back. I said, 'I swear to God, Ma, I ain't eat that food out the Frigidaire.' But in my head, I added . . . *last night.* You get it? Because God hears everything, He heard me say 'last night' in my head. So I was telling the truth!" It took me a second to catch on, but when I finally did, I was amazed by his brilliance. He had found a way to beat the Bible.

Around this time, my oldest brother, Carl, an introvert who always had his head in a book, leaned over the bunk bed one night and asked me, "Where you goin when you die?"

"If I'm good, I'm goin to heaven," I said. "If I'm bad, I'm goin to hell."

"Suppose there ain't no heaven or hell?" said Carl, who was in the sixth grade and beginning to question things. I'd never even considered that idea. What did it mean if there wasn't no heaven or hell? The question never left me.

Unlike my mother, Daddy wasn't so big into the religion stuff, but he liked to look sharp on the holidays, same as everybody in the neighborhood. One day before Easter, Daddy took me with him to go pick out a new suit for himself. He had his own style, which was influenced by the South. He chewed apple tobacco and snuff and cut a striking figure walking through the streets. Wherever he went, you could feel people's eyes on him. Daddy was fly for his day, a good-looking man with an arrowhead nose from his Mohawk Indian mother and wavy hair. You'd get seasick from just looking at those waves. Growing up, we always used to say, "Daddy, how you get your hair like that there?" He would show us his tools of the trade—a brush, Murray's Pomade, and a stocking cap. Water and grease hair, we used to call it. He'd even let my sisters braid it while he fell asleep watching baseball games.

By the time he met my mother and had us kids, he'd settled down, but the family legend is that Daddy was a wild child back in his youth. He'd tell us stories of his New York glory days working in a wood mill upstate and helping to build the railroad in Nyack, how he'd get into big barroom brawls and knock Irish guys off stools. He was such a crazy, hard-drinking young man that, eventually, he wound up in Bellevue Hospital, where the loonies went, strapped to a gurney in a straitjacket. It was an experience that changed the course of his life, because from that day forward, he never touched alcohol again. When he married my mother, who was fourteen years younger than him, Daddy was already in his early forties and working as a longshoreman. By that age, I think he was mature enough to realize the importance of taking care of himself and his family. He'd lost his parents young and didn't keep in touch with his kin back in Virginia. He was devoted to us. We were his whole world, and he treated us that way.

Daddy and I hopped on the train, paid our fifteen cents each for a token, and made our way to Ripleys Clothing, a popular department-store chain known for well-made but reasonably priced men's suits. When we arrived, a salesman came by to help us out. In the mirror, Daddy turned this way and that in suit after suit, shooting his cuffs. When he finally found the one he wanted, a navy-blue pinstriped number, he nodded, satisfied. He knew he looked good. The salesman nodded because he knew it, too. But I could already see the worry starting to form on Daddy's forehead.

"How much it cost?"

The salesman was ready. "We're having a special rollback on all men's suits. It's on sale for only $39.95."

That may have been affordable for others, but it was a fortune to us. Daddy nodded and began to slip the jacket off his shoulders. "Thank you for your time."

The salesman seemed sympathetic. "If you can't pay it all at once, we have other options."

"Other options? Like what?"

As the salesman brought us over to his desk and sat us down, Daddy explained that, even though he liked the suit, there was no way he could afford it at that price. We just didn't have the money. The salesman reasoned with him. Maybe he couldn't pay for the suit all at once, but the store could offer a very generous payment plan: several smaller installments over a period of time. With only a few dollars down, we could walk out with that beautiful new suit today and be the envy of the neighborhood. It sounded like a perfect solution. The salesman reached into his desk, pulled out a contract spelling out the terms of the agreement, and placed it in front of my father.

Daddy shifted uncomfortably in his chair. Daddy came to New York at the age of twelve, an orphan with only a third-grade education. He was from a place called Emporia, Virginia, a town of only about a thousand folks near the North Carolina border. His father, my grandfather, had been born into slavery and, like so many in bondage, had been forbidden to read and write and most likely died not knowing how. Although it wasn't unusual for kids—ten, eleven, twelve years old—to come up from the South on their own, it amazed me. I'd always ask about it. "Damn, Daddy. How come you left so young?" He'd just shrug and spit his tobacco. "They were too good to me," he'd say, cryptically. He'd done nothing but hard labor most of his childhood and all of his adult life. Railroads, mills, docks. Later, I'd learn that his experiences weren't so different from those of a lot of black people after Reconstruction and that the real reason he'd left home was to escape racist violence, which had claimed the life of a young girl he'd known. Manhood came earlier back then. Now Daddy tried his best to make sense of the words and numbers on the contract in front of him, but most of it escaped him. I tried to read along beside him.

"I'll just need you to sign at the bottom," said the salesman, handing Daddy a fountain pen. Daddy wrapped his fingers around it, two of which had been sawed off in a mill when he was in his twenties. "Take your time," the salesman said, rising to assist other customers and leaving us with the agreement.

"Thank you," Daddy said, holding the pen over the page.

As I read, my eyes came to a section about something called interest. I was in third grade at the time and tried to remember lessons from Ms. Harris's math class. I knew enough about percentages to know that there was more to this agreement than met the eye. I did the math in my head.

"Daddy, hold on."

I broke it down for him. I knew how much money he made every paycheck. I knew how much extra we had. Every month, they were going to charge him money on top of the price of the suit, and if he missed a payment, which might happen, they wouldn't give him a pass, like when a friend loans you money. The payments would keep going up and up. If he signed this contract, he'd be paying off the suit for damn near the rest of his life. I put my finger, tiny beside his big hand, next to the section of the agreement in question. Daddy nodded slowly, beginning to understand.

I loved my father. He was my role model. He worked so hard and never complained. He had every reason to be cynical and cruel, but he was good and kind. It was painful to realize that, even at that young age, I could read better than him. He deserved that suit. He didn't deserve to be bamboozled.

But, "Boy, you can *read*," Daddy said. "You can really read." I could see he was on the verge of tears, but not because he was sad. I saw in his eyes that he was filled with pride. This was why he'd left the South, why he worked so hard all the time. He wanted his children to do the things he couldn't, be the people he never got to be. Even though we didn't walk out of the store that day with a new

Easter suit, I walked out with something much more valuable—
recognition of my father's hope for me. And just as important, I
came away with a new appreciation for words. Words were power,
and reading—reading closely and carefully—had kept us from losing our power. That was the moment I really saw the importance
of analyzing and questioning everything. Reading could save you a
lot of pain in the long term. And that's remained true throughout
my seven decades on this planet, from my street days to my fashion
days: there's no problem I can't read my way out of.

After my brief time at Catholic school, I went to Public School 24,
a big four-story brick and limestone building on Harlem's east
side. All my siblings went through PS 24, as did James Baldwin
and all his siblings. While he was a student at PS 24, Baldwin wrote
the school song, which was sung at every graduation until the
school closed years later:

> *Farewell, farewell, to Twenty-Four,*
> *We shall miss you ever more.*

Though the outside world often made us feel ashamed of our lot
in life, school provided a counterbalancing force of pride in our
blackness. PS 24's motto was "Knowledge is power." My teachers
were among my most important role models growing up, the only
black people we knew who had good jobs, jobs they performed
with their brains, not just their bodies. They were brilliant people,
probably good enough to teach at Juilliard or work for NASA in a
fairer world. Teachers like Ms. Harris, who I later learned was a
lesbian and who was always dressed sharply in tailored suits. They
showed me a different reality. They made me want to be smart.
Teachers reminded us that Harlem was a place of black writers,
musicians, and artists.

I was excited by poetry early on. I saw so much of myself and the people around me in the things I was reading, especially in a poem like "Harlem" by Langston Hughes, who lived only a block away from our elementary school. "What happens to a dream deferred?" Hughes writes. "Does it dry up like a raisin in the sun? . . . Or does it explode?"

It felt like Hughes was talking about all the people I knew and all the black working people in Harlem.

Later, I'd feel a similar connection to Lorraine Hansberry's play *A Raisin in the Sun,* which takes its title from that same Hughes poem. Reading that play was a revelation. For the first time, I recognized the ambitions, frustrations, pride, pain, and dignity of people I knew. People like my parents. Not the *Amos 'n' Andy* caricatures of black people they showed on TV. Learning these great black works of art as a child and seeing so much of my neighborhood in them made me think that I might be able to create something, too.

I always thought that I could be creative. When I got left back in the fourth grade for my behavior, I came back to school the next year and won every writing award they had, just to prove a point. I even won a couple citywide writing contests. Each time, they'd display my winning pieces in the principal's office for everyone in the school to read. I also wrote all kinds of poems that they'd hang in the front of the school, including one about Christopher Columbus with a rhyme scheme I borrowed from Joyce Kilmer's "Trees."

At my mother's request, I recited it for her in the living room after school one day as she bounced my baby sister Doris in her lap:

A long, long time ago,
There lived a man everyone should know.
He sailed the seas far and wide
To see if he could get to the other side.

When I finished, she smiled with a distant look in her eyes, like I reminded her of poems she used to write. My mother never shared her poems with anybody. The only reason we know she even wrote them was thanks to the nosiness of my sister Dolores, who found a stack of them in her drawer.

While my father instilled in us the value of hard work, my mother was the one who emphasized the value of literature and education. She took it as her responsibility to be a tireless advocate for us at PS 24. This was back in the days when, if you misbehaved, your teacher would call your mother, who'd show up with curlers in her hair, holding a switch, and whip you in front of the whole class. My teachers knew us well enough to know we'd been raised to appreciate their work.

"Oh, you Lily Day's child?" my teachers used to say. "I know I ain't gonna have a problem with you."

Though she was a firm disciplinarian, someone who prized good manners and didn't tolerate misbehavior in any form, my mother also had an outgoing personality and belonged to all the neighborhood social clubs, parent-teacher organizations, and church groups you can think of. She was beloved by women up and down Lexington Avenue. Fluent in the intellectual trends of her day and never afraid to speak her mind, my mother subscribed to the black nationalist thought of Marcus Garvey, who believed in the unification and uplift of black people and called for a return to Africa. I'll never know if she harbored dreams of becoming anything other than a housewife. Whatever dreams she had for herself, she poured into us.

When my mother fled the Jim Crow South for Harlem in 1930 to live with her aunt and cousin, she was an eighteen-year-old Baptist girl from Bishopville, South Carolina, hoping for a better life. Her father had been an itinerant worker from Jamaica and an absence in her life, while her mother was the descendant of Geechee slaves who worked the island plantations off the coast of South Carolina and Georgia. Her streetwise half-brother Eddie, whom she loved dearly, was already living in Harlem when she arrived.

My mother's first years in Harlem were spent with her aunt and cousin Mary in a one-room apartment on Madison Avenue. She led a sheltered life under her aunt's strict, religious roof; her days were split between domestic work in the homes of white people and Holy Ghost worship in the house of the Lord. Only after she came of age and started a family of her own was my mother finally able to let loose with cousin Mary and go out dancing at nightclubs and drinking in bars.

With wide-set eyes, high cheekbones, and dark brown skin, my mother was a striking woman, but being dark-skinned in Harlem at that time wasn't easy. Colorism was as widespread as racism, with places like the Cotton Club refusing to hire any woman darker than a paper bag. The black-is-beautiful era was still a generation away. But that never stopped my mother from carrying herself like the most beautiful woman in the world, which to all of us she was. Lily Day was comfortable in her own skin and could talk to anybody, white, black, rich, poor—it didn't matter. She always left the house looking fabulous, often switching wardrobes three times a day. Her cousin Mary, who wound up living in the apartment above us, used to perch by her window just to see the different outfits my mother would walk out in.

I imagine my father must have been captivated by her beauty, her fanciness, and her fire, and she in turn must have valued his goodness and strength.

For all their differences, one thing they had in common was that they didn't talk about the past around us. It wasn't until much later that I found out my mother had been married to and widowed by an older man and that she'd had an affair and two children with another man while married. The only evidence we had for any of this was a stack of old letters my sisters found in her drawer alongside her poetry, and the fact that my brothers had different last names—Carl Collins, Cary Collins, James Edwards—from me and my sisters.

My mother and father married in 1943, but it's still a mystery how they first met. If I had to guess, I'd say it must have been at some poker party; her cousin Mary and older brother Eddie were both regulars on the Harlem poker circuit.

Looking back on it, I see now that there musta been some loneliness and pain underneath the extroverted personality my mother showed the world. We never heard about her dead first husband or met the man she'd had an affair with, who fathered my two oldest brothers. And I can only imagine what indignities she'd experienced as a young woman working as a domestic in the houses of white people. Then, a housewife spending her days alone with seven kids, with a husband who worked all week and played poker all weekend, she must have felt isolated and left craving companionship, which is why she sometimes sought the friendship of other men in the neighborhood, something I used to hate back then but understand now. To keep herself busy and interacting with other people, she picked up part-time jobs wherever she could, waitressing at restaurants and working as a barmaid at the Mona Lisa, a nearby watering hole where her friends congregated. Drinking became a way to cope, a release.

Kids are often more sensitive to the harsh power imbalances in the world than we give them credit for. Through my parents' experiences, I was beginning to understand the kind of reality I'd been born into. And naturally I began to question it. How come I never saw any black police officers? Or black garbage collectors? How come we didn't know anyone with a good job? How come no white people lived around us? How come my friends and I were always hungry? How come, elsewhere in the city, it seemed like people had a lot more than we had uptown?

I must have been thinking something along these lines, staring off into space, trying to write another essay for class or a poem to recite for my mother, when RC burst through the front door of our cramped apartment. RC was a relative of my mother who came and stayed with us from time to time. He had a special glow about him on this particular day.

"Hey, Danny Boy, what d'ya say?" said Uncle RC. We called him "uncle" as a term of respect, but really he was Mary's brother. I noticed he was carrying a briefcase. Even at eight years old, I knew RC wasn't exactly the briefcase-carrying type.

"What's in that?" I asked him.

"Oh, you wanna see what I got, huh?" That's when Uncle RC flicked the latches, opened the briefcase, and showed me the biggest pile of cash money I'd ever seen in my life. I didn't even know a person could have that much money at one time. My jaw must have hit the table. *Got damn!*

"How you like that?"

My mother tried to protect us from the fast life of the men on her side of the family, like Uncle Eddie, who was a cardsharp, and my second cousin Joe Thomas, who lived upstairs with Mary and was always in and out of prison.

But that day Uncle RC turned my whole world upside down. There was nothing deferred about the dream I was looking at. I was beginning to understand that there must be another way to success than what they were teaching in school. Maybe I didn't have to slave three jobs like Daddy. Maybe I didn't have to be good in school like my mother wanted. No matter how hard they worked, we still struggled, we'd still go to bed hungry some nights.

I loved writing, and I knew it brought pride to my mother that I was good at it, but it didn't take William Shakespeare to see that the real winners were not literary types like my mother and our teachers, or working stiffs like my father. It was the hustlers who were winning. I began to wonder, *Did Langston Hughes ever walk around with a briefcase full of cash like Uncle RC?*

Much later, I'd come to find out that Uncle RC was a safecracker. He'd go on to serve a number of bids in jail, all of which my mother covered for, telling us, "Oh, your uncle RC just re-enlisted in the service." She'd keep saying this well after it was clear that he was too old for the military.

I didn't know any of that at the time. All I knew was what RC was showing me in that briefcase, and whatever I'd been thinking about before—poem, essay, whatever—I wasn't thinking about it no more.

CHAPTER 3

—

Harlem Dreams

My parents and their generation came north in search of opportunities to build a better life, but many weren't prepared for the obstacles they found. Racist trade unions in the North saw them as a threat and barred them from good-paying work. White building owners tried to keep them out, drafting racist covenants limiting the number of black people who could live and work on a property. The decks seemed stacked against us. Like I said, many blacks returned to the South. Most of those who stayed were forced to live with the frustration and anger of deferred American dreams.

But there was another type of person who refused to defer the dream, who was desperate for the dream, who took the risk to operate outside the system and, if need be, in opposition to it.

Now that my eyes were opened, everywhere I looked in my life there were pool sharks, cardsharps, pimps, drug dealers, and moonshiners. Hustling was a normal, often lucrative, line of work.

Men like my father, who held a good city job until his retirement, were the rare exceptions. But whether you worked aboveground like Daddy or underground like my uncle RC, you had to have a special determination to survive in Harlem. The neighborhood weeded out the strong from the weak during the Great Migration, and it did the same for the next generation. Harlem became home to the crème de la crème of hustlers.

And in our neighborhood, no hustlers were more powerful or revered than the numbers kings. The drug game took over in later years, but when I was a kid, it was the numbers that controlled neighborhoods like Harlem, and it was the numbers kings and queens who held all the power in the community. The numbers was a lottery game, just like state-sponsored lotteries today, where people bet a small amount of money on a three-digit number in hopes of that number getting picked. Gambling historians say that black people in Harlem invented the modern numbers game in the 1920s, lowering the entry fee for their poor clients and coming up with innovative ways to cut down on paper use. Early on, though, the Italian Mafia took control of the numbers racket, and it wasn't until legendary Harlem boss Bumpy Johnson won it back that we started booking our own numbers.

For most of the twentieth century, the numbers game in New York was a major industry and employer for black people. Some estimate that by the 1970s the black-owned numbers racket was raking in over a billion dollars annually and employing as many as 100,000 people in the five boroughs. As folks in the neighborhood tossed nickel after nickel into the wishing well, dreaming of a jackpot, the numbers runners grew richer and more powerful.

My mother played the numbers every day. It was her harmless vice, nowhere near as expensive as her taste in furs and clothes, or as costly in the long run as her deepening dependence on alcohol. She might be on her way to the grocery store for Corn Flakes and spot the numbers man on his rounds. She'd place her usual bet: "Let me get one-fifty straight." That was her lucky number, and still the number 150 has special significance to the Day family. The numbers man would take her coin, take out a sheet of paper, scribble a secret code on it detailing bettor info, stuff the paper discreetly back inside his suit jacket, tip his hat, and be on his way to collect more money for bets from around the neighborhood. It was mostly poor people like my mother who played numbers, wagering a nickel here, a dime there, hoping for that 600-to-1 payout. You'd pick a three-digit number—playing it "straight" meant the numbers had to hit in order. Playing it "combination" meant the numbers could hit in any order for a lower payout.

Depending on which crew was running the game, numbers would be drawn off the random results of horse races in Queens, or daily treasury report figures in Italy, or the legal weekly lotto in Puerto Rico. The reason why legal lotteries make so much money for governments is the same reason the numbers racket was so lucrative: if your chance of picking a three-digit number is 1 in 1,000, and the maximum payout is 600 to 1, the house is never losing money. The only thing influencing profits is the popularity of the game. The more people play, the higher the payouts, the more the bosses made—that simple. Being in the numbers racket meant you were making money, and if someone got caught, which was rare, punishment was a slap on the wrist. Even after paying off the overhead of accountants, police bribes, and runners, who got standard commission on all bets and generous tips from winning customers, a numbers boss was making more money in a year than almost anyone, black or white, in the five boroughs, especially in Harlem, which had the highest concentration of players in the city.

On the rare occasions when my mother's number hit, there would be new shoes for us. The neighbors knew it wasn't normal for the Day children to suddenly be wearing brand-new shoes when they'd seen us just yesterday with linoleum-patched holes. We'd see the looks on our block from people like the Martin family. The Martins were a little more well-to-do than us, which isn't saying much, but they lived in the projects, which was where the middle-class people lived. Compared to the tenements where we lived, they were in luxury housing. Not long after my mother's number had hit, my siblings and I were outside playing when the Martins caught sight of us. When they passed by, they took one look at our new shoes and I heard them say, "Oh, Lily Day musta hit the number."

Everybody gambled. My mother played her numbers, my father had his weekend poker binges, and my uncle Eddie was a legendary card hustler. Later, when I started to make a living as a professional dice gambler, I never thought about whether it was legal or not. Gambling was just a normal part of life and a viable way to make a living on the streets. And like other parts of life, there were winners and losers, so the challenge was figuring out how to be one of the winners.

My friends and I all looked up to the numbers kings. They were the underground celebrities of Harlem. They were charismatic and slick, but also fearsome if they needed to be. They had larger-than-life reputations, and they were smart businessmen, too. What they made from the numbers racket allowed them to float above poverty. They owned property and legitimate businesses and storefronts. With their wealth came influence in the community. Numbers kings gave out turkeys for Thanksgiving, gifts on Christmas, spreading their money around the neighborhood in charitable ways that made our love for them grow. They influenced elections, throwing their support behind government leaders who were willing to protect their interests.

When I was growing up, Bumpy Johnson was the hustler we admired most. He was a little younger than my father but, like Daddy, had made the migration up to New York as a young boy. He was dirt poor, from South Carolina, but he'd taken the hustling route, starting off as the muscle for legendary numbers queen Stephanie St. Clair. He'd been in and out of jail, but eventually gained lasting fame in Harlem when he brokered the deal to take the numbers racket back from the Italians. We couldn't believe a

black person could cut a deal with the Italians. Somehow, Bumpy
Johnson had done it. He would go on to control the streets of Harlem for four decades, and we would read in *Jet* magazine about his
comings and goings, rubbing elbows with entertainers like Lena
Horne, Billie Holiday, and Cab Calloway. He was our hero. My
friend Curtis and I used to shoot hoops near a nondescript storefront on East 126th Street called the Palmetto Chemical Company,
an exterminating company that we knew he owned. All day long,
we'd watch him—a dignified, clean-shaven man with dark brown
skin—and his well-dressed associates pass back and forth. I'd watch
them smoke a cigarette and blow smoke for what seemed like five
minutes, noting how some of the smoke came out of their nose,
too. That's how close attention I was paying to these guys. Basketball was our excuse to gawk.

If you were a little black kid growing up in Harlem who went
out on the avenue at night to shine shoes for spare change, who
shoplifted because he was hungry, who saw his parents work their
fingers to the bone day in and day out with little to show for it, a
guy like Bumpy Johnson seemed superhuman. Curtis and I worshipped the ground Bumpy and his crew walked on, the way kids
might look up to athletes or entertainers now. We wanted to walk
like them, talk like them. And, most of all, we wanted to dress like
them. Gator- and lizard-skin shoes. Continental pants—wide-legged
with no cuffs.

As evening fell, Curtis and I would get tired of pretending to
play ball in front of Bumpy Johnson's place and wander uptown to
sit on Curtis's stoop. Curtis's place was just down the block from
the Woodside Hotel on Seventh Avenue. The Woodside Hotel was
the home of Count Basie and his Orchestra, who memorialized it
in one of their biggest tunes, a fast-paced swing called "Jumpin' at
the Woodside." Before the city demolished the Woodside and put
a housing project in its place, we'd watch buses full of jazz musicians pull up to the hotel. Cool, tough-looking guys in pinstriped
suits poured out, carrying instrument cases of mysterious shapes

and sizes. We scrutinized what the jazz guys wore the same way we did the hustlers. Along with Bumpy and his crew, Nat King Cole, Dizzy Gillespie, John Coltrane were our fashion idols. Even though everyone wore dark suits in that era, the particular zoot suits that the jazz players sported brought something different, a flair to an otherwise basic design. The tilt of the hat, the bagginess of the silhouette. Like the music they played, the clothes that the jazz musicians wore had a flow and aesthetic all their own, as bold and innovative as the music was. From an early age, I understood that black music had a sound *and* a look.

Often, we'd spot hustlers we'd seen from earlier in the day at Bumpy's mingling with the crowds outside the hotel. The hustlers would make money, then celebrate by going out and dancing at a place like the Woodside. There were bands and ballrooms everywhere: the Savoy, Moroccan Palace, the Palladium, Carnie's, Rockland Palace, the Renaissance, the Golden Gate, the Darling Casino. During the Harlem Renaissance, dancing was so popular that the authorities took notice and decided to pass the infamous 1926 Cabaret Law, which forbid dancing without a license in New York City. But that didn't stop anybody. Harlem was all about dancing, and all the old gangsters could dance. If you could dance really well, your fellas would get around you and cheer you on as you did the bop or the Lindy Hop or whatever dance craze was sweeping Harlem at the time.

Like the five elements of hip-hop, my generation had an unspoken pantheon of elements that dictated our respect for hustlers:

1. Were you getting money? Whether it be through numbers running, gambling, drug dealing, or some other hustle nobody had figured out yet, you had to be getting money to be a hustler. If you were getting money on the streets, it was a given that there was risk involved, so being a hustler and getting money, by definition, meant you wasn't no punk.
2. Were you good at dancing? I'm not talking about break

dancing. I mean, dancing to big-band music or Latin music. Hustlers used to go out to the dance halls that were all over Harlem, and women would choose a man to go home with based on how well he could dance. Which brings me to:

3. Were you a ladies' man? Being good with the ladies wasn't just an ego thing, wasn't just about being a player. Some guys were masters at hustling but didn't know how to talk to women without demeaning or insulting them. Good women could see through pigs and dogs and wannabe pimps. A ladies' man had an implicit economic advantage that other guys didn't, because if he wound up broke and out on his ass, a ladies' man had the ability to find him a good woman to live with who could take care of him while he got back on his feet.

4. Could you talk slick? A good hustler had to be able to talk that talk, be quick on his feet, charming, witty. You have to be good with words and know how to use those words to play with the egos of weaker people to get what you want. "What do you want, man, how much you want for that? Put it there, put your feet on it."

And the one I always cared most about:

5. Were you fly? Flyness wasn't about how handsome you were, although that helped, or about how expensive your clothes were, although that helped, or what brand they were. Brands weren't important. It was about something intangible. It was about style and how you carried yourself in the street. It was about your shoes, the way you wore your hat. It was about the car you drove and how fly your girl dressed. It was also about taking some new fashion risk that everyone else on the streets would be copying. Power was fly, and fly was power.

As Curtis and I sat on his stoop, watching the fashionable people come and go, I felt a dream forming in my mind. We may have been poor, but we'd been born into this place and time that was exploding with beauty. It felt unstoppable and so much bigger than us. It was cosmic. With my linoleum patches and my empty stomach, I sat there looking at all the hustlers as they mingled with the musicians and glamorous patrons of the Woodside, their polished shoes and gold watches and rings catching light from the streetlamps, and I was hungry for that magic.

CHAPTER 4

Sportsmen

We didn't get allowances. There wasn't money just lying around the house. We wanted something, we had to go out and get it. If I asked someone like Uncle RC for a dollar, he'd most likely say, "You ain't got no money? Nigga, go yell up a lamppost."

And Uncle Eddie might chime in, "Go snatch a ham."

So we did what we had to do. We snatched ham, shined shoes, picked pockets, grabbed hot dogs off grills, stole coins from the fronts of buses. We were hustling before we even knew what the word meant. Curtis, Bill, and I were what you might call the thugs of our neighborhood. In addition to stealing from the corner stores to feed ourselves before school, we were also in kiddie gangs, although calling them "gangs" would be an exaggeration. These weren't like the Bloods or Crips. These were more like after-school social clubs. There wasn't no initiation. You'd just say you wanted to be a member and then you'd be a member. Simple as that.

These clubs were like the little-league squads for future hustlers; Italian kids in East Harlem had them, too. They had names like the Red Wings and the Baldies, real *West Side Story* shit. All my brothers were in a group called the Sportsmen, so naturally I joined the Sportsmen, while Curtis joined up with the Politicians. There were different levels within the clubs, almost like the Boy Scouts. When I was still in elementary school, I became president of the Sportsmen Tots, while my brother James was president of the Sportsmen Juniors, and my brother Cary was the war counselor of the Sportsmen Seniors. We even paid regular dues as part of membership, because if you were in a certain gang, you'd have to be able to finance and buy your own sweater. That's how you knew which gang someone belonged to. The sweaters were designed in certain ways with certain colors to distinguish you from the other groups. As a Sportsman, I wore a white cable-knit sweater, with red and blue around the collar and trim, with the symbol of a cane and a top hat on the back.

Beyond dues, the only thing that was required of members was that they take part in what we called "sham battles," these little fake fights we organized amongst each other, to prepare us for real fights with other gangs. You wouldn't try to hurt nobody good, but you'd tussle. Although they weren't real brawls, the sham battles were important. I remember my brothers once beat up a fellow Sportsman for choosing church over a sham battle. They converged on the kid's church and beat him up outside while his family was praying inside.

"That's for missing the sham battle," my brothers said, smacking him with real blows. "Goody Two-shoes."

As the youngest boy in our family, I lived in the shadow of my three older brothers. Each of them had their special thing that I admired and wanted to emulate. Everybody in the neighborhood knew they were tough and cool, but they were also cultured, well-read, and politically aware.

My brother Carl was the bookworm in the family, and since he was the oldest, I suppose we all followed in his footsteps. Every week, my siblings and I would come out of the library with stacks of books as tall as us. All we did was read. *The House of the Seven Gables, Gulliver's Travels, The Three Musketeers.*

Six years my senior, Carl was an introvert and a mama's boy, devoted to our mother until the end. She enlisted him in the army at seventeen to keep him away from the streets. On account of his work ethic, curiosity, and intelligence, he quickly rose through the ranks of the military. By the time he turned twenty, he was a buck sergeant with three stripes, which was an almost unheard-of achievement. His experiences abroad—in Panama and the Middle East—helped him to think critically about his own surroundings, and he forced me to look beyond whatever was in front of me in Harlem to contemplate the world at large. Carl was the smart one, always with his face buried in a book. When Alex Haley's *Roots* was published and became one of the bestselling books of all time, a couple passages in it made Carl stop short. "Wait a second," he said to himself. "Why does some of this sound familiar?" He put the book down and walked over to his shelf, searching for a novel that he had read years before. Finally, he found it, a book hardly anyone knew called *The African* by Harold Courlander. Two years later, Haley would settle a plagiarism lawsuit brought by Courlander for stealing passages from *The African.*

Meantime, Cary, four years my senior, was the artistic one. He hipped us to art and jazz and would bring back stories from his adventures hanging out in Greenwich Village with bohemian types of all religions, creeds, and colors. When he wasn't busy drawing in his sketchbook, he was exposing us to all the latest music. Coltrane and Miles and Mingus. He had us listening to beat poetry by Allen Ginsberg and Amiri Baraka. I'd listen to his stories of downtown happenings with awe, filing away slang and new vocabulary for later use. Cary might mention something about being a "nonconformist," and the next day, I was running around proclaiming, "Naw, I ain't with that. I'm a nonconformist!" I didn't really know

what it meant. Cary thought it was cool, and that was what mattered. Those downtown happenings often involved heroin, which
all the jazz guys used and Cary started to use, too.

Like all baby brothers, I learned about the world through my
older brothers before experiencing it myself. Wherever they led, I
made sure to follow. They would school me. We might be listening
to a Max Roach record and at a particular thumping solo, Carl
would say, "Hear that? That's that African influence."

"That's right," Cary would chime in. "What did Duke say? The
root of jazz comes out of Africa."

Then they'd get to discussing the history of jazz and how it
evolved from the old slave chants and up through the blues. "It's all
got that African beat."

Carl and Cary were everything I wanted to be. They were always talking about current affairs and ideas and exposing me to
life beyond the neighborhood. Their influence on the way I see the
world is major.

My brother James, a.k.a. Big Moon, was a different story. James
was two years my senior and the neighborhood tyrant. The wild
child. The entertainer. His charisma eclipsed everybody else's in
the house. In many ways my nickname of Little Moon tells you
everything you need to know about our dynamic. I was a satellite
in his planet's larger gravitational pull. While Carl and Cary
brought in knowledge from outside of Harlem, James brought in
knowledge from outside of our doorstep. James taught me how
to dance, how to fight, and how to hustle. A natural-born hustler,
James had street smarts from birth. It was written in his DNA or
something. He knew the streets better than our older brothers did,
and even from a young age, James's gangster began to show itself.
In elementary school, he'd bully other kids to bring him candy and
cookies. Mothers would come to our door, yanking their sons by
the ear, to demand that James return whatever he'd strong-armed
from them.

Cause he was older than me, James had all the best clothes, and

I coveted them. If he didn't let me wear his clothes, I'd sneak em out the house. It got to the point that, to stop me, he would sleep by the front door so I couldn't get out the house in the morning without passing his inspection. But I refused to go to school unless I was looking right. To outwit him, I'd tell my friends Herman and Thurman, who were twin brothers, to wait on the street outside our building, so I could drop his clothes out the window, where they'd catch em and give em to me soon as I came outside.

That strategy worked for a while, until one day I was posted up in front of the school in James's flyest button-down and slacks, when I looked up to see somebody tearing across the school yard. I wasn't paying no attention at first, but as the figure got closer, I said, "Oh, shit!" It was James. And even though I took off running, he was faster than me. He caught me and made me walk in through the main front entrance, where students were forbidden to enter, into the teachers' bathroom to change clothes with him, since he'd left home in my ratty jeans and T-shirt. I was so embarrassed, I didn't even go to class. I snuck out the back of the school and took side streets to get back to our apartment.

It was James who I told about Spongey, an ugly, frightening neighborhood bully who stole my toys. It was James who told me I had to get good at fighting. It was James who marched me back to where Spongey hung out, putting that confidence in me that I could whip his butt. And it was James who clapped me on the back after I did.

Daddy must have known that he had to keep a closer eye on James than the rest of us. It was only James he took on his maintenance rounds of the Patterson projects in the Bronx. "Boy, listen," Daddy would tell him. "If you do nothing, you get nothing. I'm gonna teach you." Daddy never missed a day of work his whole career at the New York City Housing Authority. He was only late once, the day he had to walk to work through the Great Snowstorm of '47. He would never stop trying to teach his children the value of hard work and making an honest living. But James would come

back from working with Daddy and have us cracking up with stories of beating on rats the size of dogs. Daddy made it clear that
there were only three options for anyone living under his roof: go
to school, get a job, or get out. Even though Daddy only had a
third-grade education and couldn't read or write too well, he picked
his way through the newspaper every day, as well as *Chief,* the New
York civil service paper that listed all the government jobs. He'd
point out listings to James, trying to encourage him to think of a
life beyond running around in the streets. "Look here, Big Moon,
they got an opening for a postal clerk. That's a good job." But
James wasn't interested in no government jobs.

While I was still in elementary school, James, who was in his
early teens at the time, would take me with him whenever he was
hanging out with the older hustlers in our neighborhood, and they
quickly took a liking to me. No one's much of a hustler at eleven
years old, but I had a few tricks up my sleeve when it came to playing cards, thanks to my uncle Eddie, whose street name was Fish
Man because, in addition to cards, he was also a master of buying
fresh fish from the markets downtown and selling them from a
cooler on the sidewalks of Harlem. While all my male relatives
were gifted in the art of crooked gambling, no one was quite like
Fish Man Eddie. A tall, dark, well-built man, his reputation as a
cardsharp was legendary throughout Harlem, to the point that he
was barred from playing in certain poker circles.

"Fish Man Eddie is with it and ready," he'd announce as he entered our poker parties. "Who wanna lose some money today?"

Whenever Uncle Eddie came around, with his Murphy hat
tilted to the left, he'd teach us boys something new—my sisters
weren't allowed to touch cards—like how to deal seconds, which
was when you made it look like you were dealing the top card but
were really dealing the one underneath. He perfected his sleight of
hand after leaving South Carolina to travel with the circus at age
fourteen, winding up in Harlem seven years later. Uncle Eddie was
one of the most influential people in my early years, and the les-

sons I learned at his knee have stuck with me throughout my various hustles. "You paying attention?" he'd ask, looking me directly in the eye as he began to shuffle and cut the deck. "Pay attention, hear."

Since my mother forbid my three sisters from touching the cards, they had to resign themselves to sitting on the floor and looking on with envy as Uncle Eddie schooled the boys. Two years my junior, my sister Dolores was a tomboy and the moody middle child of the family. If she wasn't in the library reading out the entire black-literature section, she was playing baseball at the park and getting in arguing matches with me for calling her a "black spasm" on account of her darker complexion. She was strong-willed, proud, always spoke her mind, which meant she was often getting whooped by our mother. Despite that, my mother and Dolores always had a deep, loving bond between them, probably because their strong personalities were so much alike.

Then there was Deborah, three years younger than me, the neighborhood pretty girl all my friends had crushes on. Deborah was sensitive and gentle, wore her emotions on her sleeve, and cried at the drop of a hat. She channeled her emotions into acting, starring in a local youth theater group. Deborah and I were connected by our deep love for our father: she was the only Day child other than me who woke up at five A.M. to join Daddy downstairs at Jimmy's for his morning ritual of coffee, a newspaper, and a corn muffin.

Doris, five years my junior and the baby of the family, was the sickly one who spent most of her childhood in and out of convalescent homes battling rheumatic fever. Daddy had to take her in for all her medical appointments and long hospital stays, since my mother didn't trust doctors. Doris eventually beat the disease, but her time away from us and frail disposition made her an outsider among the siblings.

The older hustlers like Uncle Eddie found me amusing and at least somewhat capable, because soon they were putting me to work. After doing errands here and there for a numbers runner, I got my first real job working as a lookout for dice games. When the cops rolled up, my job was to say, "Cops!"

But whenever the cops rolled up, which happened every hour or so, the guys shooting dice wouldn't run. The game would pause briefly to pay off the cops. It was usually two officers. As the lookout, I was the one who collected the four dollars from the gamblers and handed it over, two dollars per badge. If it was the sergeant, though, they'd have to fork over a bit more. The sarge got five dollars. The cops would take their cut and say, "We'll see you in an hour."

Then they'd be off.

"Good lookin out," one of the gamblers would say, slipping me a dollar.

When I wasn't watching for crooked cops, I was watching the older guys shoot dice, learning the rules and trying to study the techniques, listening to what they said and how they said it, wanting to wear what they wore, how they wore it. There was real money in those games. The flyness and the money seemed to go hand in hand. I wanted to be rich and fly like them guys with their straightened hair, smoothing down their waves or slicking it back with wide-tooth combs like the white boys. I wanted to have a fly name like them, too. Beaver, Joe Slick, Big Clyde. No self-respecting hustler could call himself Danny Boy, which is what my family called me.

It was during the time of my apprenticeship as a dice lookout that a neighborhood crew robbed a factory. They'd gotten the safe out, cracked it open, and found four hundred dollars inside. You could tell they were in a good mood when they strolled up to the dice game. They passed around a bottle, beaming, offering me sips, laughing when I spit it out. Four hundred dollars was something else. As usual, I provided the entertainment, telling jokes, reciting poetry I'd written for school, making up little rhymes on the spot. They were laughing with me and at me at the same time. They must have recognized a younger version of themselves in my raggedy clothes, my beat-up shoes, my nappy hair. Suddenly, Beaver, the leader of the crew, was struck by inspiration. "Come on, Danny Boy," he said. "We gone take you to get your hair done."

Get my hair done? I had to pinch myself. Not only was I getting to make some money and hang out with these guys I looked up to, but they were gonna take me to get my hair done. I'd never had my hair done. And they weren't taking me to just any old place. We hopped in Beaver's Cadillac and drove down to Sugar Ray's.

Back then, the boxer Sugar Ray Robinson was one of the flyest and richest black men in the country. He owned a stretch of storefronts in Harlem, including Sugar Ray's Quality Cleaners, Edna Mae's Lingerie Shop, named after his wife, and Sugar Ray's nightclub, which was one of the hottest spots in Harlem. But we were headed to Golden Gloves Barber Shop, which was known for having perfected "the process," a new technique for straightening black hair. Sugar Ray himself got his hair done there, as did every fly guy and hustler in Harlem. This was the shop where Rogers Simon invented the finger wave, a hair-straightening technique that involved a lot of patience and grease.

The smell of hair oil, shaving cream, and rubbing alcohol filled Golden Gloves. I'd never been inside it before. Along one wall was a row of large circular mirrors and wood paneling. Barber's chairs with metal foot stands sat on fluted white pedestals. The barbers in their smocks stood snipping their scissors around the heads of the most well-groomed men in Harlem. The good mood of Beaver and his crew was rubbing off on me. I was about to get my hair done like Sugar Ray Robinson. Ain't nobody my age had hair like Sugar Ray Robinson. Out of sheer excitement, I must have started to dance.

"Look at Danny," they said, laughing.

"Look at him dance."

"You learn them moves from Big Moon?"

"Dancing Danny!"

Everyone agreed the name had a ring to it.

"From now on, that's your name."

Thus was I christened Dancing Danny of Harlem.

Eventually, it was my turn in the chair. The barber threw the bib around me, and Beaver and his crew told the barber what to do. When I was done, the chair swiveled around, and there I was in the mirror.

I had waves!

Let me tell you something, man. That was such a memorable experience.

I felt like I did whenever my mother hit her number and I laced up new shoes. Walking around school and the neighborhood with that hairdo made people look at me different. For the first time, I understood how deep it was to be fly. It wasn't the outside that was important. It was that thing that happened inside you that gave you strength. I felt powerful. When I went to bed that night and every night after, this is what I'd do: I would lie down and prop the pillow between my neck and the wall. It was uncomfortable as hell, but I'd sleep sitting almost upright all night. I wouldn't even move, so my hair wouldn't get messed up. I sprayed that joint every morning, fixed it up. You're supposed to go every two weeks to get a hairdo like that reprocessed, but I must have made those damn waves last six months.

I was too young to fully understand the implications of hair straightening in terms of power and white supremacist ideas of beauty. Natural hair wouldn't come into fashion for another decade. I just knew it felt good to be fly. To be getting high fives from all the fly hustlers I was studying under. I was becoming a part of something, a world was letting me in.

———

While they were still teenagers, my artistic brother Cary, who'd been introduced to heroin through the bohemian crowd, and my hustler brother James, who was tight with neighborhood dealers, graduated from our relatively innocent Sportsmen days of matching sweaters and sham battles to selling and using heroin, and watching them get wrapped up in it was breaking my mother's heart. She'd make them put their hands on her Bible like when they were kids and swear to her that they'd stop selling.

"Don't lie to me," she'd say, staring with the intensity of the Holy Ghost into their eyes.

I was only maybe nine or ten, so I didn't really know what heroin was. I just knew that my mother didn't like that my brothers were involved with it, and that whatever it was, it was making them some money. Drugs weren't widespread back then. There wasn't supply or demand the way there would be for heroin in the seventies and crack in the eighties.

In time, my mother would see all of her boys, including me for a brief and regrettable period, fall into the drug trade. There was the religious and moral dilemma—she worried about the souls of her boys. But there was also something deeper going on. My mother was an alcoholic. It started, I imagine, as a way to cope with the anger she felt working for white "madams" as a domestic and only deepened as she turned into a frustrated housewife living in a crumbling tenement with seven kids. Her dreams had been deferred, then bottled up inside her, out of reach. Helplessly, she watched my brothers turn to drugs, and in turn she grew more dependent on the bottle. Guilt and shame about her own addiction mixed with fury at a racist and colorist world and made her miserable. She must have felt the additional dread of someone who knew that addiction was often passed down to one's children.

Many a night I found myself having to drag her home from the bar where she often worked, the Mona Lisa on 128th and Lexington. The Mona Lisa's nickname was the Bucket of Blood because every weekend someone would get stabbed up. You'd see the blood on the sidewalk outside the next morning. Herman and Thurman used to go down to the Mona Lisa with me to pick up their mother, too. Alcohol wasn't frowned upon in the community, but alcoholics were. You were supposed to be able to contain yourself, hold your liquor. But there came a point, after the trials and tribulations of life, when our mothers took to drinking. My mother wasn't an alcoholic, I told myself. She was just a good woman under pressure who drank to ease her pain.

It hurt me more than I can say to see her in that bar. My mother was a strong, militant woman. She was religious and a strict disciplinarian, especially with my sisters. She had an air of undeniable glamour. If you looked in her drawers, you would see all these beautiful dresses and lingerie. She used to chase my sisters around the house wearing her furs. She would always get on our case about not embarrassing her with our clothes, joking that if we wound up in the morgue wearing dirty draws, she wouldn't claim our dead bodies. But there was nothing glamorous about the person wobbling on a barstool those nights. I would walk into the Mona Lisa, and everyone in the bar knew I wasn't leaving without her. My father, who knew how hard life could be for women, had taught all of his boys the responsibility we had to our mother and sisters. "In this family," my father commanded, "we protect our women."

Since I worshipped my father, I had taken his message to heart.

Even at nine years old, I wouldn't allow nobody to talk to me in that bar. Nothin. Not a word. I didn't wanna hear shit. My face was lit up with anger. After guiding my mother out of there, I walked her home through the darkened streets. When we finally got home and she collapsed on the bed, I lifted her limp hand and placed it on the Bible. It was the same beaten book she'd brought up all those years ago from South Carolina, when she was a teenage girl sent by her mother to live in Harlem with her aunt.

"Swear you'll stop drinking?" I said. "Ma?"

She grumbled something I couldn't hear. Her hand slipped off the Bible as she fell asleep, her lip bloody from where she'd fallen on our steps. My mother was the most Christian person in our household. Where was the Holy Ghost? Why wasn't He helping her? Maybe what Carl said about there not being a heaven or hell was right.

I couldn't have known it at the time, but the pain of my mother's alcoholism was beginning to force a wedge between us, poisoning me with bitterness. Case in point was the night Curtis and Bill finally convinced me to come rob some drunk people with them. For my neighborhood friends, robbing drunk people was a time-honored tradition. The drunks seemed used to it, too. You'd walk past the Irish bars on the east side and see drunks with scabs on their heads from having been beaten up and mugged go back inside and order another drink.

Back then, 125th Street in Harlem was a miniature Times Square. There were penny arcades and movie theaters everywhere. East Harlem alone had three major movie theaters: the Triboro, the Grand, and the RKO. On the west side were even more: another RKO, the Alhambra, and the Apollo. And of course there was nightlife. There were five bars between Lexington and Park Avenue on 125th Street, and Second Avenue, farther east, was where all the Irish bars were, white people throwing back ten-cent shots of whiskey. Often, we'd steal food out of those bars, sneaking our fingers through a cracked window to snatch chickens from a spit. Or we'd shine shoes for spare change so we could go to the movies. But this was also where some kids would wait in the shadows for careless drunk people. They'd drag them to a dark corner, rough them up, and take off with their wallets.

Curtis, Bill, and our friend Pusshead were pros at rolling drunks, but not me. I'd always walk over to the bars with them, teasing and laughing the whole way, but right before they'd go rob someone, I'd say, "Yeah, yeah, yeah," and turn back home. I didn't want to hurt nobody who didn't deserve it. But one night, the bitterness I'd been feeling over my mother's drinking must have got the better of me, because at the spot where I usually parted ways with them, I surprised everyone by saying that, nah, this time I wanted to help rip off those no-good drunks.

I was nervous. I could see the people coming in and out of the bar.

"I never robbed nobody before," I said.

"You just be lookout, man," said Curtis. "We'll go."

Drawing on my expertise as a lookout for dice games, I stood at the corner and surveyed the block, making sure the coast was clear of police and grown folks who knew me. It was just as bad to be caught by someone who knew your mother as it was to be caught by a cop. Sometimes even worse.

As Curtis and them went around the block, getting into position, I started my lookout. There was a frank stand on the corner, and the smell of the frankfurters and knishes cooking on the grill made my stomach growl with hunger. I'd stolen hot knishes right off the grill from that frank stand before, burning up my hand. Right across the street was the ticketing booth for the Metro-North train station, which ran on elevated tracks overhead.

After what seemed like forever, I saw Curtis come around the corner with a drunk white man in a headlock. Even though he wasn't a teenager yet, Curtis was big for his age. Tall, light-skinned, and good-looking, he was dating eighteen-year-olds when he was only twelve, which made the rest of us jealous. And his size was an advantage now as he dragged the drunk around back. Bill and Pusshead jumped in to help empty the man's pockets. It all seemed to be going smoothly. But as the seconds ticked away and I split my attention between them and the other passersby on the block, something felt wrong. What was taking them so long?

No sooner had I asked myself the question when I heard a shout from down the block. "Halt! Halt!"

Two police officers were coming right for them with their guns drawn.

"Oh, shit!"

In a flash, everyone scattered. Curtis ran right past me down Park Avenue with the police on his heels, their guns pointed in front of them. Bill and I dashed away in the other direction. Behind us, we heard a shot crack open the air. Bill stopped dead in his tracks. "What are you doing?" I said. "We gotta run."

Bill was so terrified, he decided he was gonna wait around for the police to come arrest him. He didn't want to die.

I was scared, too, but I wasn't about to get caught. My mother would kill me. I left Bill there to get apprehended while I walked home. I was a nervous wreck. Even though I was frustrated with my mother for drinking, I'd had enough sips of booze as a kid to know it could make me feel better inside, so I stopped at a store and bought half a pint of Thunderbird for thirty cents. "It's for Lily Mae," I lied. And as I walked home, I drank that cheap wine to calm my frazzled nerves. When I got home and crawled in bed, I pulled the covers over my head and clasped my hands in prayer. "Please, God," I said, weeping. "I hope they don't catch Bill."

They wound up catching Bill and Curtis and giving them probation. They couldn't charge them with much because they was just kids, but Curtis had to move in with his uncle out in Queens. Later, Curtis would explain to us what had gone wrong. "Man, we saw that guy flashing fifties and hundreds outside the bar," he said. "We had to get him. We woulda got that money and split, too, but when we took him around back, we emptied his pockets and couldn't find nothin. Later on, the cops told me the reason. They said, 'You dumb black bastard, he had on a money belt.'"

Encounters with the police were only deepening the bitterness and isolation I was beginning to feel. From what was happening to my mother and what would soon happen to my brothers and me, I was coming to understand that there was a darker side to the streets, one that was designed to destroy us.

CHAPTER 5

—

Firing Coffee

After my close call with the police, I saw the real danger of using violence to separate people from their cash. I didn't wanna be the kinda hustler who got money by overpowering people. I wanted to be one of those hustlers who outsmarted people. Even though I woulda whooped your ass if you called me a nerd back then, I recognize now that that's what I was: a hustling nerd.

I studied other people's hustles obsessively, always trying to find new angles and loopholes to make a buck. I wanted to create hustles no one had seen before. I paid special attention to guys like my cardsharp uncle, Fish Man Eddie, who never seemed to lose at poker but who no one ever caught cheating. How'd he do that? There was an elegance and a magic to it that I wanted to find a way towards.

When my older brother Cary was in seventh grade, he let me tag along with him to a dice game full of other seventh graders from his school. By that age, most boys were already getting pretty proficient at gambling. These kids knew the rules and might even have picked up a little strategy from their days watching lookout for older guys. I studied the seventh graders as they shook their dice and talked trash, imitating the older cats. My attention was drawn almost immediately to one player in particular, a gangly, awkward-looking boy wearing expensive-looking wingtips, who seemed to be on a different level than everyone else. I observed the careful way he held the dice, threw the dice, and placed his bets. He was beating everybody. "Must be my lucky day," said the kid, grinning like an idiot, though I could tell he wasn't dumb. Far from it. Under the mask, I sensed a knowledge. He was wiping the floor with the other kids, but just like my uncle Fish Man Eddie, I couldn't figure out how he was doing it. I watched him collect his handful of coins and bills, pocketing more money in a few minutes than my parents had given me all year.

After the game was over, Cary introduced us.

"Yo, Kenneth," said Cary. "Meet my little brother."

"They call me Killa," said Kenneth, trying to make his voice sound deeper than it was. Even then, I knew full well that Kenneth Williams wasn't no killer. I had a feeling that nobody called him Killa besides himself. It was hard to argue with his skills, though. He'd been killin everybody at dice. I needed to know what he knew, and as luck would have it, Killa wanted to teach me.

Soon, Curtis and I found ourselves official members of Killa's dice crew—the only members, in fact. "Anyone who's part of my crew," Killa told us, lifting a pair of green dice between his fingers, "gets to learn the secrets of hustling."

"Now do you wanna be regular hustlers?" Killa said, pacing in front of us, like a general in front of his troops. "Or do you wanna be Sols?" Curtis and I exchanged glances. We didn't know what he was talking about, but we nodded anyway. "Yeah, you think you're slick," he went on, staring us down. "But you don't know shit."

In hindsight, it seems kinda strange for Killa to have wanted to team up with third graders. Here was this teenager forming a crew with a couple kids. Why didn't he join up with guys his own age? Well, the respect he got from us he probably wasn't getting from older guys. We made him feel like somebody, and in turn he taught us how to get money from dice.

"You probably don't even know what a Sol is," said Killa.

He was right. We didn't.

Killa began to explain the secret world of Sols. A Sol, short for Solomon, is a street mason, somewhere between a magician and a scientist. There were only a handful of Sols in Harlem and not that many others who even knew what a Sol was. Being a Sol meant being part of a secret society passed down from one generation to the next. There was skill and technique to the dice game, Killa told us. He was passionate, articulate. A Sol was not a cheater, but a calculating mechanic, a strategist, someone who understood the laws of physics and probability, and the nuances of human psychology. A Sol had the wisdom of King Solomon. I liked it immediately. I could see that it required brains, and that was exciting. He wasn't just passing on a way to make money. He was also passing on an art form. And, though I didn't know it at the time, he was also planting the seeds for my first real career.

Even though Curtis and I had already started our own little playground hustles, card tricks I'd learned from my uncles, stealing unnoticeable amounts of reefer from my brothers and selling it at school, Killa was operating on a higher level. He schooled us on how to hold the dice, how to throw it. He schooled us about percentages and how to use mathematics to always win. "When you think of someone who gambles," he'd explain, "you think of someone who wanna get lucky and win some money. We ain't gamblers by that definition. We're Las Vegas. We gamble to make money off gamblers. That's what being a Sol is all about."

He taught us how to watch out for Ranks, players who tried to figure out your strategy and blow up your spot in a dice game. He schooled us on the art of elevation, a move which became known among Sols as "firing coffee." And just like a magician never reveals his tricks, a Sol never reveals his secrets—not even in his memoir.

"Try holdin em like Joe Jackson does," Killa said, demonstrating with his dice. When he saw our blank expressions, he said, "Hold on, y'all ain't never heard of Joe Jackson?" So of course Killa had to school us about Joe Jackson.

Known as Gentleman Joe, Joe Jackson was the grandmaster Sol of the Harlem dice world. He was a legend, the best, no one even near him, said Killa. Dice games were known to get rowdy, but Joe Jackson never lost his composure. Never raised his voice or cursed. He called everyone "sir," "Bet to you, sir," "Thank you, sir," all the while firing coffee in high-stakes games with all eyes on him. He was a true wizard, a member of the Georgia Boys crew of hustlers who'd come to Harlem during the Great Migration. Gentleman Joe knew all the angles. He could memorize numbers and percentages better than statisticians and mathematicians with advanced degrees. I was amazed to discover, much later on, that Joe Jackson couldn't read or write. It made his mastery that much more remarkable.

Joe Jackson became my hero, the hustler I looked up to the most, the one I learned the most from observing, standing at the edge of games to watch him work. Here was this legendary dice player who never drank, never smoked, never got high like the other hustlers. I only got the chance to meet him once, years later, when he came to watch me beat a hustler named Mr. Wonderful out of fifteen thousand dollars. I would have loved to fire on Joe, but we never got the chance to battle each other. From his example, I first recognized the power of self-discipline, style, and the true definition of cool. Joe Jackson was one of the flyest, most unprecedented men in Harlem.

Pointing to his nice wingtip shoes, Killa told us that any Sol who was gonna be part of his crew had to dress fly. "They dreaming about winning these shoes off you so bad that they start getting careless."

Killa gave Curtis and me a dismissive once-over. With our busted shoes and raggedy clothes, we were nowhere near fly. But we wanted to be. We already dreamed of dressing like Bumpy Johnson and his crew, but Killa schooled us on a new reason for flyness: it was a psychological advantage in the dice games. Guys at the dice game would see the nice shoes and clothes, and their egos would start getting the best of them, throwing them off balance. The strategy was to distract them with our flyness. If you flyer than the next guy, he wants to win you, not the game. I needed to get them to want to win me.

Killa scrutinized the outfit I had on, one of those colorful button-down shirts and creased jeans, a popular look which all the junior high kids were sporting at the time. I thought I looked slick. As the baby boy, I was always trying to dress older than my age, which meant dressing like my brothers. The only thing was, my parents couldn't afford to buy me the real button-down shirts and the jeans with the creases in them. So we'd take a pair of regular jeans and sew creases into them ourselves, and to replicate the shirts, we'd go down to the Garment District and buy Tintex fabric dye to renovate our plain white polos. We'd cut a hole in the collars, buy some buttons, and sew them on. Killa appraised the buttons of my shirt, the creases in my jeans. Then he shook his head. I got the message loud and clear.

Being a Sol wasn't only about practicing sleight-of-hand moves. I needed to dress the part. Clothes were always a means to an end. Nowhere was that more true than in a dice game. I just didn't know how I was ever going to afford the clothes.

So I started taking them. I knew the stores where Nat King Cole and Frank Sinatra and Miles Davis shopped, and I also knew where

Big Clyde and Bumpy Johnson and Joe Jackson went. So that's where I wanted to go shopping, too. The names of those stores recall a bygone era in the fashion history of the city: Phil Kronfeld, Cy Martin's, Nat Nevins, Leighton's, the Blye Shop. These were small specialty clothing stores where entertainers and gangsters went. Today, they would be considered boutiques with the same allure that Gucci and Louis Vuitton have for us now.

There was an art to shoplifting. If you had a bunch of guys, you could smash windows, knock over displays, cause a commotion, and run out with armfuls before they could catch you. But if I was going to shoplift alone in a particular neighborhood, at a particular store, I knew I had to be a little smarter than that. There was a store in the Bronx called Hearns, and next door to Hearns, a little farther up the street, was Alexander's. Alexander's was where we really wanted to go.

First, Curtis and I strolled into Hearns and asked for a shopping bag, just an empty bag. Hearns was a busy department store. They never questioned us, probably thought we were using them to cover our textbooks or something. We left with our Hearns bags, puffing them up with air on the way to Alexander's. We used the balloon effect to make it look like there was already something in it, so that when we walked into Alexander's, they thought we'd just come from shopping at Hearns, which put them at ease, because would a thief go shopping at Hearns before stealing clothes at your store? "Those young fellas look like normal shoppers to me," we imagined the clerks saying to themselves, paying us no mind. So we'd stroll into Alexander's and steal sweaters. This was long before sensor tags that would go off when you tried to leave. Soon, I had a whole collection of sweaters from Alexander's with a little area in our crowded bedroom at home dedicated to them, which I would keep real clean, real neat. When my mother asked how I managed to afford the sweaters, I'd say it was from selling newspapers and breathe a sigh of relief when she ain't make me swear on the Bible.

Now that I had the look, everywhere I went I carried two pairs of dice in my hand, determined to master the art of firing coffee. It took a crazy amount of skill and a lot of patience to become a Sol. In the years that followed, I never went *nowhere* without dice. I'd be standing on the subway platform, practicing my elevation technique. If they fell outta my hand onto the tracks, which occasionally happened, I'd go in my pocket and get my other pair. I used to stand in front of the mirror at home for hours, practicing and practicing and practicing. Over and over again, all day long, I'd repeat the moves until they were written in my body, committed to muscle memory. And it paid off. I was becoming proficient, dominating the little dice games in my elementary school and, later on, the games in junior high. I was on my way to becoming a Sol.

For a while, Kenneth was a good mentor to Curtis and me. I got a lot of jewels from him. One night, I didn't show up to a game because I'd gone to the movies with a girl. The next day he saw me and said, "Never let your dick beat you hustling." In his crude way, what Kenneth meant was never let your sexual appetite interfere with your goals in life. I never forgot that. After that, I started getting more cold-blooded when it came to chicks. "Lust has been the downfall of many men," Killa advised. "Even *great* men." Nothing came before hustling, not even relationships.

There are a lot of universal truths you pick up in the streets. Self-discipline as a path to enlightenment was something I'd learn about as an adult in my spiritual readings, but it's a lesson I first got from Killa.

Still, for all the street knowledge and dice skills I learned from him, Curtis and I were already surpassing Killa as dice players. I'd mastered all the moves that he knew and was even seeing new strategies that he wasn't picking up on. I think it helped that I was so young. I didn't have any preconceived ideas or limitations. Kids have a creative way of seeing things that older guys sometimes can't. I had fresh eyes and excitement about being a Sol. I wanted to take my craft to the next level. What other tricks could I learn? How could I make myself unbeatable? It was almost like I was possessed. Like I said: I was a hustling nerd. I had questions, and I needed to know the answers—*if* there were answers.

I started making trips to a shop in the Bronx that catered to Sols. I bought my first pair of crooked dice there, a set of Door Poppers, designed for rolling sevens and elevens in craps, which were winning first rolls. On one of my trips, I was shocked to notice another young kid browsing the goods. He was black, about my age, and he was looking over the books and paraphernalia with the same nerdy intensity as me. It was uncanny. There we were, two little black kids, way too young to be in a place like that. There was a certain type who would go to this store and they weren't no twelve-year-olds. They were middle-aged casino grifters. When the other kid and I caught eyes and nodded, I could tell that he'd never seen someone like me in that shop before, and he could tell that I'd never seen someone like him before. We were two of the youngest people who probably ever set foot in that store. We didn't talk that day, but years later, I'd come to find out that the kid's name was Russell. He was a Harlem cat like me, and in addition to becoming one of the most successful dice hustlers in Harlem, he'd also become my best friend and gambling partner. But that was still a long way off.

I was trying to perfect my craft, applying my knowledge in neighborhood dice games with other kids, beating them out of pocket change. Every now and then their fathers or grandfathers would try to hop in and get a piece of the action, wanting to teach me a lesson maybe, and I'd end up cleaning them out, too. I also had a group of younger kids that tagged along when I was playing and tried to learn the ropes from me. One of them was Joe Hammond, who became a street basketball legend, once famously arriving late to a game against Dr. J at Rucker Park then dropping fifty points on him in the second half. Guess who drove Joe to that game?

Ever since I'd read the fine print on the contract for Daddy's Easter suit, I knew that there was power in reading carefully. So to take my dice skills to an even higher level, I went to the Countee Cullen branch of the New York Public Library and read all the books on gambling. I said to myself, *I got to know everything.* The history, the percentages, the casinos. I familiarized myself with John Scarne's in-depth guides to gambling, studying each new edition inside and out, sharing my discoveries with Curtis. I paid close attention to the subtle differences between the information in the old gambling guides versus the new guides. There was a whole world of knowledge at my fingertips that no one had ever brought to the street dice games of Harlem.

The better I got, the more insecure and jealous it made Killa, who was sixteen now and, like my brothers Cary and James, had dropped outta high school. I saw that come out in the way he treated his girlfriend, accusing her of cheating and abusing her physically. Kenneth also started to snort heroin, the beginnings of what quickly became a life-altering habit. Killa couldn't even control himself no more, never mind the dice crew. So we went our separate gambling ways.

By the time I started attending Benjamin Franklin High School, on the far east side of Harlem, I wasn't that interested in getting a formal education anymore. All those years in school, and what had it gotten me? What had it gotten any of my brothers? Not long after Carl came home from his travels abroad, cutting a dapper figure in his uniform, Cary introduced him to heroin, and Carl got hooked. Then he went AWOL. In the end, military police came to the house and locked him away in Fort Dix, New Jersey, before he finally received a general discharge and left the military. If he wasn't home reading a book and chain-smoking Camels, Carl was out somewhere getting high. Cary had dropped out of school without a diploma and was living at home, drawing in his sketchbook and staying high. James had dropped out, too, and was living at home, using heroin and hustling, just like Cary and Carl.

My family was still poor. It crippled us how broke we always were. We couldn't afford food, clothes, vacations, nothing. My mother was drinking more than ever, and her drinking was taking a toll on her marriage. Things were so hard for everyone. I didn't want to have to depend on my family or ask them for anything. The pain of our poverty made getting money the only thing I cared about. The long-term benefits of getting an education seemed abstract at best and a lie at worst.

So I didn't go to school, I went around school. Each morning, I'd wake up, get my shoes shined, head to Benjamin Franklin, and start the dice games outside. No one knew I was a Sol: part of the code was secrecy. By sophomore year, I'd officially dropped out. I was making a good salary shooting dice outside the high school, around fifty dollars a game, the equivalent of four hundred dollars now. With all that cash, I was finally able to buy myself some new clothes. No more hand-me-downs from my brothers. No more sewing buttons and creases. No more shoplifting. My reputation was on the rise, too. Everyone in Harlem was starting to know me for three reasons. First, there was my dance moves, which had landed me with the name Dancing Danny. Second, there was my style, always looking fly. And lastly, there was my skill with a pair of dice.

Observing one of those dice games was a sharply dressed older hustler known for his chops on the tenor saxophone. Everyone knew him in the neighborhood as Dapper Dan, but when he saw me firing coffee outside the high school, with my shined shoes and Continental pants and collared shirt, an admiring look spread across his face. He waited until I'd finished collecting my winnings to ask me what my name was.

When I told him my street name was Dancing Danny, Dapper Dan shook his head. "From now on, I want people to call me Tenorman Dan," said the man formerly known as Dapper Dan. He pointed to me. "You the new Dapper Dan now."

PART II

—

MIDDLE PASSAGES

One three centuries removed
From the scenes his fathers loved,
Spicy grove, cinnamon tree,
What is Africa to me?

COUNTEE CULLEN,
"HERITAGE"

CHAPTER 6

———

The Cursed Game

The drug game is cursed. I say that to anybody who'll listen. I'm a broken record about it, but that's because I've seen what it does to people: to my brothers, to my friends, to my community. And I know what it did to me. Ever since we've been free, black people in cities have suffered from addiction epidemics. Before crack, it was heroin, and before heroin, it was alcohol.

But back in the fifties, the drug game was on the outskirts. People saw it as a fringe hustle, another way people made a buck in the underground economy, less lucrative than numbers running or fencing stolen goods. There were numbers kingpins, but no drug kingpins, and you didn't have shooting galleries and addicts lining up for dime bags in broad daylight like we'd come to see later.

Like alcohol, drugs have been a part of life for most of American history. Dope is as old as America itself and still used in every hospital as a painkiller. A medicine man traveling on the *May-*

flower allegedly had some dope on him. Thomas Jefferson was such a fan of dope that he grew poppies at Monticello. After the Civil War, people gave mixtures of morphine and alcohol to kids, called them "soothing syrups," and sold them legally over the counter in stores.

When I was growing up, there wasn't a huge underground market for cocaine or heroin, nor was there widespread awareness of their effects. We knew about junkies and pushers, but we didn't have the language to describe addiction, dependence, recovery, relapse. Most of the drug dealers in the neighborhood were known to snort a little cocaine or heroin every now and then. They were party drugs. Selling and snorting your own supply was an accepted part of the hustler lifestyle, as normal as taking a sip of whiskey. But as I moved through junior high and high school, the underground drug trade slowly began to take over my family and the streets of Harlem like some kind of biblical plague.

My first early teachers in the streets all got high. I used to run errands here and there for a hustler named Sonny Bishop, a real gangster, and he was always high on drugs. Being the inquisitive type, I used to ask Sonny why he did drugs, but he never answered. I kept asking him, until finally one day he said:

"Come on with me."

This was 1953, and I musta been nine years old, still worshipping the ground these hustlers and gangsters walked on. So I followed Sonny down into a dusty, musty basement on 129th Street. "Sit right there," he said, pointing to a turned-over crate. I sat, and Sonny took a seat right across from me. I didn't say nothing. Just sat there, watching him take out his little baggie of heroin and cook it with his cooker. I watched him pull it into his needle. I forced myself not to wince when he plunged the needle into a vein in his arm. The whole time, Sonny never said nothing.

Immediately, though, I began to see the transformation take place. Sonny started changing. His body changed, his eyes changed, his everything changed. He was nodding and fidgeting. I said to myself, *I guess that's what he's telling me.* That was the first time I ever saw someone cook up heroin. It wouldn't be the last time.

A few years later, when Curtis and I were in Killa's crew and I was starting to become more serious about being a Sol, Curtis had his first experience with heroin. He'd been gambling with Killa, the two of them secretly working as a team, as we sometimes did. I wasn't with them, but according to Curtis, this is what happened that night:

We were in front of Nick's Bar, shooting craps outside, and we were working together that night. Killa make a bank, I put up some money. We just trimmed everybody, nobody's got no money but me and Killa. After the game's over, I see Killa walk off with this junkie. Well, that's what he was, but I didn't know it at the time, because I was only thirteen. And this guy that Kenny walks off with is filthy-looking. I said to myself, *Why is Kenny going with this dirty-looking guy?*

So I followed them. They had the bleachers up there on 128th Street, where the ballpark was. And I watched Kenny and the junkie go up under the bleachers, and I kept sneaking up on him, because I wanted to know what was going on, what's he doing with this filthy guy. I mean, this guy looked like a mess. And me and Kenny, we stayed looking sharp from the money we made at dice. We wore fresh, nice clothes. We looked good.

When I snuck up on the two of them, they was shaking something up in a bottle top. They got the bobby pin on it, and they were holding lit matches.

I said, "What the fuck is that, man?"

Kenny said, "You don't want none of this here."

Now let me tell you how stupid I am. I said, "Well, what you doing?"

Killa tried to warn me again. He said, "Man, I'm telling you, Curt. You don't want none of this here."

I said, "Just give me a little taste."

Now, I'd tried reefer and sniffed cocaine before, but I had never even seen nobody cook up before. I said, "Give me a little bit." So that's what he did, before he tied up, Killa stuck me in the arm, gave me a skin bump, a tiny bit. And then he tied up and mainlined the rest into his arm.

All of a sudden, I felt sick. I got so sick that I regurgitated all night long. Couldn't keep nothing down. It was terrible. I said, "There's no way I'm trying this shit again." But when I woke up, I was nodding.

The first time you drink, you get sick. The first time you smoke cigarettes, you get sick. And the first time you use heroin, you get sick, too. But that next day, I started feeling the full effect, and it was different. I was oblivious to every-thing that was going on around me. I could escape reality. And I think that's what I liked. That's what got me.

By the time I got to high school, all three of my older brothers were deep in the drug game, having brokered a deal to get their own supply of French-connection heroin and their own little territory on Madison Avenue to sell it in. This was in the late fifties and early sixties, when heroin was starting to penetrate deeper into America, and the main source of product came through the Italian Mafia's supply chain, which ran from the Middle East and South Asia through France. The number of American heroin addicts would more than double in the ensuing decade, which many at-tributed to economic decline and soldiers returning from war in Vietnam, where heroin use was prevalent.

When they were first starting out, I'd often hang out with my brothers and their crew on the corner of Madison and 132nd Street, dancing, telling jokes, and trying to act like I was older and slicker than my age. They were pulling in good money, and now that I knew the powerful effects of heroin firsthand from having watched people around me shoot up, my brothers and their crew gave me an education in how to sell it.

One person to take the money, another for the handoff. Undercut dealers in nearby territories to grow your customer base. Never let a junkie start a tab. Never answer any questions from police, even if it's about other people. Just mind your business.

My charismatic, dancing-machine brother James, who'd been making a name for himself in the streets since grade school for his toughness and street smarts, was becoming a real player in the booming heroin trade. James was watching the older guys around us begin to turn a huge profit off the drug game, getting really rich, even richer than the numbers guys. Now the drug guys were the ones buying property, owning stores, driving big Cadillacs. James knew we needed to be right here in Harlem, watching and learning from them. All of Daddy's efforts to steer him away from the streets proved to be in vain. All those days spent polishing floors, the gentle nudges to get a good civil service job, the speeches about the value of honest work. James wasn't hearing it. He grew up to be such a force to be reckoned with that people in the neighborhood gave him the name Cesar, because it seemed like he was on his way to building his own empire.

While people like our sisters sought to leave Harlem and better their lives through education, the Day boys had other ideas.

"We gone stay," said Cesar. "And we gone rule."

At least, that was the plan.

When my father gave my older brothers his ultimatum—school, job, or get out—he was serious. Though my parents loved them, they couldn't stand to see their boys falling to dope. So when they finally got booted from the apartment, my older brothers started living in a rooming house not far from the spot where they sold drugs, a run-down building with cheap rooms, shared bathrooms, and bars on the windows. Their crew used to hang out there with them. Because I missed having them around the house, I would sometimes spend the night over there, too.

One night, alone in their shared room, I got an unintended peek at the wicked side of the drug trade, my first real glimpse of the curse.

I was reading a book for class, about to fall asleep, when one of my brothers' crew, this tall, light-skinned cat named Rico came barging into the room. It didn't surprise me that Rico had a fine lady on his arm; he was known to be a ladies' man. They wanted a place to be alone together. I could tell that they were both high. So I left the room for them and sat outside in the hallway, waiting for them to finish. Some time passed, then Rico opened the door with sweat on his forehead and his shirt buttons wrong. He had this blank look in his eyes I'll never forget. He walked out of the building and returned with two of his friends, Calvin and Shorty, who looked just as stoned as Rico. All three of them walked into the room and closed the door behind them.

I heard them taking turns with the girl. Then I heard her start to cry. When they were done, they came out into the hallway, laughing like it was a big joke.

Shorty must have caught me staring at them, must have sensed the fear underneath my expression. He pointed to the door and said, "You want some, little man?"

"Yeah, c'mon, take you a turn," said Calvin.

I was ten years old, a long way from even thinking about sex, and they were asking me to join them in a gang rape. I barely even knew what it meant to have sex or what had really been going on behind that door. "Nah," I said, trying to talk my way out. "She crying and stuff. She making too much noise."

That must have been a good enough excuse, because they

stopped bothering me. They let the girl go, and she disappeared out into the night, weeping, a transformed version of the lady who'd walked in earlier on Rico's arm. With her cries replaying in my head, I closed the door. It took a long time to fall asleep, and I don't know how long I'd been out before a series of loud blows shook my door.

Boom boom boom, like a big fist was pounding on it from the other side.

Oh, I said to myself, rising from where I slept. *This ain't good.*

When I opened the door, I was standing in the towering shadow of a police detective, and behind him Rico's girl and a man I didn't recognize. He turned out to be the girl's husband. The police officer was big, black, and mean-looking. He flashed his detective badge and started asking me questions. Did I recognize this woman? he asked, pointing to Rico's girl. Did I know who raped this woman? This was my first face-to-face encounter with a police officer. I remembered my brothers' lessons about minding my own business and keeping my mouth shut. Truth is, I didn't even really understand what rape was. I told the detective that I didn't know nothing.

But that wasn't enough for him. He grabbed me by the throat and lifted me off the ground, pinning me hard against a wall. My heart raced. My feet dangled in midair.

"I don't know nothing!" I cried. "I wasn't in the room!"

The detective let me go and started searching the other rooms in the building. Calvin had left already, so they couldn't do nothing to him. And Rico, even when they caught him, couldn't be charged because his encounter with the woman was judged to be consensual. But when they searched the rest of the building, they found Shorty unsuccessfully trying to rip the burglar bars from a window to make his escape. The cops took him away in cuffs, and he wound up taking the whole rape case himself and going to prison.

I was haunted by the way the detective had treated me and by the way those guys had treated that girl, like she was a toy, like she was less than human, offering her up to a ten-year-old boy. I was seeing what men in the neighborhood were doing to women— getting them strung out, abusing them, cheating on them. The way women were treated on the streets was deeply troubling to all the men in my family. We knew how vulnerable young women could be. We knew how they could be manipulated, traumatized, and forgotten by men, especially with heroin and cocaine so ingrained in the street lifestyle. If a girl was a drug addict, there was usually a man nearby who had gotten her hooked. Whatever we did in the streets, we made sure it never came anywhere near our sisters. We had to be vigilant. We had to be strong.

From the time I was old enough to fend for myself, around eleven or twelve, my parents put me in charge of my younger sisters. My brothers didn't live at home anymore, my mother was battling her own demons, and Daddy—nearing sixty—was too old and busy to keep track of the comings and goings of three black girls in Harlem. I took my father's mantra about protecting our women to heart, maybe a little too forcefully.

When my sisters got to be in their teens, my protective instincts went into overdrive. I knew the guys my sisters had crushes on weren't worth shit, even if my sisters didn't know.

I didn't play, and the boys in the neighborhood knew it. If I wasn't around when a boy came knocking to see Dolores, Deborah, or Doris, he didn't want word getting out that he'd spent time in the house with any of them without me present.

I can imagine one of them greeting a boy at the door, inviting him in.

"Is your brother Danny home?" the boy might ask.

"No," my sister would say, annoyed.

And that boy would be running from the building at full speed.

If you were trying to get with one of the Day girls, it meant you had to pump the brakes and back off. If a boy so much as mentioned one of my sisters in passing, that boy was getting his ass whooped. My sisters nicknamed me El Dictator. But I behaved like that because I felt that there were no men in our environment who were good enough for them, real men, men that they could build a life with. All the guys they knew, including me and all my friends and all my brothers' friends, we were in the streets experiencing the curse of the drug game firsthand.

I might have been a dictator, but it came from a place of terror at what happened that night with Rico's girl. I was seeing terrible things happen to women in the streets, smart, beautiful black women whose lives were ruined by falling for the wrong guy—and addiction was almost always part of the tragedy.

My sisters were dreamers, and my parents encouraged them to dream. My mother and father never said, "No, you girls can't do that." My sisters had their sights set beyond Harlem. They loved my brothers and me, but they needed to get away from us and become their own people, which they went on to do. All three wound up going to college, getting advanced degrees, breaking glass ceilings in the corporate world (Deborah), teaching (Doris), and community organizing (Dolores). But my brothers and I were seeing all these men hustling, getting money, buying real estate, driving big cars. That's what we wanted.

Our glass ceilings were a lot lower.

CHAPTER 7

——

Too Easy

From the outside, the hustler lifestyle might look glamorous and exciting. But it's all a lie. My early days in the streets, when I was learning the hustle and looking up to those older street guys, admiring the way they looked and acted and even held a cigarette, that was the most fun part of my entire hustling career. My hustling life after that was all pain, paranoia, and trauma that I'm still recovering from. The stress associated with the street—every true hustler wants to be away from that. The ones who might like the lifestyle are the ones who get high. They medicate to buffer themselves from how they feeling. But most real hustlers hustle in order to amass enough money to never have to hustle again, and for their children never to know the feelings associated with that life, because those feelings are the opposite of fun.

At fifteen, I was a high school dropout earning decent money hustling dice games here and there, applying my Sol knowledge and skills. When the dice money was slow, I would sometimes help my brothers out with their drug enterprise. Every now and then, I'd share a harmless little snort with them, like bartenders taking a shot at the end of their shift. Then, I'd go back home to crash with my parents and sisters, trying to play off my high. My mother and father weren't fooled and would get into heated arguments over my presence and behavior in the house. They knew their boys were selling dope, and they knew we was using, too. Even though Daddy had given all of us the "go to school, get a job, or get out" speech, he was the one coming to my defense in arguments with my mother. He had a soft spot for me, his shadow. My mother wanted me gone. The one time she caught me high, nodding off on the steps of our building in a daze, I didn't see her coming, and she smacked me with her big hands into the middle of next year. By this point, my relationship with her had completely soured. I know she hated seeing me high, same way I used to hate dragging her off the barstools of the Mona Lisa. We didn't like each other no more—we were getting in ugly fights, saying things to hurt each other, trying to get my father on our sides. Thinking about how much Daddy cared for us both, I can only imagine how hard that time must have been for him, to see the two of us struggling with each other and with ourselves. Their marriage was coming to a breaking point, and though there was probably other stuff going on between them, I felt responsible.

What the hell had happened to me? I used to be an aspiring writer whose poems and essays won citywide contests. I was the star student whose big shoes the teachers told my sisters they'd have to fill. The one who always had his nose in a book. Now who was I? A high school dropout. A dice-game hustler. An occasional drug dealer. A junkie. I couldn't grasp how my life had come to this. I was in pain, adrift, and it seemed like everyone around me was, too. The same brothers I used to stay up late with talking about music and politics had all quit school and were selling and using dope near the seedy rooming house where they lived. And when I couldn't take my parents' fighting at home no more, I accepted Cesar's offer to come join them and start selling drugs full-time. It seemed like an easy decision. The rent was only fifteen dollars a week. The risks were a little higher than with the dice games, but so were the rewards. My brothers were making steady money, more than Daddy earned working three jobs. Soon enough, I was just as good at the drug game as I was at dice and as I had been at school. I excelled at it. As my brother and teacher, Cesar, who was the leader of our drug operation, was clearly proud.

But soon after I moved in, it became clear that Cesar's grand ambitions of building a Harlem drug empire were not proceeding as planned. He was snorting nearly as much as he was selling, and before we even knew what was happening to us, my brothers and I were all developing addictions.

I had been in junior high the first time I tried heroin; I was hanging out in the hallway of our building when I saw my friend Elmo down the way. Elmo and I were co–point guards for our basketball team. We were the two most popular boys in school, and that day, Elmo was drinking with some of his friends who lived in my building. All of them were sniffing something, too. Elmo held out a folded matchbook with some powder cradled in it and said, "Here, man. Take a hitta that." I remember taking a one-and-one, which is when you sniff the dope through one nostril, then the other one, using a folded up matchbook to hold the powder. That night, I had gotten sick and thrown up just like everyone when they first try heroin. I knew I didn't want nothing to do with it. Or so I told myself then.

Now I was snorting it on a regular basis and would be for the next few years. We didn't realize it, but my brothers and I were already under the curse. Those years were a nightmare and a blur. I lost my touch with the dice. Usually a wiz with numbers and figures, I'd sometimes lose count of the dope profits, and Cesar would yell at me. We were all off our game, dangerously so. Once, while we were both high, Cesar got so mad about something money-related, he pulled a gun on me. Cary had to hold him back. "I ain't gone kill him," he said, trying to raise the pistol. "I'm just gone shoot him in the foot."

I didn't like what my brothers and I were going through, and neither did Daddy. One day, he came by the rooming house wearing a solemn expression. I thought he was planning some kind of intervention: our hero come to save us from heroin. Instead, he had something he wanted to tell us.

"Your mother and I ain't living together," he said. "She up in the Bronx now, but I ain't leaving."

After our building on Lexington Avenue was condemned and torn down to make way for new high-rises, my family had relocated to a building across Lexington Avenue that was condemned soon after they moved in. By the time my father settled in a subsidized apartment on Lexington and my mother moved to a newer project in Mott Haven, all my sisters had left home. My mother wanted my father to join her, but Daddy couldn't see himself leaving Harlem.

Had my parents been in love? Had they been in love and then, after some incident we'll never know, fallen out of love? Or was it something more gradual? I used to get so upset whenever any of my mother's male friends from church would pay her a visit while Daddy was out the house working. She'd get so angry at me for scaring them away. I thought I was protecting the Day women like Daddy taught me, but maybe I was getting in the way of her only real moments of companionship, of something like love. Maybe I'd gotten in the way of her happiness.

I recognize that part of the problem between my mother and myself was that I never gave her a chance to show that loving side of herself to me, because I was mainly interested in getting love from my father. Probably, whatever problems existed between the two of them, I helped make worse by clinging to my father and eating up all of his love. I never once stopped to ask myself about how she musta felt when Daddy went on his weekend poker binges. Did he have other women in his life that we didn't know about? What did love even mean to folks like my mother and father? What did love mean to me?

My brothers and I weren't shocked. We knew their marriage had been in trouble for a while. As much a hero as my father was to me, I can't speak to how good Robert Day was as a husband, if he gave my mother the love and companionship that she needed. Even so, they never officially divorced, and they cared about each other until the end. My father always checked up on my mother in the Bronx, helped her pay her bills with his pension. That the separation wasn't bitter didn't make it any easier to accept. We'd grown up in a house of joy and trust. For all their arguments and drama, we knew there was real, unshakable love between them. That was gone now. It felt like life was coming apart in every direction for our family.

But Daddy was a rock. He probably saw shades of his younger self in us, the young man who'd been strapped to a gurney in Bellevue. Daddy knew that turning our lives around meant getting clean. And I knew he was right. But as every addict can tell you, it's not about what you know is right. It's about the physical pull, the desire which is even deeper than desire. The curse. There was no Narcotics Anonymous yet, but there was a voluntary program at Beth Israel Hospital that Daddy had heard about. "Go see what they talking about," he said. My brothers didn't think they had a problem, but I decided it was worth giving the program a shot.

I didn't wanna get high no more.

When I arrived at the rehab program, I met a gangster I recognized from the streets, and the sight of him surprised me. Even more, it comforted me to find out from him that my brothers and I were not alone in our struggles. Lots of guys in the neighborhood were struggling in silence. Kicking heroin was gonna be the biggest fight of my life, the gangster warned me. It was gonna take a strength that most people didn't have. Coming from a guy like him, the words were powerful. Though I only spent one afternoon there, I left feeling motivated by his honesty and vowed to quit using.

More light came into this dark period thanks to my old friend Curtis. One day not long after my brief visit to the rehab program, I met up with him at the park to play basketball. When I got there, he was sitting on a bench looking at some documents. "What you doing?"

"I'm changing my legal documents," he said and showed me the forms. He was changing his age from seventeen to twenty-two.

"And what you gonna do with that?" I said.

"I'mma get a job."

The next time I saw Curtis was maybe a year later, and he was wearing a suit. He carried himself like a different person. He looked healthy. He looked professional. He told me how he'd taken his hustling into the corporate world and gotten a job with a big cosmetics and stationery company. The streets had given him a knack for sales and marketing, and the company loved him for it. He had stopped using now and was rising through the ranks. They'd just given him control of a branch out in Queens. It was the best news I'd heard in a long time. I was happy for him.

"You should come and work with me," he said. "Get away from all this."

Curtis was living in Queens, in a home that his grandmother had bought with money from a car accident settlement. I'd never lived outside of Harlem before, but my life was going nowhere fast. Anything seemed better than what I was doing. I wasn't the only one, either; Curtis had come back to the neighborhood and offered all of his old friends jobs at the cosmetics company. He was good like that.

So I moved out to Queens, and Curtis made me his assistant manager. I ran errands, cleaned up, made deliveries. Like Curtis, I had to dress up for work, my first time wearing a suit and tie regularly. Living and working in Queens with Curtis was an education.

Curtis started taking me to parties in St. Albans, where all the middle-class black people who'd made it out of places like Harlem had gone. James Brown had a house there, as did Count Basie and the boxer Floyd Patterson. I looked around these parties, and I saw black people dressed up, looking sharp, looking clean, dancing to Smokey Robinson, doing the "Mickey's Monkey." I was eighteen years old, and I'd never seen black people like this in my life. Doctors, lawyers, businessmen. Everyone who lived there owned their own homes. They had salaries, not as good as their white colleagues', but good enough. There was a different mentality out there, different personalities. At least in St. Albans, it seemed brighter, more hopeful. Curtis and I were brighter and more hopeful, too, both clean and getting in real good with the company. We were hustlers, we were fly, and as long as we were hustling for them, they loved us.

The company wanted to recruit more people to work in these black neighborhoods selling beauty products. They wanted black managers, too, so they put me in charge of one of their new stores in Queens. Being the cocky young hustler that I was, I thought I saw a harmless, victimless way to profit off of my newfound authority. I had friends who made money from the booming drug trade in Harlem, and thanks to my new promotion, I was entrusted with making bank deposits with large sums of company money. My teenage hustling brain whispered: what if I took the company money, bought a bundle of dope, gave it to some friends to sell, made a good profit, returned the original company money, then used the profit for another bundle?

Two close friends back in Harlem, the twins Herman and Thurman, agreed to help me with my embezzlement scheme. Both of them had followed a path like mine since the days when we were nine years old and would walk defiantly into the Mona Lisa together to retrieve our drunk mothers. They'd dropped out of school and were doing what they could to survive on the streets, selling drugs, often using them. They jumped at my plan. One weekend,

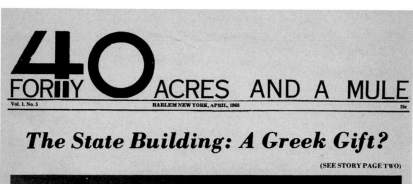

40 FORTY ○ ACRES AND A MULE

Vol. 1. No. 5   HARLEM NEW YORK, APRIL, 1968   25¢

The State Building: A Greek Gift?

(SEE STORY PAGE TWO)

My cover story for the revolutionary student newspaper *40 Acres and a Mule,* in 1968, warning my community against the danger of gentrification coming to Harlem. Later, I'd learn that gentrification is to Harlem as appropriation is to fashion.

In Accra, Ghana, in 1968, buying souvenirs to bring back to America.

Me and one of my various Peugeots, which I color-coordinated with my outfits and would ride through Harlem to find dice games, circa 1971.

Me and Dad near the Bridge Apartments on 181st Street in the early 1970s. I started buying him clothes so we could dress in the same style.

Me and Danny, Jr., in Florida around the time *Super Fly* came out, wearing our Ron O'Neal coats.

My brothers James (left) and Cary by the Harlem River in the early
1970s.

Standing in Monrovia, Liberia, next to my Fulani
tailor. He made all my clothes for me in Africa
and, years later, gave me the idea to make my own
clothes.

My first Mercedes-Benz, parked at 116th Street between Eighth and Manhattan Avenues, courtesy of my Frank Lucas gambling era.

I took this photo at the wedding of Frank "the Terror" James (far left). Frank was part of Nicky Barnes's crew. That's Nicky in the back and Big Smitty, Nicky's enforcer, directing traffic. Frank died in jail in 2018, and Nicky's still in witness protection.

Wearing one of the pastel suits I took to Africa, circa 1974. I traded this for art and new tailored clothes.

Me and my friend the kingpin New York Freddie at Western night at Club Le Cou Cou on 54th Street in the late 1970s.

Previewing the sign for the opening of the first Dapper Dan's store in 1982, with my friends Walter and Mimi Peterson.

My customized MCM Jeep, featured in LL's "Big Ole Butt" video, circa 1987. Took a week to paint and upholster.

One of the shoots Ted Demme arranged for MTV.

Photo by Wyatt Counts

not long after handing off the bundle to Herman and Thurman, I paid them a visit, expecting them to hand me a stack of bills to replenish the money I'd stolen from the company, with some left over for myself.

"We ain't sell nothing," said Thurman, handing me back the bundle.

I went back to Queens confused. Something wasn't adding up. Were they just lazy? Was the competition that stiff? The thought crossed my mind that Herman and Thurman might have been doing me dirty somehow, but I couldn't understand it. These were my friends, my brothers. When I finally got confirmation from someone else that they had in fact ripped me the fuck off—taking the original bundle, selling it, and using the money for a new bundle, which they handed back to me, pocketing the profits—I couldn't believe it. I had to find a way to replace the three thousand dollars I'd stolen from these white folks. So I started juggling money at work. I realized that this could end everything—not only for me, but for Curtis, too.

I saw red.

"Come on," I said to Curtis. "We goin over to Herman's house."

First, we stopped by Cesar's place. I needed to borrow his gun. He handed it over without hearing another word, because the less he knew the better. I tucked the pistol into my waistband, and Curtis and I headed over to Herman and Thurman's house. Before either of the twins could say a word, I pulled out my gun and held it to Herman's head.

"Don't do that," he begged. "C'mon, Danny. Don't do that."

Herman's pleading voice brought me back. I remembered how, if a bully would ever pick on one of us, we'd get the other two to come back and whoop his ass. We didn't even need to bother with getting my older brothers. The three of us would jump the bully ourselves. Together. We had each other's backs. And now here I was, standing over one of my best friends with a gun to his head. It was the same gun my brother had pulled on me not too long ago when he'd accused me of messing with his money. We were turning against each other. Brothers against brothers. Friends against friends. This was it. This was the curse.

I lowered the pistol and left.

My brief fly life in Queens had been nice while it lasted. I replaced the money, but not before an internal investigation was conducted into what had happened to the missing deposits. I lost my job. Curtis nearly lost his job, too, because of me. In the end, they didn't fire him, but they demoted him back to a worse branch of the company in Manhattan. Soon, Curtis was back uptown, hanging out in his old haunts, and he relapsed. And I found myself back on the avenues of Harlem with no better work than selling drugs, and no better way of escaping that reality than using drugs. I relapsed, too. In no time, I was back to using heroin on a regular basis. It didn't seem like things could get much worse. But they would.

Those years in the drug game was the darkest of my life. Through my late teens and early twenties, my dice skills vanished. My grasp of numbers and statistics—gone. Nothing about me was fly anymore. I had lost my way. I avoided my friends, not wanting them to see the physical toll of my heroin addiction. I was deteriorating mentally and physically.

The first time I got arrested, it was for selling drugs. All four of the Day boys were picked up by the same police officer and hauled off to jail. We later found out that one of our best customers had snitched, an older junkie who always bought his dope from us, who we thought was our friend and ally.

Daddy came down to the jail to make sure we were okay. Back then, they had these little booths for communicating with inmates, like phone booths. Daddy was running from booth to booth, checking in with all four of his boys.

"That was too easy," I told him, upset. It was too easy how they caught us all. We hadn't been careful because we was all using. Even though he didn't ask me to say it, I promised him that I'd never use or sell drugs again. "I ain't *never* doing this here."

Daddy nodded his head. Whatever we did, right or wrong, my father was there for us. Whether we got locked up or strung out or found religion, he was there. Never judged us. Never got angry. If we was letting him down or it was breaking his heart to see his children behind bars, which it must have been, he didn't show it.

Since it was my first offense, and since the severe Rockefeller Drug Laws were still a few years away, I got lucky, and they set me free soon after the arrest. We were charged with a violation of New York State Public Health Law, section 3305, for "the possession and control of controlled substances." They released Carl, Cary, and me, but my brother James, who had a prior violation, wound up getting a six-month hospital stay to rehabilitate. Back on the streets, I was walking around feeling, in the back of my mind, like my freedom was one mistake away. That sent me right back to medicating. I felt trapped in my own life. I knew the drug game was cursed and, as long as I was using, I'd be cursed, too.

I kept using. I kept making promises to myself that I'd quit.

I'd say to whoever was near me, "Yo, man, this is it for me. I'm done with this."

But for the life of me, I couldn't kick it.

Finally, I got arrested again. It wasn't a drug charge this time, but breaking and entering, which came with a heavier punishment than my first offense. I was facing up to a year in jail, possibly more. I didn't have the money for bail, so I had to wait for trial. I spent the next three months in the Tombs, which is the nickname for the Manhattan Detention Complex in Chinatown. Back then, the Tombs lived up to its name and then some. The conditions were a nightmare. A tomb would have been an improvement. There was vermin everywhere. Mice, roaches, lice. The cells and holding areas were way overcrowded. It was more than twice as full as it was designed to be. As the guards shoved me towards my cell, I passed by inmates sleeping on concrete floors without blankets.

I walked into my cell, the metal grate slamming shut behind me. I wondered if this would be my future from now on, caught in the cycle of dope and prison. The Tombs was the kind of place meant to crush the spirit, and it would have crushed mine if I hadn't found a way back to myself through the unlikeliest source of inspiration: an accused assassin locked up a few cells down from me.

CHAPTER 8

Tree of Life

I spent that first week in jail going through a bad drug withdrawal. My body wanted dope. I had the chills, the sweats. I was throwing up in the nasty shared latrine in my cell. Most of the day, I'd lie on the floor, doubled over from stomach pain. I'd never felt more depleted in my life. But as the days wore on, I started to recover. Slowly but surely, by the end of that first month in jail, I felt more like myself than I had in ages. I could feel the curse beginning to lift.

Then, at some point, I noticed a small army of guards march down our cellblock to a nearby cell. Why did they need so many guards? I watched, transfixed, as they took the inmate from down the hall past us. He was black, young. He looked about my age, clean-shaven with a wide neck and jaw. He was roped with muscles like a football player or soldier. What was most striking about him was the look on his face when I saw him pass. There were no furrows of anger between his eyebrows. He was not cutting his eyes everywhere, trying to look all hard. His face was calm, untroubled. His eyes seemed focused on something in the distance that the rest of us couldn't see.

I turned to my cellmate. "Who's that?"

"That's 3X," he said.

Then he clarified: "One of the cats that killed Malcolm."

His name was Norman 3X Butler, and he was one of three men convicted for the assassination of Malcolm X. All three of the accused were members of the Nation of Islam. I was familiar with the Nation because of their strong presence in Harlem and the onion-domed mosque they owned on 125th Street. Nation Members dressed in an unmistakable uniform of suits with bow ties. Those days, they were on as many street corners as the dealers, handing out copies of the *Muhammad Speaks* newspaper, which spread the teachings of leader Elijah Muhammad. The Nation had been around since the Great Depression. It was a black religious and political group that taught self-reliance and self-defense against whites, whom they saw as evil. But it wasn't until Malcolm X's rise to prominence that the group came into wider attention in America.

I was twenty-three now, and like almost every young guy in Harlem, I loved and idolized Malcolm. His murder had hit us all hard. He was on my Mount Rushmore of heroes, along with my father and master hustler Joe Jackson. He had been one of the most beloved and influential black leaders we'd ever had. Malcolm found eloquent, powerful words to express the rage and confusion that so many of us felt. He spoke truths about how racism was woven into the fabric of American life, from laws to news to movies to history, and he did it without compromise or apology. He taught a whole generation of us how to love and respect ourselves and how to resist the fear and self-hatred that surrounded us. A prominent young boxer by the name of Cassius Clay started making trips to Harlem to learn from Malcolm and soon changed his name to Muhammad

Ali, further spreading the popularity and influence of the Nation of Islam.

We loved Malcolm because Malcolm loved us. And Malcolm was us. He'd been a gambler, a pimp, a drug dealer. He'd spent his early years hustling on the streets of Harlem just like my friends and me, and he'd emerged from a six-year incarceration with a new sense of purpose as a member of the Nation of Islam, studying under the wing of Elijah Muhammad. But after Malcolm's pilgrimage to Mecca, Islam's holiest city, where he saw Muslims of all complexions from all over the world practicing their faith together, he realized that Islam was not a religion of hate but "a religion of brotherhood which includes all mankind." He came back, and he just couldn't see the world the way Elijah Muhammad did no more. Malcolm's realization led to an ugly, public separation. Articles started coming out in *Muhammad Speaks,* a newspaper which Malcolm had founded, calling Malcolm a traitor and implying that death might be appropriate punishment. The American government had already been targeting Malcolm. Now that he was advocating brotherhood with all, including white people, the Nation wanted him dead, too. On February 21, 1965, shots rang out as Malcolm stood to speak at the Audubon Ballroom on 165th Street.

Before his arrest for the murder of Malcolm X, Norman 3X Butler had been a lieutenant in the Fruit of Islam, which was a combat and security detail for the Nation. The Fruit of Islam were martial artists. These were guys you didn't want to mess with, which is why it took so many guards to escort him from our cellblock. Although he wasn't caught at the scene, authorities claimed he'd helped mastermind Malcolm's assassination, and they charged him with first-degree murder. To this day, Norman 3X maintains his innocence. He certainly didn't look like a man who was going to spend the rest of his life in prison. It was one thing to hear about a guy like 3X on the news; it was a totally different experience to see him in person.

Although he was not much older than me, Norman 3X com-

manded respect. Guards, inmates, lawyers, even the warden himself would come pay him visits. I'd never seen white men show a
black man, let alone a convicted murderer, that much respect before. I attributed it less to Norman 3X's alleged crime than to that
inner strength he seemed to give off. He had a glow to him, a quiet
commanding way of moving through the Tombs. It was like he
wasn't concerned with earthly affairs, but focused on something
higher.

Every now and again, a corrections officer would come by our
cell.

"Uh, listen. Mr. 3X wanted me to pass along a message to you
fellas," the guard muttered. "He wants you to know that Allah is a
most merciful God and that, if you get a chance, go read the Koran.
Okay?" I couldn't believe it. He had the guards delivering mes-
sages on his behalf about converting to Islam!

Now that I was through detoxing, I became fascinated by 3X
and curious about the teachings of the Nation. I'd never stopped to
fully consider my spiritual life. With time to think about something
other than hustling, I began to have those kinda questions. I attributed 3X's power to the fact that he didn't drink, smoke, or do
drugs, as the Nation of Islam expected of all its members. I started
to think about the power of self-discipline, and the more I thought
about it, the more I recognized its spiritual importance. What did
all my heroes have in common? Daddy, Gentleman Joe, Malcolm?
None of them drank or got high. The message sunk deep into me.
I started doing calisthenics in my cell. I said to myself, *You know
what, man? This is it. When I get out of this place, I'm living clean. I'm
eating healthy. I'm not drinking ever again and I'm not going nowhere near
dope. I'm gonna just endure. I'm gonna just be patient. I'm gonna just not
have.*

That's how a place called the Tombs started bringing me back
to life.

———

September 27, 1967. After three months in the Tombs, my day in court finally arrived. I saw my father sitting quietly in the rows behind me. We exchanged somber glances as I entered. Before the judge even took the bench, I'd already accepted my fate, and when my verdict on the breaking-and-entering charge came down as guilty, I started mentally preparing myself for my prison sentence. *Here it comes,* I thought. I was looking at more months, maybe a year, in prison up on Rikers Island. They told me to rise as the judge read out my sentence.

I was hereby sentenced to a term of three months in a correctional facility, which I had already served; therefore, I was free to go.

The judge had a look on his face like, *And don't come back.*

As the surprise and relief wore off, I hugged my father, my first real human contact in a long time. I couldn't wait to get out of that place. They returned my pants, my jacket, and what few dollars I had at the time of arrest. After I was processed, I hurried outside of the courthouse and drank in the air. It was a warm, beautiful day. I was free. But "freedom" was not just a legal term. To be truly free, I knew I had work to do.

I walked back uptown and didn't stop until I reached the Tree of Life bookstore on 125th Street. After seeing the spiritual intensity and commitment of a guy like Norman 3X Butler up close, I was inspired to seek out a path towards my own truths. Why had it taken me so long to address my inner life? Having grown up in my mother's Holy Ghost church, I associated spirituality with organized religion, which I'd been turned off to from observing the corrupt ways of local Harlem pastors. I believed in the power the Holy Ghost had for some people, but I didn't feel it the way they did. I wasn't spooky, meaning I didn't believe in walking on water, turning water to wine, and all that. If I was going to find a path to a higher or deeper truth about the universe and my place in it, I'd have to make it myself.

I had so many questions now about my purpose, and what it meant to live a good, strong, healthy life.

———

If there's one thing I knew, it was that I'd never settle for less than a full explanation. I'd have to interrogate everything, the same way I'd learned how to master a pair of dice and become a Sol. I'd have to be focused and deliberate. I'd need to read my way through this. My life felt like it depended on it.

When I opened the door of the Tree of Life bookstore, I was only vaguely aware that I was starting out on a search for enlightenment that would take me through the world's major religious texts, philosophical movements, and scientific insights, a spiritual quest that continues to this day. I have found ideas linking the philosophers of ancient Greece with the gurus of India, symbols in Judeo-Christianity that resonate with the freemasonry of ancient Egypt. Every science or spiritual book I've read has provided a hint about understanding the great mystery of existence. God or science or soul, I needed to define that mystery for myself.

Tree of Life was an intellectual bastion in Harlem. In addition to books, they had a space in the basement where speakers like Dick Gregory and veganism pioneer Viktoras Kulvinskas would hold readings and lectures. The main space was packed to its high ceilings with books. New hardcover novels sat in bright, well-organized piles on the tables. There were African wood carvings tucked into every corner and on tabletops, as though keeping guard over the merchandise. High atop the walls were framed black-and-white photographs of black heroes, and dominating your field of vision when you stepped in was a nearly life-size oil painting of Malcolm X. He towered over the shop, standing at a lectern in a suit and narrow tie, two leather-bound books tucked under his arm.

Tree of Life had a small curated section on health and spirituality that I immediately gravitated towards. I bought three important books that first day out of jail. Since the inner strength of Norman 3X had made me interested in the Nation of Islam, I bought two of Elijah Muhammad's books, *Message to the Blackman in America* and *How to Eat to Live.* I reached for another book whose title intrigued me: *Man's Higher Consciousness* by a white alternative healer and mystic named Hilton Hotema. I'd never heard of him before, but I flipped through the opening pages. "Poverty, Want and Sickness are the work of man. They are the products of his habits which correspond with his desires. He increases his burdens as he multiplies his wants. The less man needs the more complete he becomes." There it was again. The message of power over self. Hotema took it to another level, saying that people could live hundreds of years and didn't need food to survive. Why do we eat meat, Hotema asked, if most animals with teeth like ours are herbivorous? I bought the book, and it started bringing everything together for me. Hotema's work became one of my most important spiritual guides.

My time in the Tombs getting clean also had me thinking about how drugs had harmed so many of my relationships, particularly the one with my mother. We hadn't been on the same page for so long, but now that my mind was clear, I could see that it was our shared pain that was at war, not us. Upon my release, she agreed to let me stay with her in the Bronx while I got back on my feet, my first attempt to truly understand her as a person.

I found her in a bad way. My brother Carl, who was thirty years old and had never stopped using drugs, was living in the apartment with her. Neither of them left the house much. Carl stayed in his room, chain-smoking and reading books, while my mother laughed and drank in the next room with her girlfriends. For all her outward displays of normalcy, she was a shadow of her old self and getting frailer and sicker by the day. Somewhere along the line, the world had broken this charismatic, glamorous woman. I thought about the part that my brothers and I played in that, how much it must have hurt her to see us fall to addiction, just like her. But I also knew this might have been a truth too painful for her to admit to herself. I thought back to the poems I'd read to her in elementary school and thought about my mother's deferred dreams, the dreams she had for herself and for us. I was glad for the time with her, but it was hard to see her like that, especially at a time when I was so focused on my own physical and metaphysical health.

On my next visit to Tree of Life, I picked up *Malcolm X Speaks,* a book of Malcolm X's speeches. One line in particular hit me. "If you want to understand the flower," said Malcolm, "study the seed." In other words, if you wanted to get to the bottom of something—a question, a problem—you had to go below the surface. You had to look at the roots and work your way back to what was in front of you. Studying the seed meant looking into myself, and it also meant reading history.

The drug game was threatening to destroy my life and the lives of my brothers, but we barely knew what heroin was or how it originated. I wanted to understand it, especially after coming across a passage in *Man's Higher Consciousness* about the "poisonous properties" of the "dangerous narcotic from juice of poppy." I started reading my way under the surface of the problem, trying to find the seed. I read about how opium had been around since ancient human civilizations, who called it "the plant of joy." The Egyptians were the first to mass-produce it and had a drug empire across North Africa and Europe. King Tut was a kingpin, too.

I kept reading, learning about how heroin became one of the building blocks of the Western world. When British companies colonized India and started exploiting the Indians, they took control of the drug game, setting up a dope pipeline from India to China, America, and Europe. The profits were so outrageous, Wall Street jumped in. John Jacob Astor became America's first multimillionaire thanks in part to drug money. Europeans fought to maintain their drug monopoly in China, which led to a bloody war called the Boxer Rebellion, an anticolonial uprising that the colonizers brutally put down. I started to think about the greed and destruction that seemed to follow the drug game throughout history. The drug game was cursed. History just confirmed it.

Because the Nation of Islam recognized the drug game for the curse that it was, I started attending regular meetings while I was living with my mother. I was happy to have found a community who encouraged my spiritual growth. My brother Cary, who had joined the Nation and changed his name to Omar, wanted me to go all the way. He wanted me to convert. But at the time, I was also reading a lot of Eastern philosophy and other metaphysical books. When I measured what I was reading against my environment, what struck me most was the difference between what black people in America was going through in the sixties compared to white people. People like the Beatles and Janis Joplin were rebelling against the social and spiritual structure, helping to raise the consciousness of white people in America. You had people going to India, studying Transcendental Meditation. White people were seeking out their spiritual roots, outside of religion, while we were seeking out our cultural roots. We weren't challenging the core of ourselves and the universe the way they were. To me, we should have challenged the church, but we didn't. Our community was so focused on understanding and asserting our own identities as black people that we missed out on the deeper spiritual liberation. Right or wrong, while we were looking for this physical blackness, white people were finding this metaphysical thing. I said to myself, *I can't let this spiritual stuff pass without understanding it.*

Metaphysics is the last stage in the evolution of any cultural form, and those who understand that are the ones who push culture forward. When Coltrane started getting metaphysical with an album like *A Love Supreme*, I said to myself, *Oh, that's where I need to be.* Jazz went to such a high level that it lost something and had to die and start all over again. Now we're watching rap begin to strive for the metaphysical. When I look at a song like Kanye West's "Jesus Walks," I say to myself, *That's it! That's where we need to be. That's what we need to gravitate towards.*

I thought there were some flaws in the Judeo-Christian and Muslim ways of thinking, and I had problems with the Nation of

Islam's mythologies about white people and their emphasis on them as biological devils. That never rang true for me. But in their own way, the Nation got me thinking seriously about my place in this world as a black person and what freedom truly meant to me on a cosmic level—more flowers I wanted to understand, more seeds I needed to study. So I questioned and read and began to feel myself change from the inside out.

CHAPTER 9

—

Home

Even as I reached for a higher purpose, there was still a part of me that I struggled with: my love life. Which is so complicated it could be its own book.

When it comes to love, the first thing you gotta understand about me is that I'm a street nigga. That don't mean I don't respect women. Of course I do. It don't mean I never fell in love before, either. Of course I have. It just means that I came of age with a different mentality about romantic relationships, one that's long been in conflict with my spiritual development.

See, when you a street nigga, and a popular nigga in the streets like I was, and you ain't a junkie or a deadbeat or an abuser, and, on top of that, you dress the way I dress, which is to say flyer than almost everybody, you definitely gonna have women coming after you saying, *I wanna have his baby*. A lotta the women I knew were the kinda women my mother didn't want my sisters to become—

girls who were part of the street life. Those kinda women wanted a man that they could trust to provide for them, even if they couldn't trust that man to be faithful. At least, that was the way I saw it at the time.

When I met my wife, June, in 1968, I was in the middle of turning my life around. I had crashed an Omega Psi Phi fraternity party on the campus of City College in West Harlem. The party was full of bougie black coeds, and as a recovering heroin addict and high school dropout recently released from jail living with his mother in the Bronx, I felt like a fish outta water. I didn't have but two pairs of pants and some dice to my name, but I still went to the party looking as fly as I could. Navy-blue blazer, gray pants, and a crisply ironed white shirt. Though June didn't know it at the time, those were the only real clothes I owned. She says now that it wouldn't have mattered to her.

We danced and got to know each other. June lived on Avenue D in the East Village with her mother. She had an interest in technology and studied data processing early on. She'd even been accepted with a full four-year scholarship to NYU, but somehow that had fallen through and she'd ended up focusing on bookkeeping at community college. I asked for her number, and she gave it to me. It took me about a week to finally call her, but once we started talking, we never stopped.

June would invite me over to her mother's house for food. "I'll fix you something," she would say, and I'd bike down to the East Village. I've never been an eater. Years later, when I was nonstop busy running the shop, I used to get angry that I had to take time out to eat. I always wanted to be like the Silver Surfer, who could just look at the food and absorb it through his eyes. But June's food was something else. There'd be rice and peas, grouper, yams, collard greens. No soul-food place in the world could touch them meals. I'd go down there, stuff myself, lie on the couch, and pass right out. I loved those meals so much I took pictures of them. She didn't tell me until much later that it was her mother who was really doing the cooking.

Love is partly good timing. When June and I met, I was just getting sober and spiritual and beginning to turn my life around from the inside out, and because of that, we developed a special connection. The daughter of strict Caribbean immigrants, June had the same humble goodness as my sisters—smart, kind, a gentle sense of humor. I wanted a better future than my past, and June was part of the future I saw for myself. We had a daughter, Danique, the following year.

Before I met June, I had already fathered two little boys—Chuckie and Danny, Jr.—with two different women. Part of the reason I had to hustle so hard and make so much money gambling was so I could send my two sons to private school, an agreement I'd made with their mothers. It would have made things a lot easier if I coulda remained faithful to one woman. But I couldn't—not even to June.

After June and I had Danique, it would be another ten years before we moved in together. During that time, I went on to have three more kids—Daniella, Ayeisha, and Malik—with three other women before June and I had our second child, Jelani, in 1985. My final experience with fatherhood was my youngest child, Tiffany, the result of an affair with a dancing partner.

I've been clear with every woman I've ever been with how I feel about sex and relationships and procreation. I consider sex a deeply spiritual and meaningful act. Before each of my kids was born, their mothers and I had an agreement about the way I wanted them to be raised. Based on my reading of *Prenatal Origin of Genius* by Raymond Bernard, I wanted them all to be raised vegetarian until they were old enough to pay for their own food. They would all be sent to private school. I made sure they would always have a house. And thanks to a life insurance policy I took out, they had a large sum of money coming to them in the event of my demise. Part of the reason I hustled so hard was so I could provide for my children in ways that my parents hadn't been able to for me.

I'm deeply proud of all my children. But looking back on the decisions I've made, I know I could have done better by them and their mothers. As a father, I've wanted to play a role in their lives, but I'd be lying if I said it wasn't complicated. As much as I've tried to provide emotional support and guidance, I wasn't always there for them when they needed me. If there's any mending that I have to do with what's left of my life, it's to leave a legacy that my children and their children can tie into and feel good about. I know that's the hole in my soul these days.

My promiscuity is tied to the fact that I still wrestle with the macho mindset of the street and maybe also the traumatic generational memory of slavery, which used our desire against us, tore families apart for profit. I don't mean that to sound like an excuse. I'm sorry for the way I've treated the women in my life. The last frontier is always mastery over self, in particular what the sacred teachings call the lower self. For men like me, that means understanding your own sexual desires and relationship to women. As much as I tried to follow spiritual teachings and conquer my lower self, I never succeeded. My mentality hadn't quite transformed into a better version of myself. The spiritual stuff had set down, but it hadn't fully spread out.

Even though I've fathered children outside of our relationship, June is the one woman I've shared my life with, the one I pooled my money with to move into our brownstone together, the one I trust with my secrets, the one who kept encouraging me to go into fashion and leave gambling behind, the one who stuck by me, the one I call my wife. But I can't tell June's story. I can't pretend to tell the story of any woman I've been with. As someone who understands the indignity of appropriation, of having your life and contributions erased by those with more power, I'm not going to sit here and do the same thing to the women in my life.

——

I couldn't go back to selling drugs, but I had to figure out a way to support my two young sons, Chuckie and Danny, Jr. The only other hustle that had ever put steady money in my pocket was gambling. It was time to hit up the dice games again. Now that I wasn't using drugs, I got my touch back in no time. I kept current on the latest Sol literature. Anything about hustling, I would read. Some books had stories about old-fashioned techniques, and I had the real-world experience, so I worked on putting the two together: my book knowledge with my street knowledge. I applied those old-time hustles and con games to street craps and kept switching it up so no one caught on to what I was doing.

My relationship to hustling had changed. The books I was reading about religion, science, and spirituality were showing me that it took self-control to succeed. The power you brought over yourself from inside was what made the difference. That applied to any aspect of life, whether you were a civil rights leader, a fashion designer, or a hustler. The only difference between a master dice hustler like Gentleman Joe Jackson and a community leader like Malcolm X was that one was in the streets making money and the other was onstage making change. Point is, they both possessed a self-discipline that set them apart, a power over themselves that separated them from their surroundings. I began to aspire to that, too.

While I was still at my mother's apartment, I rode my Peugeot bicycle all over the Bronx, dropping in on dice games and trimming guys left and right. Almost all the guys I was gambling with were drug dealers. They were the only ones in the streets who had that kind of money to bet. With the dope game booming, there was more cash in each new game. I wasn't specifically targeting the drug dealers, but I didn't feel remorse about hustling them, either. I was throwing with purpose: to support my kids and save up to make my next career move. The more I saw dice as a means to an end, the better I got. I knew that the same big egos that made the guys I gambled with good drug dealers could also make them vulnerable in a game that relied on strategy. I started thinking about how I could use their lack of self-knowledge against them. In addition to the other tricks I had up my sleeve, playing mind games gave me an advantage. I had a newfound appreciation for the psychology of a dice game, and as a result, I was becoming unstoppable.

I needed to find a way off the streets, but until I figured out what that would be, I was content to hustle dealers out of their drug money. For the next ten years, as I slowly found my way towards the fashion game and money from the drug trade flooded Harlem, dice became my primary income, my main hustle.

One day, riding my bicycle through the Bronx and down into Harlem, dice-game proceeds stashed in my sock, I caught sight of a group of young guys I recognized from my school days hanging out in front of a nondescript storefront. I slowed my bike down, sensing another hustling opportunity, but they weren't playing dice. A guy who looked like he coulda been a hustler stood before them.

"Dig this," said the guy. "I been in your shoes. I know y'all left school and don't see no point in this education shit, but I'm telling you, this here's the way to a real future. You wanna future, young-blood?"

It turned out he wasn't just some old head trying to hip us to a new get-rich-quick scheme. He worked for the Urban League, a nonprofit that helped connect poor people in the community with education and employment opportunities. But this guy didn't sound like no teacher. He was speaking our language. He was dressed like guys we knew and he wasn't talking down to us, like we was dumb. He was trying to connect. I leaned my bike against the building, and a few of us followed him inside the storefront to hear him out.

The program was called Harlem Prep, and before mismanagement forced it to close a few years later, it was a cutting-edge experiment to get alienated young people like me off the streets and put us back on a path to college. While it lasted, it was one of those rare success stories in Harlem, luring street kids into casual educational sessions like the one I'd just stumbled into. No pressure, no strict timetable. People like legendary history scholar Yosef ben-Jochannan was among those who taught at Harlem Prep, instilling students with a sense of pride in their African heritage. Once we were ready, we could enroll in a more rigorous course schedule to transition towards enrollment at Newark Preparatory School, a private high school in New Jersey. I signed up on the spot and, at twenty-three years old, started attending regular classes at the storefronts to get my high school diploma.

The Urban League also put out a monthly newspaper called *40 Acres and a Mule,* run by students in the Harlem Prep program. It'd been a long time since I'd thought about writing, but the opportunity to express myself was appealing. The young people on the staff wrote poems and essays and made illustrations about issues affecting the community. I was coming into a greater consciousness about myself and my reality and had a lot to get off my chest. So in addition to taking classes, I started writing for *40 Acres and a Mule.*

The name of the paper symbolized its black radical spirit, a reference to Abraham Lincoln's promise of land redistribution to freed slaves after the Civil War, a promise that the government retracted. It was an angry name befitting our angry times. At the end of the civil rights era, my generation was seeing the same empty American promises all over again. Following the assassinations of black leaders like Malcolm X, Medgar Evers, Fred Hampton, and Martin Luther King, Jr., we were waking up to the lies of the American dream, and we refused to keep quiet. By giving students a forum to write and think about the issues of the day, *40 Acres and a Mule* took the message of black self-reliance and self-defense to journalism. They were giving us a voice.

The year I joined the paper, construction had begun on a new building on 125th Street, a nineteen-story development that would become the tallest building in Harlem. Proposed by the state as an attempt to revitalize the neighborhood with government jobs, the Harlem State Office Building seemed to me like an old-fashioned con job. Although the word "gentrification" hadn't yet come into fashion, people were already feeling a lotta bad blood about government attempts to change the community, especially when our needs were always kept in the background. My editorial about the new building landed on the cover of *40 Acres and a Mule,* with a picture of the architect's model of the building reimagined as a Trojan horse. "Why should we struggle to get Harlem rehabilitated for the sake of being integrated?" I wrote. "We in Harlem should first try and get our Harlem controlled by us: by increasing Black business ownership and having more voice in the school system."

I was writing and publishing pieces for the newspaper with regularity. I wrote about drugs, the Bible, whatever was on my mind, often inspired by my spiritual readings.

I won't conform to society
Think what you want of me.
I can't adjust to a country
unless I'm totally free.

In every new issue, at least a couple articles, opinion pieces, or poems had the Daniel Day byline. I was surrounded by other passionate young people from the community looking to express themselves and turn their lives around. One of them, Victor Hernandez Cruz, would go on to a distinguished literary career as a member of the Nuyorican poetry movement. When I was promoted to the editorial board, I started to think, *Maybe this journalism game ain't half bad.* Writing was something that came easy, something that gave me pleasure, and I was encouraged to believe that there might even be a future in it for me.

As part of the street academy program, which had the sponsorship of big corporations like Chase Manhattan Bank and Pan Am Airways, we had access to professional people in the mainstream world for the first time. All these black scholars, white publishing professionals, and people from major media companies would come and teach us how to write and edit. I got to spend a day tagging along with a reporter from *The New York Times,* an opportunity that put me in the room with Mayor John Lindsay. I began to seriously wonder if journalism was gonna be my way off the streets.

The Urban League definitely seemed to think so. After my first year in the program, a couple of the organizers took me aside. They said that they'd been admiring my work on the paper. They had contacts at the Columbia School of Journalism and wanted to know if I'd be interested in attending a summer program for emerging journalists. Not only that, they were offering to pay my way.

"What do you think, Mr. Day?"

What did I think? I didn't know what to say, but yeah. *Yeah yeah!*

I thanked them and rode my bike home, back to my mother's place in the Bronx. I found her in the living room with one of her drinking buddies. When I told her and Carl that I was going to attend a program at Columbia to help me become a journalist, they congratulated me, and she smiled the same way she used to when I would read her my poems.

Whatever had broken my mother's spirit seemed like it had moved on to destroying her body. She was fading before our eyes, and since she hated doctors, she did her best to hide how sick she really was. Within a year, there'd be nothing any doctor could do to save her. My father, who was retired but still taking on odd jobs, would visit regularly to drop off money and beg her to see someone about her health. So would my sister Dolores, who was living in an apartment in Harlem and working as a secretary at Chase Manhattan Bank.

Otherwise, Omar had a life in the Nation of Islam that kept him busy, while Cesar was still out there running the streets, hooked on heroin. We didn't see much of them. We didn't see much of my sister Deborah, either, who had a civil service job and a two-year-old baby girl with her high school sweetheart. My youngest sister, Doris, moved out of my parents' house when she was sixteen, fed up with the chaos of our family and growing sick of city life, and would soon leave New York permanently for Virginia.

But it didn't matter who was there for my mother or who wasn't. There wasn't nothing we could do to stop her from sitting alone all day long, dressed immaculately as always, drinking the hurt away.

Despite the sadness I felt watching her health deteriorate, things were starting to fall into place for me. By focusing on self-discipline and using my reading and writing to rise above the world around me, I was already seeing positive things start to happen. Hadn't I always loved writing? Hadn't I been winning awards since elementary school? This was my destiny.

Wasn't it?

Shortly after I was offered that journalism scholarship, a first step in my newfound career, this cool-ass white boy started talking to me about Africa. His name was Bill Stirling, and he was an English teacher for Harlem Prep. Later, he'd go on to become the mayor of Aspen and a Democratic delegate for Colorado, but back when I knew him, he was an idealistic twenty-six-year-old—only two years older than me—who had already volunteered with the Peace Corps in Kenya and was fluent in Kiswahili. Because of his first-hand experiences in Africa, he was heading a new program to take a group of black students on an immersive, three-month, all-expenses-paid trip to the motherland. "Black Americans," he said at the time, "feel a compelling need to discover a heritage that has been denied them for centuries." Thus was born the 1968 African Summer of the New York Urban League.

Harlem was in the midst of an Afrocentric phase. There were shops all over the neighborhood selling Ashanti fabrics, Igbo sculptures, Ethiopian crucifixes. We were reading books that revealed suppressed histories of African contributions to science and civilization, like George G. M. James's *Stolen Legacy*. A new generation of young black parents were giving their newborns African names. When I was growing up, America had us really brainwashed to be ashamed of Africa. We were ashamed of our skin, our features, our hair. We called ourselves "colored," not "black." Back when I was young, if you called someone black or someone called you black, you'd get in a fight with them, because the term was seen as an insult.

But now here was James Brown and here was Malcolm X and here were so many others saying black was beautiful. The generation that came up in the late sixties and early seventies were the first African Americans to embrace the term "black" for themselves. You could see the transition in hairstyles, too. People who used to straighten their hair started growing big Afros, and all the light-skinned guys who had the pretty hair stopped using product. Unlike the people in my generation, my children would not grow up using "black" as an insult. Black was loud. Black was proud. Black was beautiful.

Black consciousness hit me as hard as anyone. So when Bill and the director of the newspaper told us about the Africa trip, I recognized it for the once-in-a-lifetime opportunity that it was. You know, when you're looking for a reason to substantiate your blackness and who you are, it takes over all your other ambitions. I needed to understand my full identity as a black person. Africa held a key.

Just one problem. The dates of the trip conflicted with my Columbia scholarship. I could do the journalism program, or I could do Africa. But I couldn't do both.

———

Best believe I chose Africa.

My sponsors for the journalism scholarship seemed confused when I told them my decision. Did I know that an opportunity like Columbia didn't come around every day? Was I sure I wanted to pass it up? The way I saw it, the Columbia School of Journalism was just down the street from where I'd been my whole life. If I wanted to, I could check out Columbia any day of the week. It would be there when I got back. But when would I get the chance to go to Africa again? My whole life, all I'd known was Harlem. I needed to see the motherland and experience it for myself. I needed to study the seed of my own existence and the seed of all humanity.

Imagine, twenty-five young black guys who'd known nothing but the streets of New York City, all of us standing with our bags near the Pan American World Airways ticket counter. Bill, our tour director and chaperone, stood with our passports, waiting for our tickets to be processed and printed. Pan Am, one of the Urban League's major corporate sponsors, had donated the tickets. But soon we heard Bill's voice take on a frustrated edge. I saw a supervisor for the airline make an apologetic face. Something was wrong.

"Well, guess we ain't goin to Africa," someone muttered.

Quickly, our tour leaders hopped on the phone, trying to pull some kinda strings. It turned out that when US government officials discovered that a group of radical black students from Harlem were planning on traveling through Africa for eleven weeks, they had applied pressure to Pan Am to stop us. They'd canceled all our reservations a few days prior, but they'd waited until we got to the airport to tell us.

Furiously working the phones for the next hour, our tour leaders were able to secure the money for airfare from an anonymous benefactor, a rich black man in upstate New York whose name we never learned. Without him, we woulda never been able to get on that plane. We ran through the terminal to catch our flight, tickets in hand, no thanks to our government or corporate sponsors. It wasn't until long after that we learned the depth of what had happened and how close we'd been to missing out on the trip entirely. That wasn't even the end of our suspicious travel difficulties: once our plane touched down in Ghana and we were processed through customs, all our passports magically disappeared, only to reappear a few days later at the American embassy in Accra. It seemed like our country didn't want a bunch of young radical journalists going anywhere outside the United States, especially not on a trip to Africa during its revolutionary socialist years. Recently, one of the organizers of the trip whom I'm still in touch with told me something that probably shouldn't be surprising: secretly, the CIA had someone follow us the whole time.

In the lead-up to the trip, I'd been studying African history and politics. The entire continent was in the midst of sweeping change. Over the past twenty years, African people had united from Senegal to Zimbabwe, Congo to Angola, to overthrow their oppressive colonial shackles. A generation of revolutionary black leaders like Kwame Nkrumah in Ghana and Julius Nyerere in Tanzania and Jomo Kenyatta in Kenya were founding a new black African identity. Their examples were already inspiring us from afar, but to be there as a young black man at that point in history was truly unforgettable.

Oh, man. This trip was something. We went everywhere: Tanzania, Ethiopia, Sudan, Egypt, Ghana, Uganda, Kenya. Every country we went to was a live-in situation with other students and their families. We were experiencing life as it was lived by everyday Africans. I sent June an excited postcard from every country on the trip. In Kenya, I stayed with a family in a small rural village two hundred miles northwest of the capital. That level of intimacy allowed me to see firsthand how the things I'd read about in books and newspapers were playing out on the level of people's lives, unfiltered by Western media. Watching the transfer of power from European to African hands was fascinating. While living in rural

Kenya, I noticed what President Kenyatta did to dismantle the divide-and-rule strategy of the colonizers: he broke up all the tribes, like the Lua and Kikuyu, placed them among each other, and divided up resources equitably. He knew that for his country to survive after he was gone, they needed to be united by something greater than tribe. I contrasted the Kenyan success in removing foreign business interests with the Ugandan failure to do the same. Kenya took it slowly with legislation, allowing Kenyans to learn from Europeans and Indians before taking more control, while Uganda did it quickly, with force, leaving both foreigners and their own countrymen in disarray.

One of the most important things I learned from that trip was during my stay at a school in Tanzania. A few countries away in South Africa, the people were still suffering under the brutal racism of apartheid. But at this Tanzanian school, they were training South African refugees to fight back in their home country. When I struck up a dialogue with these South African refugees, I got a clearer picture of just how brutal the colonial regime in their country was. To hear them talk, to see their desperate attempts to fight back, I witnessed the same anger that we were feeling in the streets of New York.

Everywhere we went, we felt connected with the African people. We never held back from speaking our minds, either. Early in the trip, all of us was eating at this restaurant in Accra, when we heard someone yelling. When we turned to look, we saw the manager of the place, a white man, yelling at a member of the waitstaff. I don't even remember what their conflict was about, but the white manager raised his hand and smacked the black waiter across the back of the head. When we saw that, our Harlem came all the way out. I'll never forget. Oh, we had a fit in that restaurant. Almost caused a riot.

"What?" we shouted, rising to our feet.

"Why you smack him?"

"He didn't do nothin!"

"What you say?"

We bugged out in there. Believe it or not, the name of the restaurant was Uncle Sam's.

Whether we were starting fights up in restaurants or just walking through the city square, wherever we went in Africa, we were treated like celebrities. People would take us to their houses, to the beach, everywhere, and just parade us around: their American friends. They might have known Americans before, but they'd never met Americans like us. Americans who talked like us, dressed like us, were quick to throw down like us.

Not only were we there, meeting the local people and witnessing firsthand these things we'd only read about, but we also got to talk to the mayors, the governors, even the presidents in these countries. When we reached Kumasi in Ghana, the Ashanti people's ruler, known as the Asantehene, sacrificed a cow for us. We went through the whole ritual. During the month that we stayed in Ghana, we went all the way up to Bolgatanga in the far north of the country and met with a fetish priest, a traditional holy man who was said to have spiritual powers. I was especially excited about that. The fetish priest took us down to a river and performed a ritual to summon a crocodile. When the holy crocodile emerged, the fetish priest told us, "Don't do nothing." But one of the young guys on the trip with us was this troublemaker from the projects. He took a rock and threw it at the crocodile, making it turn away. The priest jumped up and down, did some kind of stuff, and that night, the guy who threw the rock caught a case of diphtheria.

One other important thing happened to me on that trip: I fell in love with African clothes. The tour coordinators had given each of us a stipend to live on, but I ain't come back with no money. I came back to Harlem with nothing but African clothes. I'd sold all of my American clothes at the markets and exchanged them for traditional robes and garments. I also had some tailors make me new slacks and suits done in African tailoring styles. They fit me better than anything I'd ever bought or shoplifted from a store in New

York. Man, I was fly, and I was fly in a way that made me feel good about myself on a deeper level. I'd been told so many lies about what it meant to be black. The truth I witnessed in Africa was that we were doers and makers. We were strong and knew how to fight for freedom and we knew how to win. That trip, seeing all those skilled artists and tailors in all those different countries making beautiful things with their hands, had a permanent impact on me.

Looking back, I realize that was what really changed me and my whole concept of fashion. It went deeper than I'd ever realized. Though I didn't know it yet, that was the seed I went to Africa to find.

CHAPTER 10

Mind Games

After that summer in Africa, I came back to New York ready to move forward. I'd graduated from Harlem Prep's storefronts and was now enrolled in a private school out in New Jersey. Classes were going well. My trip to Africa had me excited about world history. I was back to my elementary school days of being a star student. But it wasn't easy. The guys in the program alongside me didn't have the same ideas about self-discipline that I had. Every day on the bus back from Newark, they'd be drinking and smoking reefer and trying to get me to stop reading and join in with them. I'd dropped out of the streets to achieve a different kind of life, and I wasn't about to go back to my old ways. Those bus rides were torture, but I stuck to my principles.

The following year, once I finished my studies at Newark Prep and got my GED, the Urban League offered me an academic scholarship to get my bachelor's degree at Iona College, a four-year

Catholic school in New Rochelle. Iona was only sixteen miles north of Harlem, but it felt like a different world. I was the only black person in a lotta my classes, which was new for me. One of the first college courses I took was a lecture on protohistory, or the study of human culture right before recorded history. The professor was a man named Bohdan Chudoba, a Czech immigrant who was among the most popular teachers on campus. Since I'd gotten back from Africa, I was considering history as a major, possibly focusing on African history, and the chair of the history department had encouraged me to take his class.

There I was, struggling to keep my eyes open one morning while Dr. Chudoba began to lecture about the scientific study of prehistoric man. I'd been working myself into the ground. I was back at hustling dice games and saving up to move out of my mother's apartment. I needed a place of my own and money to pay for private school for my two sons. On top of that, June had just given birth to our daughter, Danique. Trying to balance college and all-night dice games to support my family meant I barely got any sleep. I was always tired.

"In order for man to have survived during those ancient times," Dr. Chudoba said in his Eastern European accent, "he must have had powers that he doesn't have now. The only people that could possibly still have these powers today are the black and brown people on the planet. . . ."

When I heard him say that, I sat straight up in my chair and thought, *Hold up*. This is one of the most esteemed scholars at Iona College telling a packed lecture hall that black and brown people were the only ones on the planet who still had spiritual powers. How come this was my first time hearing about that? I looked around. I was the only black student in the class. I wasn't tired anymore. He had my full attention.

Dr. Chudoba went on to talk about this UCLA graduate student in anthropology, Carlos Castaneda, who had spent time among the Yaqui American Indian tribe in northern Mexico and the Southwest. Castaneda, Dr. Chudoba said, had studied with a shaman, or "man of knowledge," who claimed lineage with the ancient ways of the universe and tried to become a man of knowledge himself. Castaneda wrote about his experiences in a book called *The Teachings of Don Juan: A Yaqui Way of Knowledge,* which was based on his master's thesis at UCLA and had just recently been published. The book would help trigger that whole psychedelic era, where white people went off to find their identity by smoking peyote and eating mushrooms. Spiritual quests through psychedelic drugs became a way to understand the universe, thanks in part to Castaneda's book. As I listened to Dr. Chudoba lecture about the spiritual powers of black and brown people, I said to myself, *This is what I need to know. This is how I need to formulate myself.* I wanted to become a man of knowledge and was particularly fascinated by the mysterious gray areas between history and the spiritual world, science and religion. After that lecture, I chose history as my major.

Though college was intellectually stimulating, I felt like a fish out of water at Iona. Most of my classmates were white and younger than me and came from middle-class homes. Their biggest worry was over what major they'd pick. Still, I went to class looking sharp, always living up to my street name even if I wasn't in the streets. That was the era of bell-bottoms and platform shoes, and when I mixed those with the exotic clothes I'd brought back from Africa, I was a sight to be seen. My outfits excited people on the campus of Iona as much as they did on the streets of Harlem. Clothes have a power that cuts across social and economic lines. On campus, I looked like any other free spirit expressing himself through his wardrobe. On the streets, I looked like a hustler who knew how to get his.

For a while, I had a foot in both worlds, the academy and the streets. I was rubbing elbows with scholars by day and drug dealers by night, and it was proving to be too much. I was reading books trying to attain a higher level of consciousness while hustling dice games to provide for myself and my family. I'll never know if I woulda made a good historian, or if I'd have gone on to study something else. Soon, my GPA was too low to keep the scholarship, and without the funding, I couldn't afford to stay in school. So I went back to the streets full-time, doing what I did better than anyone else. I might not have been cut out for the academy, but I was still the best dice player in Harlem. Or as I came to find out, one of the two best.

The early 1970s was the peak of my gambling career in New York. I was twenty-seven years old and banging the drug crews every day from 115th to 112th. My morals wasn't right: I'd sometimes bang guys making money off angel dust, beat them out of all their money, and then let them bet the dust, which I'd win and sell to my dealer friends.

Not coincidentally, that was also the peak of the dope era, and New York was the dope capital of America. Endless cash was flowing through the streets of Harlem as a result of the drug craze. Each day crews were walking away with literal shopping bags of money. Heroin had started as the drug of choice for jazz musicians and beat poets before it made its way to people in the streets, and once the whole hippie thing made drug experimentation a symbol of countercultural rebellion, even mainstream people began to use dope. You'd see suburban white boys with New Jersey plates roll through Harlem, looking to cop.

The war on drugs had done nothing to stop the demand for dope. By targeting poor black and brown communities across the country, all that Nixon's disastrous policies had done was slow the supply of narcotics, which was a huge financial benefit to dealers brave enough to risk the new tougher drug laws. There were open-air drug markets around the neighborhood where people would literally line up around the block the way they do outside of sneaker shops nowadays. The ones who'd cornered the market, hustlers like Nicky "Mr. Untouchable" Barnes, Frank "American Gangster" Lucas, and Richard "Pee Wee" Kirkland, were pulling down many millions a year through sophisticated strategies that helped insulate them from punishment. This new generation of careful, organized Harlem kingpins had taken control of the dope game from the Italians and were maximizing profits by manufacturing, packaging, and distributing the product themselves. Like the numbers kings before them, the drug kingpins became the new power brokers in the neighborhood. They were the ones dressed in expensive suits, driving fancy cars, bankrolling businesses, dating the flyest women, and giving out turkeys at Thanksgiving. Now young hustlers in the neighborhood dreamed about building their own drug empires.

But not everyone looked up to the dealers. Churchgoers prayed for God to punish dealers. Local black politicians ran on antidrug platforms. And if you were a member of the Nation of Islam or the newly formed Harlem chapter of the Black Panther Party, you were starting to think about taking matters into your own hands. Ever since I'd returned from Africa, I'd been an on-again, off-again visitor at the Nation of Islam's No. 7 Mosque, and I'd also started attending regular meetings with the Black Panthers. Like many others at the time, I saw the Panthers as our version of the successful independence movements that I'd observed firsthand in Africa. With their militant socialist message of taking power back through armed self-defense, voter registration, and health and food programs for the poor, they seemed like the new hope for black liberation in America. To the Panthers, our biggest shackle was the drug game. In secret, they were devising a plan to combat it.

At one meeting, they closed the door, made sure no one was out in the hallway listening, then they passed around a sheet of paper with a list of names on it. It was a hit list. They was gonna kill all the drug dealers in Harlem, starting with every name on that list. I took the sheet of paper and read the names to myself in silence. My blood ran cold. I recognized the name of a good friend of mine, a guy I'd grown up with who'd turned to dealing. I couldn't condone that kind of violence. I passed the sheet back, left, and never went to another Panther meeting again.

Later that year, the drug curse hit my sister Deborah with a life-changing tragedy. None of us knew it at the time, but Deborah's husband, her high school sweetheart, had gotten hooked on heroin. He'd become negligent and abusive towards her, and one day, while Deborah was at her civil service job, he drowned their three-year-old daughter in the tub. We'll never know if it was intentional or an accident, but he wound up serving two years in prison and, from all I know, was a broken soul after that.

My sister was never the same, having suddenly lost a child and a marriage. I stayed with her for a few weeks, taking care of her, and passing along wisdom from my readings. With the encouragement of our brother Omar, who brought her into the fold of the Black Muslim community, she began to read the Koran and embarked on a spiritual journey after the death of her child that would eventually take her to India to study Hinduism and finally to an ashram in Jamaica with her second husband, a devout Hare Krishna.

I didn't like my own role in the drug game as an enabler, but at least my Robin Hood approach avoided violence. It relied on skill and strategy, not bloodshed. I would go wherever they was selling drugs and gamble. In this way I made a living, saving up money until I was finally able to move out of my mother's place in the Bronx into an apartment of my own back in Harlem.

I was at Deborah's when I heard someone ring the bell and a voice come through the intercom: "Yo, it's Scotty!"

"Lil Scotty!" I said and buzzed him inside. Lil Scotty was a good friend of mine, but he was the kind of guy who was good friends with everybody. He was getting money in the drug game through a connection he had with the East Harlem Purple Gang, an independent crew of Italians who had a powerful grip on heroin in the neighborhood. That day, Lil Scotty was as excited as I'd ever seen him.

"Maaaan," said Scotty, as he came into the apartment trailed by his pal Ricky Duke. "We was just down on 115th Street with the Mota Boys. Those kids over there getting crazy money, man! They got a dice game started. They was coming out with fat rolls out they pockets, man. Come on over there!"

Like everyone in my part of Harlem, Scotty knew I had a special way with the dice and was excited about seeing me play against these Mota Boys. I sensed a golden opportunity. So I told Lil Scotty I'd meet him down there in a few, and I got myself together. Put on my flyest pair of platforms and bell-bottoms, stuffed a wad of playing money in my sock, hopped onto my bicycle, and made my way over to where the Mota Boys and their crew were hanging out. Sure enough, when I got there and parked my bike against a lamppost, I saw a big old dice game well under way. And just like Scotty had promised, there was money everywhere. I was looking at hundreds and hundreds of dollars on the floor.

"Everything down is a bet," someone hollered. "Everything down is a bet."

There was guys all over the place, drinking, smoking that strong Mota Boy reefer that people were coming from far and wide to buy in those days. I found an opening in the crowd and reached into my sock.

"Yo! What up, Dap?" someone shouted, recognizing me.

"Yeah, tryin to get this money," I muttered coldly. Little did they realize it, but my strategy was already in motion: with the cash I was flashing, the clothes I was wearing, even the reputation that preceded me. They was playing cee-lo, but I was playing mind games. Nonchalantly, I counted out five hundred dollars and called out bets I wanted to make, bets that sounded like easy money to them but were rigged in favor of me by the simple law of probability. "How much you want on that four or better?" I said. "How much you want on that beat the deuce twice?"

"Forty bucks says I beat the deuce twice," said one of the Mota Boys shaking the dice in his fist. To say you trying to "beat the

deuce twice" in cee-lo means you believe you can make at least one
die come up with the number two in two consecutive rolls. With
three dice in hand, it's a bet that sounds like easy money, but it
ain't. If he stopped for a second and did the math, he'd have realized that the odds, over time, were against him two-to-one. I liked
to think of these more as mind bets, because it's a bet that chal-
lenges a man's ego—that he won't be able to roll the number two
again.

"You got a strong wrist?" I said, egging him on. "Lemme see you
fuck that deuce up."

"Come on," said the Mota Boy, taking the bait.

"Beat the deuce goose!" I jested, waving the bills.

"You crazy?" he said. "I tear that deuce up."

He got lucky and beat the deuce on his first roll, which got everybody excited and ragging on me. Knowing full well the power
of self-control, I paced myself, putting down careful mind bets. I
was prepared to be there all night. Games could go on for thirteen
hours straight. "I know you want some of this!" I said, flashing
more cash, all the while talking slick and playing the part of the
sucker with money to burn. Usually, I never touched the dice. My
strategy was to convince them to make dumb bets with me on their
rolls and wait for the law of averages to break them.

Like clockwork, guys started playing into my strategy, egos
clouding their judgment in the moment. They was trying to shut
me up, trying to see me humiliated and broke. Meanwhile, no
one's paying attention to how much I'm winning. They trying to
win me, I'm trying to win the game. My strategy was so effective
that even Lil Scotty, who was gambling, too, started to get frustrated with me. He was making impulsive decisions. He wasn't following my lead. I pulled him aside at one point and tried telling
him to wait until I told him to bet. But he wasn't hearing me. After
this went on for a while, Lil Scotty nodded his head, indignant, and
stepped away from the game.

"That's all right," he said. "I'm bringing my man over here. You niggas ain't getting all the money."

His man? Please. Lil Scotty could bring whoever he wanted, but wasn't nobody about to beat me.

I was a master with the dice, been practicing and playing and honing my skills since I was a kid. I was Las Vegas. Nobody stood a chance. When Lil Scotty came back a while later, he had someone with him. "Hey, let my man play," said Scotty, pulling his friend into the fray. "Let my man play. He gone ice all y'all niggas."

I glanced over. I'd never seen Scotty's friend at any of the dice games I'd been at before. He looked to be about my age. All of a sudden, I had some crazy déjà vu. I knew this cat's face from somewhere. Then, like a bolt of lightning, it hit me. Back when I was twelve, still goofing around in Killa's crew, I had visited that Sol shop in the Bronx to get my first pair of trick dice and seen a kid there—black, young, too young to be in a store like that.

It was him! Only older now. He looked at me funny, squinted.

"Man, I remember you," he said.

"Yeah," I said, playing it off. "Everybody knows Dapper Dan."

"I'm Russell," he said, eyeing me carefully.

I was keeping my cool, because this was my profession. It wasn't no time to get nostalgic or overly friendly. I had my guard up because I knew there was no loyalty, no true friendship on the streets. I wanted to see what this cat was made of. If he'd been honing his craft the way I had, he was gonna be trouble. For the first time in my gambling career, I was nervous.

People who gathered around us seemed to already know him off reputation, but somehow I'd never seen him before. If you're a Sol, you can spot another Sol immediately, as much by what they do as by what they don't. Once we started playing, I saw that he was tracking everything I did, but he wasn't ranking me, either. It was like he and I were communicating on a level that none of the other guys gambling with us understood. And we were breaking everybody else, but we were letting each other kinda take turns, profiting off each other's bets. I'd never played with anyone who had the same level of proficiency as me. Game recognized game.

After that uncanny meeting with grown-up Russell, I realized the huge advantage that he and I could have in future dice games. Being the two most talented dice players we'd ever met, Russell and I crewed up, hitting all the street gambling spots together every day, trimming these drug dealers and splitting the profits. Russell and I were like the hustlers in that movie *The Sting*. I was more the patient Paul Newman type, and Russell was more like Robert Redford. He would always wanna go at em. I would observe till what I thought was the most opportune time, but Russell would get impatient and say, "Man, let's *get* these lames." When it came to the dice, Russell was the only one I felt completely comfortable with on the level of skill and strategy. We shared trade secrets, techniques we'd never reveal to anyone but each other. He was from the west side of Harlem near Abyssinian Baptist Church, adopted by a friend of his mother because she was too busy working as a domestic and raising three other children. He grew up with the same holes in his shoes and the same admiration for the numbers guys as me, and, just like me, he had the same love of reading and hunger for information. He was amazing, a hustling nerd like me. The world was our ATM. That's how we started running together. And we been best friends ever since.

CHAPTER 11

―――――

The Rumble

Dig this here, all the old-time Sols was busting everybody in two-dice games, but they wasn't paying me and Russell no attention because I never stepped foot inside the gambling clubs in Harlem. There was Sols in there, and the Sols knew who each other were. And once you went in a gambling club, people could read your game, because you can't bet inside the club one way then come on the street and bet another way. They'd say, "Nah, something's up with this dude."

So I played pure sucker.

Out on the streets with the drug crews, two-dice craps was falling out of fashion and cee-lo, which is played with three dice instead of the standard two, started taking over. The thing about cee-lo that every old-school Sol knew was that there is much less complexity to gaming the odds when you add a third die. In other words, it is easier to get caught cheating with three dice than with two. So the other Sols stayed away from cee-lo in favor of regular two-dice craps. But then I came up with the angle to break the cee-lo game, and Russell picked up on it right away.

My biggest mentor in the dice game was an older Jewish guy named Hymie, who ran a magic shop in midtown. He was a legend among Sols, and his handcrafted dice were on another level than everyone else's. Completely undetectable. Hymie treated me like a long-lost son, which may have been because he had a son also named Danny. I just hung around him as much as I could, soaking up all his knowledge surrounded by the machines, drills, and presses of his workshop. Sometimes, I'd take June with me and we'd spend hours at Hymie's shop. He taught me about the structure of dice. The way they were made and how they could be manipulated. It's amazing how the most subtle modification to the shape of a cube can change the odds. Hymie taught me the ins and outs of making dice, the physics, the probability, the engineering. Russell and I was buying all our special dice from Hymie, but at eleven dollars a cube, they weren't cheap, especially because we needed three dice for cee-lo. So we took all that we'd learned from Hymie and started manufacturing our own special dice, making them out of a new substance that even Hymie hadn't thought to use.

To this day, the kind of dice techniques me and Russell invented during that time period haven't hit the street—*to this day*. That's how far ahead of the curve we were. We had all the cee-lo games in Harlem to ourselves. Lining them up, breaking them like crazy. It's hard for me to explain how good we were. We never got caught. Often, we wasn't even using the special dice. Just math. I never played the same game twice, either. Customizing. Improvising. Russell, too. We were on another level. We were even breaking other so-called master gamblers. There were these two Sols who called themselves the Crap Priests who held dice games up near Yankee Stadium in the Bronx. Russell and I went up there once like we were suckers. We'd say, "Bet you don't throw over seven."

And we'd just keep breaking them. Russell'd go break em for a while, and then he'd leave and I'd go break em for a while.

At our height, Russell and I were putting in sixteen-hour days from spring to fall and each of us could clear twenty thousand dollars in one good week, mostly shooting with Nicky Barnes's crew, who were the biggest hustlers in the neighborhood. These guys had ten and fifteen thousand in their pockets to gamble with. It didn't hurt them at all to drop a few thousand in one night at a dice game. My money went to my children and their education and then towards maintaining a lifestyle befitting a man named Dapper Dan. My outfits, my jewelry, my penthouse apartment in the Bronx overlooking the Long Island Sound: all of that was a form of theater. I didn't want or need those things. I simply saw them as extensions of my professional life. I had to dress and live like a big-time hustler. That way, I could target the big-time hustlers to step up and challenge me in high-stakes dice games. My whole lifestyle was bait for guys with big egos and deep pockets, and I was just living from one dice game to the next, no longer thinking about a career.

It was a far cry from where I thought I'd be just a few years before. Instead of working at *The New York Times* or the *New York Amsterdam News,* interviewing politicians, writing reports, dreaming about Pulitzers, I was putting in long days with the kind of people I didn't want to be around. Russell felt the same way. He was too smart to be doing what we were doing. Like me, he'd been a hungry reader since before he even started kindergarten. We were both natural observers of the world around us, and when we weren't working on new dice techniques, we sat around talking metaphysics. Russell had been deeply influenced by a book of Hermetic philosophy called *The Kybalion* by Three Initiates, which argued that "all is mind" and that one could bring the separate spheres of mental, physical, and spiritual life into harmony. Many of the ideas that stuck with Russell resonated with what I'd already been reading in *Man's Higher Consciousness.* We shared books and took time

out to discuss higher things. We knew that there had to be something beyond this world. Not just a world beyond the dice games,
but a world beyond the physical itself.

In 1971 my uncle and hustling role model, Fish Man Eddie, died of
sclerosis of the liver. Like my mother, his half-sister, he'd been a
lifelong drinker who also shared her distrust of doctors. It broke
my mother's heart and probably gave her more reason to drown
her sorrows. The year after Uncle Eddie passed, I got a call from
my sister Dolores that our mother was laid up in Harlem Hospital.
That's how I knew it was something serious. With her Southern
distrust of white people and their medicine, my mother had never
stepped foot in a doctor's office or hospital her whole life, not once
during her seven pregnancies and home births. I knew she musta
been real sick. I wasn't wrong.

When I arrived at her room, I saw tubes coming out of her from
everywhere. I hated seeing her like that. Dolores sat holding her
hand beside the hospital bed.

The doctors said it was cancer, already too far along to do anything. I couldn't fit the lively, healthy woman I remembered from
childhood with the withered body and white hair lying immobile
on the bed. Two weeks later, she took her last breath.

She was only fifty-nine years old.

My father took it with a stoic demeanor. "Lily Mae died because
of that drink," he said to me on the day of her funeral. Though she
had drowned in sorrow, he vowed not to do the same. "I'mma take
care of myself."

The grief hung heavily on all of us. Most heavily on my brother
Carl, who had been devoted to our mother and had been living in
the Bronx with her through the final years of her life. He seemed
shattered by the loss. His grief musta been part of what killed
him in the end. Within a year of my mother's death, Carl was di-
agnosed with throat cancer, the result of years of chain-smoking,

and a few months later, at only thirty-five, he succumbed to the disease.

It was the middle of a dark, grief-filled period for my family. The loss of my niece, Uncle Eddie, my mother, and then Carl—it was all so heavy. I don't know how anyone deals with losing a loved one, let alone so many in such a short time. Right or wrong, my response has always been to avoid death. Avoid thinking about it, avoid talking about it. Because it's not something any of us will ever be able to fully understand. There's nothing you can do with death but mourn. So we mourned for those we'd lost so soon. I mourned my mother and the hole in her heart nobody could fill, that South Carolina Geechee girl with deferred dreams, who loved her gospel in the morning and wrote poetry in secret and tried to make sure that we would make it in a cruel world without her.

Ever since that first student trip to Africa, I felt a strong desire to return and see more of the continent, and the deeper I got into hustling, the more I dreamed about it, but with my week-to-week existence, it felt like yet another dream that would be deferred. Until one day, when Russell tossed me the sports section of the newspaper and said, "Heard about the fight?"

There was an article about the upcoming heavyweight championship boxing match between George Foreman and Muhammad Ali, one of the most anticipated boxing matches of all time. We had all been waiting to hear where it was gonna be. I read the article with surprise: it was gonna be in Africa, and they were advertising it with the playful but racist name "Rumble in the Jungle." A little-known promoter named Don King had arranged a deal with the government of Congo, securing a massive stadium in the capital city. King brokered the deal with a brutal, Western-backed dictator named Mobutu Sese Seko, who'd recently renamed his country Zaire. No one had ever held such a high-profile sporting event in an African country, and for two black athletes at the height of their powers to compete as the eyes of the world were on them, it felt historic. Especially since one of them was the Greatest.

Not since Sugar Ray Robinson had there been a boxer as captivating as Muhammad Ali. But unlike Sugar Ray, who was Ali's hero growing up and one of mine, too, Ali didn't straighten his hair or wear pink suits. Instead, he kept his hair natural and preferred the toned-down wardrobe of a practicing Muslim. Sports are always bigger than just the competition, and in the case of Ali, he had become the athlete of my generation who stood for something greater than himself. With his fiery critiques of American racism, he embodied the radical, antiestablishment spirit of black dignity and excellence. His freedom and strength felt like ours. When he fought, he fought for us. When he won, it gave us hope that we could defeat the forces set against us, like Joe Louis's fight against the German Max Schmeling in 1938. Watching Ali's physical grace and speed inside the ring, and his wit and intelligence outside it, was liberating. The way he danced and struck and dodged, the way he spoke out in interviews against racism and the Vietnam War. As an Ali fan, I wanted to be there to watch history.

As if I needed another reason, it soon came out that people in the music business were planning an epic concert before the fight: Zaire '74: International Black Music Festival, a three-day musical showcase of African American and African musicians. "Black America's greatest strengths at present are sports and music," said the R & B singer Lloyd Price, who coproduced the event. "We want to combine them and help blacks in America, strangers in an alien land, to grasp the strand of the motherland—the musical beat." It was like Woodstock for black people, a cultural showcase of excellence unlike anything the world had ever seen before. James Brown would be the biggest draw, but thirty other performers were scheduled, including Bill Withers, B. B. King, Celia Cruz, Sister Sledge, the Spinners, and over a dozen African acts, like world-music icon Miriam Makeba, who was married to Black Panther and writer Stokely Carmichael at the time. I knew that it couldn't hurt my image as Dapper Dan the high roller if people found out I went to Africa for the fight and rubbed elbows with all these A-list celebrities. But more than anything, I was excited to see another part of Africa. I'd never been to Zaire. At the time of my first trip, it was still known as the Democratic Republic of the Congo and had been recovering from a bloody five-year proxy war between Western-backed and Soviet-backed forces that left hundreds of thousands dead, including freedom fighter and former prime minister Patrice Lumumba.

So I went back to Africa. This time, I wasn't some twenty-three-year-old in a program with a stipend. I was a grown man nearing thirty, a Harlem gambling legend with money to burn, going on his own steam, and had the wardrobe to prove it. I went to Zaire *Super Fly*–style. I had all them pastel suits packed in my suitcase: pink pastel suit, powder-blue pastel suit, mint-green pastel suit. All with matching hats and platform shoes. I got there a couple days early, too, to soak in more of the country: the people, the art, the clothes, the history, the culture.

The atmosphere around the music festival was unreal. To see all those black musicians and dancers and flavors coming together, and to have it in Africa, that was amazing. There was James Brown in his flamboyant velvet and silk getups, with customized lettering that read "GFOS" (God Father of Soul), jamming in a stadium filled with Africans who didn't understand the words but understood the funk. And there was Muhammad Ali's crazy cornerman, Drew Bundini Brown, walking around Kinshasa blowing his reefer smoke in the face of every white guy he saw, something he said he started doing once he found out that all the police in Africa were black. Man, the parties we had in Africa!

It wasn't until after I got to Zaire that news broke about George Foreman's injury. He'd gotten a bad gash on his brow only a few days before the fight, when his sparring partner caught him with an elbow during training. Word was, the sparring partner was so terrified of Foreman's thunderous power that, when he went to cover up his own head, he accidentally landed an elbow above Foreman's eye. The match had to be postponed for five weeks. That meant everybody who'd been expecting to enjoy the fight after the music festival would have to return home and watch it on TV like the rest of the world. Understandably, a lotta folk was upset about that. But not me. It just meant I got to spend more time in Africa.

I'd stay in Africa for a month waiting for the fight, waiting for Foreman to heal. Back then, they had a great deal where you could get off the plane and get back on with no extra charge, so wherever the airline flew in Africa, I could go for free within a forty-five-day period.

I said to myself, *Wherever this plane stops, I'm getting off.*

Because of the language barrier, I visited the places that spoke English: Nigeria and Liberia. I got off in Lagos, Nigeria, first. From my hotel window, I looked down at the street below and saw a stand of local artists selling their goods: beautiful fabrics, paintings, wood carvings, statues, masks. I dropped off my bags right away and went down to do some shopping.

At one stand, I said, "Damn, I like that painting."

The artist looked me up and down. "Man, I like your clothes," he said.

"You wanna trade?"

"Yeah, let's trade."

I ran up to my suitcases in the hotel, took out all my pastel suits, and came back down. I didn't leave Lagos with nothing but African art. To this day, I still have those statues and paintings lining the walls and mantel of my brownstone in Harlem. But by the time I left Nigeria, I realized that my impulsive decision meant that I was running out of things to wear. I needed some pants, jackets, suits, and shirts.

Fortunately, my next stop was Liberia, where I could use my American currency to purchase new clothes. I was looking forward to finding a store and picking up some new suits to last me until I returned home. When I landed in Monrovia, the capital named after US president James Monroe, I became fascinated by the historical connection Liberia had to African Americans. Liberia was colonized during slavery times by a group of Americans wanting to resettle free blacks in Africa. In the years before the Civil War, nearly twenty thousand free African Americans and Afro-Caribbeans boarded ships and resettled in Liberia, where they ruled over the indigenous African people until the end of the twentieth century. William Tubman, the long-serving president who had just died when I arrived, was a descendant of those early African American settlers.

I had difficulty finding anything I liked in the clothing stores in Monrovia. Even though blacks in America were becoming fascinated with traditional African clothes, the Africans were mostly into Western clothes. They weren't wearing the dashikis. European tailor-made polyester suits were the trend, and all of the cuts and designs were based on that Eurocentric aesthetic: tapered legs, muted colors. That wasn't the hustler look I was going for. I needed someone to make me something fly. "Go to a tailor," one of the shopkeepers told me. "They will make you a suit."

As I continued on through the market, I heard a voice say, "Are you Fulani?"

I turned, and there was a man standing with a tape measure around his neck.

"No," I said. "American."

"You look like Fulani."

His name was Ahmed, and he was a tailor. But he wasn't a tailor in the American sense of the word. He wasn't some guy who made your slacks bigger when you put on weight. No, Ahmed didn't just alter clothes, he made clothes from scratch, starting with raw rolls of fabric, scissors, sewing machines, and templates. He was from Guinea, a member of the Fulani ethnic group, a seminomadic tribe spread throughout West Africa who were known for their distinctive mixed features.

I'd never met a black person who could do what Ahmed did. Back in the day, Harlem only had one real custom-clothing shop, run by a black tailor named Orie Walls, who catered to high-paying clientele but ultimately drank himself out of business. Other than that, we were forced to buy all our clothes from the same big department stores as everyone else.

Ahmed showed me around his shop, pulling out suits and blazers, designs he'd recently finished.

"I like the material on this one," I said, pointing to a pair of pants. "But could you flare out the leg?"

Ahmed could do that.

"What about the color? Can you make it a pastel?"

"I can do whatever you want, brother."

Ahmed was blowing my mind. With his help, I altered the cut on pants, changed the color on a blazer, and added lapels and flares to resonate with the trends back on the streets. I couldn't remember being as excited about anything as I was when I placed my order with Ahmed. No one in Harlem had ever seen the designs and materials I was about to have. I knew it was going to wow people. It was gonna be African, but also European, but also street. Those clothes I collaborated on with Ahmed were my very first Dapper Dan original fashion designs. I started thinking about Orie's old custom clothing shop in Harlem and how his business had gone under years ago. Ever since then, there'd been a void in Harlem. I began to think, *Someone could fill that void.* Not just making suits, like Orie had, but making anything. Pants, jackets, shirts, sweaters.

Working with Ahmed to design my own clothes was a revelation, but with all the money I'd spent at his shop, I couldn't afford to stay in Africa for another three weeks waiting for the Rumble in the Jungle back in Zaire. So after six inspiring days in Liberia, I hopped a flight back to New York with an entire new wardrobe of all original pieces.

In the end, I wound up watching Ali's amazing victory at home in Harlem. Ali laid back against the ropes, protecting his head and letting those thunderous shots from Foreman glance off his body. People thought Ali was done for, or maybe that he was intentionally throwing the fight for money. Or that he was scared. No, it was all part of his genius. When the time was right, once he recognized that Goliath had truly worn himself out, David came off the ropes with a flurry of lightning and struck sharp, precise blows that sent Foreman spinning to the canvas. "Ali, boma ye!" the crowd chanted in Lingala. "Ali, kill him!" Although I missed out on witnessing what many consider the most strategically brilliant heavyweight boxing fight in history, I found something on that trip that changed my life forever: a love for custom tailoring and inspiration for a brand-new hustle.

One of these days, I'mma need to track down Foreman's sparring partner and thank him, because if it wasn't for him accidentally injuring Foreman's eye, I probably woulda never made my way to Liberia and met Ahmed and decided to dedicate the rest of my life to making people look fly.

CHAPTER 12

Hubba Hubba

The reaction I got in Harlem to my new clothes was incredible. I came back from the motherland fly as what. They'd never seen the kinds of designs Ahmed and I had come up with. One of my favorite suits Ahmed made was a two-tone beige African print jacket with matching beige flared-leg pants. They wanted to know where they could buy something like that, too. I kept the truth close to my vest. I was thinking more and more seriously about the clothes game, though I didn't know where to begin. On top of all my life expenses, the money it would take to open a storefront and grow a business was still out of reach for a dice hustler.

But I was getting tired of the dice and knew I couldn't stay in the streets trimming drug dealers for much longer. It was an unhealthy career and I felt like I was stagnating. Plus, there was never a guarantee that I'd walk out of any game unharmed. The rewards were high but so were the risks, and both were getting higher and higher.

My hustling mentality grew increasingly dark. I wasn't about to go broke from fear. If someone didn't like me winning, they was just gone have to kill me.

The city itself was breeding that kind of desperation. More guys were serving longer prison terms on drug charges. Old Harlem was dying, too. You didn't see no more pushcarts in the street. No more horses and buggies. No more guys like my uncle Eddie selling fish on the corner. If it wasn't prison sending men away and breaking apart a family, it was the city developers breaking apart whole communities, tearing down buildings to make way for high-rise public housing. Now people got thrown into one big, chaotic pot.

Between 1965 and 1975, New York's homicide rate skyrocketed, and in the years ahead it would only get more and more murderous. That was a grim, lonely time for the city. It was also a grim, lonely time for me. Unlike most everyone around me, I didn't drink or get high, I was a vegetarian, I read books from the Theosophical Society. I had all this stuff going on in my head—spirituality, philosophy, all my memories of Africa, alongside street knowledge. Russell was the only one I could connect with, and him and I were both secretly miserable all throughout our gambling years. It was difficult to admit that maybe we weren't *just* doing it for the money. Maybe a part of us, that was more important to us than we wanted to admit, was doing it for others. We wanted to be perceived in a certain way. We wanted to be seen as a certain type of guy. Though we said we understood the line between our true spiritual selves and the hustler personas we presented to the world, sometimes the line blurred, and we weren't too sure where our souls ended and the streets began.

And Russell was starting to get caught up in it. He was spending more and more time with the guys in the drug game, guys who would sniff a little cocaine every now and then. He was partying with those dealers and started using coke with them, too. One day it was just casual use, something done in a social way. There wasn't the stigma that's attached to it now. You'd see a friend and say,

"What's up, man? Gimme a bump." There was a glamour to cocaine, a freedom and power and confidence it gave the user. It was
expensive, too, so to be able to afford it was a status symbol. White
boys on Wall Street were doing it, and the money men in Harlem,
the movers and the shakers, were the ones who could afford to use
it around our way. I saw what had happened with me and my brothers before happen to Russell now: the drug curse. He wasn't able to
understand how or why or even that it was happening. It just did.
Slowly and then all at once, it started taking over Russell's life.

While Russell spent his free time partying with his dealer
friends, I was feeling even more alone. Even though we were still in
each other's lives, it was clear that he and I were setting out on different paths. But it was the birth of a destructive new era that we
were all heading towards. None of us saw the violence of the crack
era coming. None of us imagined the effects that this new drug
would have on our communities. Russell lost his dice touch and his
sharpness as a Sol. Girls would steal from him. He started owing
money to support his habit. A lot of money. And users who owed
money would often wind up dead. More than once, I'd be breaking
a drug dealer at cee-lo, watching these guys gamble away money
that I knew they owed other people, money that if they couldn't
pay would get them killed. If you know your activity is contributing
to a person possibly losing his life because of money, how you going
to be happy with yourself?

Something had definitely changed. The value system was deteriorating. I'd see my friends who were still running in the streets,
and how they didn't have no relationships with their own children.
A new generation of dealers was coming of age, more hopeless and
angry than mine. More money to be had, but more brutal policing,
too. The stakes were getting astronomical. As a hustler who prided
himself on his intellect, I was feeling like a relic in this dawning age
of kidnappings and shoot-outs.

Even though I'd always played dice against guys who dealt

drugs and weren't afraid to pull a gun or a knife on you, I had never been afraid for my physical safety. I came from a strong family of gangsters and hustlers and usually gambled with a friend-slash-bodyguard to watch my back and add to my mystique. I didn't have to worry about jealous retaliation for my success, because if you lost the money fair and square, it was on you. There was a code. My back was straight. But more and more, the dice games I was taking part in were starting to unnerve me.

The dice game that made me want to quit for real took place at what used to be a jazz joint called the Hubba Hubba. The ownership had changed hands and the Hubba Hubba became an underground hangout for the crew of one of Harlem's biggest kingpins, Frank Lucas. Lucas had made his fortune by going around the French Connection middlemen and buying kilos of heroin directly from producers in Thailand. That bold move meant he could net a profit of $100,000 for every kilo of heroin that made it to the US. His crew was a cliquish group of young guys with big egos making stupid money. I'd once seen a sixteen-year-old member of their crew make 1,700 hand-to-hand sales of quarter bags of heroin in one day of work, a hustling record that netted $42,500 cash in broad daylight. Hundreds of thousands of dollars were exchanging hands in their dice games, so you know I had to find a way in. I had a friend named Earl who was down with them, so when I heard about a big dice game happening over at the old Hubba Hubba, I stuffed a wad of starter money, $10,000 cash, in my sock and hopped on my bicycle to roll on over to their spot. I didn't know Lucas's crew as well as I knew other crews, but that had never really been a problem before. Just in case, I brought my friend Moon, who worked as a bodyguard for the other major kingpin in Harlem, Nicky Barnes.

The Lucas crew was an insulated bunch. You had to know everybody to even get through the door. Their guard was up from the moment I walked in.

Immediately, the aggressive questions started flying.

"Who's he?" said someone, pointing at me. "We don't know him."

We hadn't even started putting down bets yet. Not a good start.

"They good, they good," said Earl, vouching for us.

I knew these guys had a reputation for being clannish, but there was an additional undercurrent of hostility. Staring in awe at the piles of cash on the floor, I stayed. "Okay, man, too many people down," said one of them. "Five hundred dollars and up, per bet."

That meant the minimum you could bet on a single dice roll was five hundred dollars. That was the craziest thing I'd ever heard. I thought it was a move meant to intimidate any timid gamblers and also to feel me out, see if I was serious, but all of a sudden all of these young guys started dropping Gs—a G here, a G there. Like it was nothing. I'm talmbout *everybody* got money. The whole crew had stacks and stacks—I'm talmbout *stacks* of money. And they all looked like they were still in high school.

Can you imagine what that was like for me? I was in *heaven*. Oh, man. I felt like the only rat at the biggest picnic in the world.

Once the game was under way, guys started coming at me even more aggressively. Every now and then, someone would interrupt and ask, "You gone bet? What you betting?" Trash talk was a normal part of every dice game I'd ever played. They say something fly to us; we say something fly back to them. Sometimes, an upset gambler might take out his gun and fire off shots in the air in frustration. But at the end of the day, there had always been an understanding, a certain code that nothing shady would go down, otherwise it would ruin a guy's reputation in the streets, jeopardizing his entry into future games. Every single day, right as we speak, people are going to casinos. Losing money. Do they fight the owners? Do they demand their money back? Nothing happens. It's the same mentality. Our gambling had its rules, its respect, its cultural understanding.

So I ain't pay these guys no attention with all their nasty talk. I'd never won like I was winning. It was already the most money I'd ever held in a single game of dice in my life.

But they kept asking, "Who y'all with? Who y'all with?"

They already knew Moon was down with Nicky Barnes, and I felt sure they wouldn't do nothing to him because everyone was petrified of Nicky, but they kept wanting to know more about me. I said something slick and kept my focus on the game. Egos were flaring, just as I hoped. They trying to win me as usual, while I'm trying to win the game. I was planning to keep breaking them as long as I could, when I felt Earl slide up behind me and lean in close to my ear.

"Danny, man," he whispered. "Please, please, don't say nothing else."

When I saw the fearful look on Earl's face, I understood that I was in more danger than I'd realized. Keeping my composure, I slowly gathered up most of my winnings and hit Moon on the arm. "Follow my lead," I whispered.

"Hold this bet for me," I said, putting down five hundred dollars. "I gotta take a leak."

Moon followed me out the front door.

And we was gone.

When I got back to my apartment and counted it all up, I had over fifty thousand dollars—from one dice game. I hardly knew what to do with it. The next day, I went down to a dealership on Forty-second Street and drove a new blue Mercedes-Benz 280S off the lot, paid for in cash. I rode down to that game on a bike, and I left in a Benz.

When I ran into Earl later that summer, he told me that it was a good thing I had left when I did because Lucas's crew had been planning to kill me and Moon that night and leave us in the basement. I knew he was telling the truth because news had just come out that they'd found other bodies down there. Mine could have easily been one of them.

———

Without a partner like Russell beside me, the stress of making a living as a solo dice hustler in this new bloodthirsty environment was wearing me down. My wife, June, knew this better than anyone. "I don't wanna gamble no more," I would always tell her. "I really don't wanna do this." I didn't like the people that gambling put me around. I didn't like the mentality of the street. I didn't wanna be that. I was looking for a way to get money without it affecting my conscience.

Once you reach a state of awareness, you start seeing your friends and what they're doing, the experience that's hurting all of us together. The pain that we're inflicting upon each other. I was even thinking about coming out with a T-shirt that said "I've seen the enemy. And it's us." It's like in that movie *The Pawnbroker* with Rod Steiger. His character is a Holocaust survivor running a pawn shop in East Harlem, and he sees what's happening to the blacks and Hispanics in the community and realizes what's happening to them, because the same thing had happened to him in Nazi Germany. Now that I'm bearing witness to the decimation of my people, how I'm going to be so friendly with them knowing what they're doing to the community? All of this was punctuated for me on a quiet night that found me sitting on a stoop talking to Shawn, a young woman who was the sister-in-law of a drug dealer I knew named K. K had started out working under Lucas but then broke off and began making trips to Asia himself to source the heroin.

"You heard K and them got locked up over there?" she said.

I hadn't heard that. I'd been cool with K and his crew and gambled with them before. They was getting money like crazy from branching out on their own. Shawn told me they were in Thailand when authorities kicked in their hotel door and gave them eight years in prison. Only K made it back home to Harlem in the end. One of them died over there in Thailand, while the other one got addicted to drugs.

Shawn's baby sat in her lap, sucking its thumb. Though I wasn't best of friends with K and his crew, I felt a sense of loss for them.

"Damn, K got busted over there, huh?" I said, still processing the news. At the very least, I was a witness to these young lives and the tragedies that so often occurred around me in Harlem. Despite the fact that so many of her friends and family had gotten involved in the drug game, Shawn herself had stayed out of it. I had a great deal of respect for her. Which is why what she said next hit me with such power.

"That's what happens to people," she said, "who make money off other people's sorrows."

She was right. As much as I tried to rationalize what I was doing, stealing from these dealers, I was still making money off of sorrow. Those words on that night, from the lips of that woman, was what made me walk away from gambling. That was it for me. Whatever I did in life, I knew it would have to be something that wasn't creating victims. Soon, a chance encounter on the streets would plant the seed for a brand-new hustle that would provide just that: a hustle with no vics, a hustle more lucrative than any dice game I'd ever played, a hustle that eventually gave me the capital I needed to go aboveground and leave the streets for good. I ain't even talking about selling clothes yet.

CHAPTER 13

———

Aruba

What Shawn said about profiting off other people's sorrows was still ringing in my ears. At the same time, I had a family to feed. I started selling clothes out of the trunk of my car, but fashion was still only a side hustle, and all the goods was coming from a creep-thief who sold them to me after boosting them from department stores. I wasn't yet convinced I could make a living from clothes. So I kept swallowing my morals and going down to the drug corners and shooting dice. A lot of the guys I grew up with had become bosses of their own crews. They knew my reputation, but their crews didn't. They'd often warn their younger members about playing dice with me.

"Y'all don't want it with him," they'd say, laughing. "Leave Dap alone, man."

But the younger guys would let their egos get the best of them, and I'd just be spanking them and spanking them.

That's exactly what was happening on West 116th Street when a guy who'd just used the last of his cash pulled out an envelope from his coat pocket. He said he'd knocked off a FedEx truck the other day, and he handed me one of the packages from it. Inside the envelope was a bunch of credit cards. They were supposed to go to some executives at a big company downtown.

Credit cards had been around since the 1950s, but they'd never been part of my reality or the everyday lives of most people I knew in Harlem. That was for the middle class and wealthy. But there were some hustlers who specialized in the paper game. That's what we called everything from kiting checks to credit card fraud—the paper game. Since dice had been my main focus, I'd never really thought about the paper game before, but now that I was looking for distance from gambling, I got curious. I'd heard a rumor about some guys in the Nation of Islam who were masters of it. I had a hunch that I could maybe do something with these stolen cards, even if I wasn't sure what.

"So?" he said. "Can you use em?"

"Yeah," I said. "How much you sellin em for?"

"Fifty a piece," he said.

He had half a dozen cards. I took all of them joints.

The next thing I did was call up my friend Hasan, who was in the Nation of Islam and knew all about the paper game.

"Can we do anything with these cards?" I asked him.

Hasan said, "Yeah, man, we can make a killing with this."

"Yeah?"

"You know Amir, right?" said Hasan.

Man, Amir and I went way back. We used to be in the same Harlem Academy program, taking the bus to and from prep school out in Newark. I knew Amir's whole family.

"Yeah, I know Amir."

"He the one with all the science about the credit cards," said Hasan. "You need to talk to him."

So I called up Amir. In the years since our Urban League prep school days, Amir had joined the Nation and was even one of the people indicted but never convicted of the high-profile murder of an NYPD officer inside the No. 7 Mosque, which drew national attention. Since then, Amir had had a falling-out with the Nation and left the organization after Minister Louis Farrakhan had risen to power. As a devout Muslim, Amir was a man of discipline and self-control, so I knew he'd make a good partner for any paper-game job.

Amir was sharp, one of those guys who was three steps ahead of everybody else, and when he and I met up with Hasan to discuss what to do with the stolen cards, Amir's expertise was apparent. His plan was to get us some fake IDs to match the credit cards. Then we'd buy as much expensive jewelry as we could before the credit card companies caught wind. Then we'd sell the jewelry and make a killing. "But we ain't gone get it here," Amir explained to me and Hasan. "We gone go out of the country and get it. If we go out the country like South America and the islands, man, we can play this to the fullest." That part of the world was virgin territory for credit card fraud. Store clerks and local authorities wouldn't be able to pick up on the game, and by the time they did, we'd be long gone.

A job like that meant we needed a team. Besides Hasan, Amir, and me, we wanted someone who could speak Spanish, because we were planning to visit at least a couple Latin American countries, so Amir enlisted a friend of his named Nabil, a Puerto Rican Muslim. I was tight with a couple Dominican women from my time spent dancing in the Latin dance halls, so I enlisted them for the trip. They could provide a certain amount of cover, making it look like we were some black executives on a honeymoon with our spouses, not a crew of con artists pulling a credit card scam. Since I was the one who'd bought the cards and was footing the bill for the trip, I made whatever I made plus half of whatever everyone else made.

A few months later, IDs ready, we hit the road. Our first stops were in the Caribbean: we hit St. Croix and Curaçao, busting the cards out at the jewelry shops and buying gold rings, gold chains, gold nuggets, gold coins. We was island-hopping like crazy, going everywhere, busting the paper. None of the store clerks was catching on to us. But once we got to Barbados, I started to have a bad feeling. For starters, the two Dominicanas I'd brought along were becoming a distraction. I'd always kept in mind what my former mentor Killa had said—"Don't let your dick beat you hustling"—so I never let women mess around with my work. Neither did Amir. But Hasan was having himself a good time. He was taking the girls back to his hotel room every night, having sex with them on the terrace, making all kinds of noise, breaking champagne bottles. After one of his wild nights, we had a meeting.

"Yo, these girls messing up the situation," I said. "They gotta go."

But even after we sent the girls home and started using our cards again at the jewelry stores in Barbados, I still felt uneasy. It seemed like every store we hit something went wrong. The clerks weren't acting normal. They'd take our cards in back and ask us to wait. I worried that, somehow, people had gotten wind of what we were doing. I said to the other guys, "Something ain't right here."

We didn't stay too long in Barbados after that. We'd already hit three or four stores by that point, so to play it safe, I made a side trip to St. Thomas, where June's mother lived, and dropped all the jewelry I'd bought so far with her, cleaning up shop. After that, I flew to Venezuela to meet up with the team and continue the journey.

On our first day in Venezuela, police pulled us over on the highway. They weren't just regular police. They were soldiers with automatic rifles, and they didn't speak English at all. Luckily, we had Nabil, who spoke Spanish. The soldiers made us get out the car. I didn't know what was going on. Later, we'd learn that the soldiers in Venezuela were notorious for robbing people, especially well-dressed foreigners like us. They took us over on the side of the road. They were talking in heated tones with Nabil. Meanwhile, they had their rifles aimed at us. It seemed like Nabil was trying desperately to reason with them. All I heard was *Baba-baba-ba.*

"What the hell is going on?" I said under my breath.

"Man, I don't know," said Amir.

We had no idea what the police were saying to Nabil or what he was saying back to them, but the fear in Nabil's face was unmistakable. I was thinking it must be some kind of mistaken-identity thing. They must think we was some kind of killers or CIA operatives or something. After a while, Nabil managed to talk them down with some American dollars. They pocketed the bribe and let us go.

Back in the car, I said, "We gettin the fuck up outta here." So we turned right back around and drove our asses to the airport. Only later did we find out that Nabil was begging the soldiers for our lives. "They was gone kill us," said Nabil as we sat waiting for our flight. "They was gone kill us, take everything we had, and leave us there."

It seemed like whatever luck we'd started with on the trip was running out. I was feeling like our next stop, the Dutch Caribbean island of Aruba, should be our last one before we took our earnings and caught a flight back home. Our only plan there was to meet up with R & B singer Patti LaBelle, whom we met by chance earlier in the trip. She'd expressed interest in buying some jewelry from us when we got to Aruba. The plan was to sell her the jewelry and take off back to the States with the cash, but we couldn't resist making a few more purchases while we was there.

To look less suspicious, we split up from our hotel in Aruba into two-man groups. Amir and Nabil went to one side of the island, while me and Hasan went to hit up the stores on the other side. We agreed to meet back up at the hotel for lunch. The Aruba merchants seemed easier than the ones in Barbados. We put on our charm, made small talk. They ran our cards and sold us jewelry, no questions asked. A few hours later, Hasan and I gathered up what

The second boutique location on 125th, with a new awning.

From left, my good friend Walter, aka Cha-Cha, who used to tear up the Latin dance clubs with me; his brother Gene; and a friend, all in my stuff, late 1980s.

Big Daddy Kane (center) and customers next to my MCM
Jeep, which I kept parked outside the store.

Me and NBA players (from left) Derrick McKey, Olden Polynice, and
Jerry "Ice" Reynolds. Part of my early celebrity and athlete clientele.

PAPER magazine's "Women in Hip-Hop" photo shoot in 1988 featured four of my fits: Sparky D (back row, far left) has the navy and gray Gucci dress; one of her dancers (front row, far left) has the brown Louis suit; and her other dancer (middle row, far right) has the pink Fendi tracksuit. Synquis (front row, far right) has the navy Fendi tracksuit. Logomania at its finest! *Photo © by Janette Beckman*

Salt-N-Pepa decked out in Dapper Dan at a photo shoot for their label in 1988. *Photo © by Janette Beckman*

LL Cool J in the Gucci crisscross jacket, circa 1987. *Photo by Drew Carolan*

Jam Master Jay of Run-DMC in a Louis Vuitton bomber tracksuit, on the set of the music video for "Tougher Than Leather," circa 1986. *Photo © 1986 by Glen E. Friedman*

Sparky D, a pioneer MC
in the hip-hop world,
dressed in a Dapper
all-leather Gucci
dress in 1988.
Photo © by
Janette Beckman

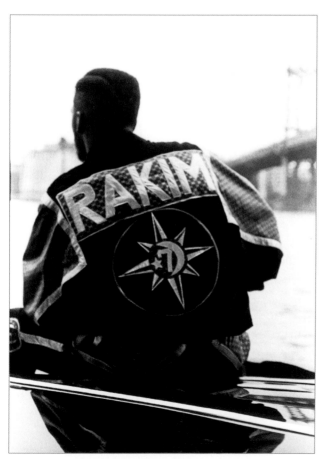

The famous
Gucci ensemble
I made for
Eric B. & Rakim's
album shoot.
Photo by
Drew Carolan

The notorious Mike Tyson vs. Mitch Green fight at my store. Mike shakes hands with Mitch before they took it outside, four A.M., August 23, 1988.

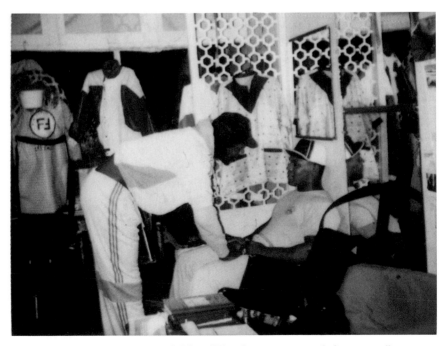

Mitch starts antagonizing Mike. "You know you ain't beat me."

Mitch follows Mike outside to his Rolls-Royce, still not letting up.

Mike finally has enough and knocks Mitch out.

Posing in Harlem for a photo shoot, showcasing my designs for the 2018 partnership with Gucci. *Photo © by Janette Beckman*

we'd bought and headed back to the hotel, but when we arrived, Amir and Nabil wasn't nowhere to be found. We got in our car and started going around the tiny island looking for them. Before long, I noticed a sound coming from behind us.

Sirens.

A cavalry of police cars came whizzing past at top speed. While we kept searching for Amir and Nabil, we kept seeing these same police cars screaming back and forth around the island. Aruba's so small that they'd zip by where we were going one way, and then a few minutes later they'd zip going the other way.

"Where they going?" said Hasan.

I had this bad feeling that they was looking for us.

Something told me we needed to get out of Dodge with the quickness. But we didn't know where to go. It was an island, after all. So we pulled over, walked down to the beach, and stood there ripping up all the paper we'd accumulated from the trip, tearing up dozens of carbon-copy receipts and trying to toss them into the ocean. As we were doing that, two cop cars pulled up to us with sirens blaring. We were surrounded. The only escape woulda been swimming out. They told us to turn around, then slapped on the cuffs, and took us into custody.

We didn't know when, we didn't know how, but somehow our paper game must have blown up. We knew it for sure as soon as we got to the precinct. Sitting alone in the holding cell were Amir and Nabil. The job was officially over.

Luckily, the charges against us seemed relatively minor, and our court-appointed lawyer kept assuring us that we'd be out in thirty days for such a victimless and unheard-of offense as using stolen credit cards. But thirty days passed with us just sitting in jail. I sent letters home to my family telling them about the situation. With all the tragedies our family had been through the past few years, I could tell from my sisters' letters that my imprisonment in a foreign country was hitting Daddy real hard. After the episode in Venezuela, I didn't trust that we wouldn't be abused or mistreated, so I instructed the mothers of my children to make sure to send me a letter every morning so that these people knew there were folks back in America who were watching. The other guys were sending frantic letters home, too, asking for assistance: "In the name of the Most Honorable Elijah Muhammad . . ."

By then, our exploits had hit the local papers in Aruba. *Islamic criminal gang has been operating on the island.* Forty days passed. Then fifty. We sat in jail for two whole months before they brought us before a judge, but when we finally had our day in court, I assumed we was gonna have an outcome similar to my first arrest back home, when I lucked out and got time served. It seemed like there was a good chance that they'd just let us go that day, and our lawyer agreed. He kept assuring us that the charges were minor, very minor.

But he was wrong. They threw the book at the four of us. The judge sentenced us to nine months in a *huis van bewaring,* the Dutch term for prison. Later, the warden would admit to my wife that the harsh sentence was likely rooted in religious prejudice. We'd be locked up in Aruba for another two-hundred-some-odd days.

The prison in Aruba was as small and relaxed as the island itself. It had a little courtyard next to the cells—one step out and you were in it. We slept three to a cell or one to a cell; they didn't let us sleep two to a cell. Me and Amir and some white boy, Nabil and Hasan with another white boy. In the middle of each cell, on the back wall, there was a shower stall where you'd shower, and in the middle of the shower stall, there was a hole where you'd shit. No toilet, no seat. When I came back to America after nine months of squatting over a hole, I couldn't even use the toilet right. My thighs were so built up from squatting, I'd just hover.

It was chill as far as prisons go. The guards carried around six-shooter pistols, passed by once a day, and used a skeleton key on the doors to let us out. In the mornings, we got a cup of coffee and bread, and later on we'd get a bowl with everything in it that we were going to eat for the rest of the day. Since none of us ate meat based on our beliefs, we insisted that they give us a vegetarian diet, so we had a vegetarian diet. For nine months, I ate nothing but tropical fruits and fresh vegetables. I was a fruitarian. Two of the mothers of my children came to visit, bringing me money so I had something to spend. If we complained, the warden would come see us, plus the American consulate by law had to come see us once a month because we were in a foreign jail.

What made the experience even more unique was that we were the only black people in there, which is the other reason I think the sentence was so harsh. There were other Americans in there but they were white boys. Who knew all these white boys were in prison in Aruba? And these white boys weren't like the white boys we knew from New York prisons. They were all pilots and college graduates. As fellow countrymen, we struck up a friendship with these white-boy pilots.

"How long they give you?"

"Thirty days," they all said. "Failure to file a flight plan."

After we'd finally been in there a while and seen all these different white boys from America come and go thirty days at a time from the *huis van bewaring* for failing to file a flight plan, we started getting curious. There had to be more to the story. Soon we got the full scoop: they were working for a drug-smuggling ring called the Black Tuna Gang based out of Florida. Like Frank Lucas had done with heroin, the Black Tuna Gang were innovators of large-scale reefer smuggling that would pave the way for better-organized South American cocaine cartels in the 1980s. They was gutting out old DC-3 airplanes, the kind used during World War II, and filling them up in Colombia with reefer. The DEA estimates that the Black Tuna Gang smuggled over five hundred tons of reefer during the seventies before they were finally caught.

One of our cellmates was a middle-aged guy who said he'd made over a million dollars making flights between Colombia and airstrips in Florida. "Just to give you an idea," he said, "the guy who unloads the plane for me gets fifty thousand each trip."

But how'd they wind up in Aruba?

He broke it down. Whenever they'd fly back from Colombia with a shipment, they had guys, soldiers working at small airstrips, who let them land. They'd call down from the plane: *Carlos, open the gate.* That was the code word for turning on the airstrip lights and letting them land. But sometimes their guys wouldn't be in the tower when they arrived, so they'd have to turn the plane back around. The planes didn't have enough gas to make it back to Colombia, so they had to dump the entire shipment of drugs into the sea and find somewhere else to land.

"We can't land in Cuba anymore because Castro's been giving us a hard time lately," he explained. "So we've been landing here in Aruba."

Since they'd already dumped the drugs into the water, the authorities in Aruba couldn't charge them with anything but a minor violation: failure to file a flight plan, which came with a sentence of thirty days.

Hasan was fascinated by what these white boys were doing with the drug game. He sat for hours and hours learning from them, asking questions. And later, once we made it back stateside, he'd take what he'd learned in Aruba and start up his own South American import business.

For my part, I used the time in Aruba, like I had in the Tombs, to reconnect with my spiritual self. There's not space for much self-reflection when you're hustling. This was the first and only time in my adult life that I didn't have to worry about nobody. I was exercising every day and, after my family sent me my spiritual books, I was reading every night, diving even deeper into Hilton Hotema's collection. I was completely at peace. The only real conflict I encountered was the heated philosophical debates I had with Amir, Nabil, and Hasan, whose hard-line Nation of Islam views clashed with my perspective. (There might have also been some animosity left over because the whole credit card trip had been my idea in the first place.)

We got into a discussion about Elijah Muhammad's interpretations of scripture. My self-guided comparative-religion studies made me less rigid in my interpretations. I took the words of scripture metaphorically and tried to connect them with other ways of thinking. The other guys didn't like that. When Muslims go to jail, they can get *real* spiritual. They stopped talking to me. I said, "Yo, okay, just wait until the books get here." I had my whole collection sent over, and they started reading and reading and reading. This was the first time in their lives they heard about the higher forms of Masonry, Eastern religions, the chakras, discourses by Hotema, Helena Blavatsky, and Amos Bronson Alcott. And I had *Man's Higher Consciousness* there, I had *The Secret of Regeneration* there, I had *The World's Sixteen Crucified Saviors* there. Their whole mindset changed, and peace was restored.

The teaching went both ways. While Hasan was learning about the smuggling game from the Black Tuna pilots, Amir was sciencing me out to the paper game, since he knew more than anybody about it. He was part of the reason why they used to blank out the numbers on the cards in credit card commercials, because Amir and his crew were taking them directly off the TV. Now that he wasn't affiliated with the Nation, he'd been branching out on his own, trying other angles. He broke down the whole history of the credit card industry and how they was playing it. Every night I would ask him questions. And every night he would break it down to me. As I got my PhD in the paper game, I started seeing a lot of potential.

There wasn't no question too stupid for me to ask. What kind of plastic they use? Where do they get it? How they come up with the numbers? Amir knew it all. The more I learned, the more I blamed myself for putting us in this situation. I hadn't done enough reading on the credit card game. Before we'd decided to hit up the islands with our fake IDs and stolen cards, I shoulda studied more, learned the history, the ins and outs, backwards and forwards, the way I'd mastered gambling with dice. I'd gone out on a limb with this trip and fallen on my ass. Next time, it'd be different. Next time, I'd make sure that no one saw me coming.

CHAPTER 14

Remakes

When we finally left Aruba, we were on needles and pins because we thought we was gonna get arrested when we got back home. Fortunately, getting arrested for the same crime woulda been double jeopardy, so there was nothing the US authorities could do. When we got off the plane, we was cool, and thanks to Amir's schooling me on the credit cards while we were locked up, I was ripe and ready to bust the uncharted territory of the paper game wide open.

But I was broke. Even though I vowed to do something other than gamble, the long sentence in Aruba had set me back to square one. Compared to the dice, the paper game felt like a bigger risk. There was an unknown factor to it, it was so new. I decided to go back to the safe money of the dice games, at least for now, though I knew I couldn't take part in any of the big games without at least five Gs in my pocket. I had to figure out a new way to hustle up some gambling funds in a timely manner. I needed to do some flatfoot hustling.

My first stop was the boosters, who had been providing the clothes I'd occasionally sell outta my trunk before Aruba. The boosters I worked with were often in need of drivers to take them to department stores around the city. They wasn't the kinda guys who could afford their own cars, so they always had to have a driver there to get them out in a jiffy.

I started taking out two boosters every day. I drove them down to wherever they wanted and waited out front with the engine running. They'd give me fifty dollars each, and on top of that, I also bought whatever they'd stolen that day for 25 percent of retail. Then I took the clothes and sold them to my hustler friends for 50 percent of retail. I had all the dealers back uptown buying boosted clothes from me.

My first thirty days, I knocked up a hundred dollars a day just from the driving, plus whatever profit I turned from selling the boosted clothes. And I spent as little money as humanly possible. I didn't have no bad habits, and some days I ain't even have to eat if I didn't want to. After a month, I'd saved up five Gs and was back in business, ready to hit the dice games again outta sheer necessity. But word had gotten out in the neighborhood about my adventures in the Caribbean. A lot of the guys I knew would come around flashing stolen cards and offering to sell em to me—guys like Slim, a friend from around the way.

"Yo," said Slim, flashing a credit card. "I got these for sale."

But I didn't pay him no mind. I'd rather take my chances gambling with the drug dealers than risk getting locked up again. "I don't mess with the cards no more," I told him.

"These ain't regular, though."

"Looks like a regular card to me."

"It's a remake."

Slim told me how he'd gotten it from some white boys who'd started producing their own credit cards. They took a regular card's numbers and somehow, through some process that Slim didn't understand, switched them to numbers that they had stolen from other people's discarded carbon copy receipts. In other words, you didn't have to steal someone's credit card to draw funds from their account, you could just get their numbers and create a brand-new card.

"How they change the numbers on there?" I wondered.

Slim had no idea.

My gears were turning. I couldn't help myself. I started reading up on credit card plastics. Although there was a law for stolen credit cards, there wasn't anything yet on the books about stealing the numbers and creating new cards, as far as I could tell. Plus, the credit card companies wouldn't know what was going on if charges started showing up on a person who still was in possession of their card. Remakes were a way I could bust the paper game wide open. But the big mystery I needed to figure out was the process of putting the numbers on the plastic. I became obsessed.

I locked myself in the house, experimenting, then experimenting, then more experimenting. I baked the card, I boiled it, I melted it. I thought of every way I could to remove the numbers off a credit card and plant new ones on it. I didn't do nothing for three straight weeks but experiment, only leaving the house to get food and come back. I wasn't getting nowhere. But even though my DIY approach wasn't working, I didn't quit.

As in times past, I set about reading my way towards a solution. I picked up manuals that the credit card companies used. Soon, I realized that a visit to Pitney Bowes was in order. A major American technology company, Pitney Bowes were the ones who created the first bar code equipment for retail use. They also manufactured the technology for making credit cards. Pitney Bowes's offices at the time were in the old Twin Towers, so I threw on a suit and tie, got real fly, and went down to the World Trade Center to discuss their machinery.

I sat there across the desk from the sales representatives and put on my best business persona. My story was I worked for a small bank that wanted to offer a credit card. "Where might one find such machines?" I asked.

"Well, sir, most hospitals do use a similar one to produce staff identification."

"So hospitals, you say?"

"Yes, sir."

"Quite interesting."

Now, it wasn't as easy as putting cash on the table and walking out with a credit-card-making machine. There were all kinda reasons why I couldn't just buy one. Instead, I took every informational brochure and pamphlet and document they had to offer. "I'll certainly be in touch, my good man," I said, shaking hands and bidding them good day. I stuffed all the documents in my briefcase and headed all the way back uptown. Soon as I got home, I called my man Lonzo, who worked at a hospital. If Pitney Bowes said I could find similar machinery in hospitals, there was a chance that Lonzo could get me one.

I started to describe it to him.

"Yeah," he said. "We got one at the hospital."

My man Lonz!

I paid Lonzo to knock it off. He crept in through the window after hours and got that joint. The fact that it was not the typical thing anyone breaking into a hospital would ever think to steal meant there wasn't a serious investigation. And when Lonzo asked me what I needed this weird machine for, I was evasive about my plans. Soon as I brought it back home, I started my experiments up again. This time, the numbers came on and off the cards with ease.

Uh-oh, I said to myself. *It's on now, goddammit!*

Now that I had the key to manufacturing my own credit cards, I needed to assemble a new team to start putting them in play. What

I was doing existed in such a legal gray area at the time, I had a feeling that this was going to make me a killing for as long as I could stay under the radar. With the money I stood to make off this hustle, I needed a crew of people I could trust around me. I needed my oldest and truest friends. I needed Curtis and Russell.

There was a part of me that hoped having them close would keep them from getting into trouble on the streets, because the streets was becoming extra murderous. A fifth of the city was living below the poverty line, while the wealthy and powerful refused to acknowledge the depths of our despair. You had historic prosperity on one side of Manhattan and unprecedented suffering on the other—1980 was the most lucrative year in Wall Street history and the worst year of crime in New York City history, with over 2,200 murders. Dudes we knew were dropping like flies all around us. I'm still not over so many of those losses. Curtis hadn't been able to shake his dope habit, and Russell's coke use was putting his own life in serious jeopardy. I was scared for him, especially after what had happened to our friend Lil Scotty.

Lil Scotty who wore his hat broke off at an angle, cocked "ace deuce trè" as we called it, Lil Scotty who first brought Russell and me together at a dice game a decade before. That Lil Scotty had started selling coke, but he'd been using it, too, like Russell. Soon, he was hooked and messing up the work. He fell into debt with his suppliers, started lying to them about the money they were front- ing him. They wasn't dumb, they figured it out, and when they did, they had a friend of ours kill him.

I'd heard that Russell was getting into similar danger. I didn't know how deep the danger was until one night I heard someone pounding frantically at my door, so loud it woke everyone in the building up. When I went downstairs and opened it, Russell was standing there looking terrified. His face was covered in sweat, his pupils dilated.

"Hey," he said. "Can I come in? I got problems, man."

Of course I let him in, because this is Russell, my brother, my partner. I trusted everything he said. He took out a brown paper bag from his coat pocket and held it towards me. There was thirty-five hundred in the bag, and he wanted me to hide it for him. I tried to follow his train of thought as he explained to me the seriousness of the situation, but I was having trouble. "Shhh!" he said, all of a sudden. I sat there in the silence of my living room, my ears perked up, trying to hear what he was hearing. But I couldn't hear anything. Russell stood and put a finger over his lips and dragged me towards the bathroom. He whispered, "They in the vent."

"Who's in the vent?"

When we got to the bathroom and locked the door behind us, Russell said it again: "They in the vent!"

"Oh, shit," I said. "They in there? Damn."

It seemed like someone had been following or spying on him. Maybe some other gangsters or maybe the cops. I didn't know what to do, trapped in the bathroom with him. "I gotta hide this," said Russell, and he went into his brown bag and started stuffing big bills into the tank of my toilet. This was a guy I trusted with my life. I wasn't used to the paranoid side effects of heavy cocaine use. I was thinking Russell was for real. And whether it was real or he was just hallucinating, he was putting me in danger. That's why you hear me talk about the danger of a weak friend. Weak friends are worse than strong enemies. An enemy can't tell me nothin, but a friend like Russell could tell me something and I'd trust him. Now I've got to watch out for him. He could come to me with a story that was sheer paranoia and, because he was my trusted friend, it could catch me out and put my life in danger. I hung on to the money for a few days and gave it back to him after he'd calmed down.

Russell and Curtis didn't deserve to waste away on the streets. Neither did so many other friends and family we knew. I had to get them away from the curse of the drug game. So I gathered them at my place and explained the logistics of our new hustle. We'd go downtown at night dressed real fly in suits, so no one would see us coming, and we'd go inside the trash cans—

"I ain't going in no trash can," said Curtis. "I ain't no bum."

"Let me finish," I said, and continued explaining that what we were looking for wasn't no scraps of food or leftover cigarettes. We were looking for credit card receipts. We'd take the credit card numbers off the receipts and put the numbers on our blank cards. If it worked the way I thought it would, we was gone make a killing.

They was down.

I started taking Russell and Curtis out every day with remade cards, collecting receipts and using the remakes to get cash advances and purchase expensive goods to sell on the streets. But because of their addictions, they was in worse shape than I realized. I'd have to take them to get high and then make them use the toilet before we went out on the town for a score, because I couldn't trust them to handle themselves without it. I hated doing that, but I didn't see no better way.

While we drove around, I'd also take out that record "The Gambler" by Kenny Rogers and put it on the cassette player. *You gotta know when to hold em, know when to fold em, know when to walk away, know when to run.* I was trying to school em. I told Russell and Curtis, "Hold your money. Don't spend none of your money."

But they ain't listen.

From the time I was thirty-five until I was thirty-seven, I ran the remake hustle full-time, and man I was killing em. Just killing em. I wasn't spending a dime of the money I was making, neither. I saved it all up. I knew the more we spent, the faster we'd get caught. I also knew that there was only so long that we could run this game before the authorities started getting wise, so best to play it hard but play it safe.

As for the specifics of how the remaking process worked, I wouldn't tell nobody. Not Russell, not Curtis. I mean, nobody. I kept the game to myself. I didn't want it to spread too quickly or it would risk bringing us all down. Even though I trusted both of them guys with my life under normal circumstances, they were compromised by the drugs, and I didn't think there was anything I could do besides put money in their pockets and keep them close. None of my team knew what kind of machine I had or where I'd gotten it from. All they knew was that somehow I'd figured out how to take a credit card and put numbers on it so that it worked like a real one. They knew the what, but not the how, and I kept it that way for a while. For two years, I was setting everybody up. Not just Russell and Curtis, but Amir and others, because eventually I had to spread the joy to my other friends, and soon everybody was getting in on it. Because of the love we had with each other, I couldn't keep it all to myself. I shared the game with my brothers Omar and Cesar, too. Even though Omar had moved upstate after a street beef had made Harlem dangerous for him, he came back from time to time for a credit card score.

But like all games over time, the paper game got dusty.

When people are under the influence of drugs like my friends were, they want the quickest route to cash. Instead of doing what I told them and going to a new place each time they used a different card, Russell and Curtis kept going back to the same banks using their remakes for cash advances. I said to them, "Why you keep going in the same place? You overplaying the spot." Soon, the tellers started recognizing them and alerting the authorities.

Since I was careful about it, I was never arrested for running the paper game, but Russell and Curtis was in and out of courtrooms for years. We were so ahead of the government that the judges downtown were confused whenever they brought them in. They were used to dealing with murderers and drug dealers—we was just guys with credit cards. Russell would go to court dressed in a suit and tie, holding a leather briefcase, and the prosecutors would try desperately to explain to the judge how serious his offenses were. But the judge would just squint.

"What you saying? He made a piece of plastic?" The judge be

up there getting irritated. "Are you crazy, man? I ain't got time for all this foolishness. What is he *doing*?"

The prosecutor say, "Well, I'm trying to explain it." The people who got caught with remakes was just getting thirty days, a slap on the wrist.

That same dynamic played out in court for years before the law came out. But eventually, federal forces started getting involved and the government voted and passed a law against the kind of credit card hustles we was running. When I read about the new legislation, which switched up the technology and increased the sentences, I told Russell and them, "That's it. I'm out."

"What you mean you out?" they said.

"I made tons of money off this here. Now with this law, they cracking down. So I'm walking away. Didn't I tell y'all save your money?"

I took my credit card machine and threw it in the East River, where it still sleeps with the fishes. I didn't want nothing to get back to me. I wouldn't even go around Russell and Curtis during that time.

The remake game had been more lucrative and safe than any other hustle I'd ever run. I was in my late thirties, coming up on forty. I'd been doing my gambling thing for more than a decade and the paper game for a couple years. I hadn't stepped on anybody's toes, which wasn't easy. I'd had some close calls. But somehow I got over. The fact that I managed to survive made me an exception. Whatever the future held for me, I knew I couldn't let the talents and skills I'd cultivated thus far in life go to waste. But before I could walk through the next door, I first had to walk away from the streets.

PART III

THE SHOP THAT NEVER CLOSED

And because I had been a hustler, I knew better than all whites knew, and better than nearly all of the black "leaders" knew, that actually the most dangerous black man in America was the ghetto hustler. Why do I say this? The hustler, out there in the ghetto jungles, has less respect for the white power structure than any other Negro in North America. The ghetto hustler is internally restrained by nothing. He has no religion, no concept of morality, no civic responsibility, no fear—nothing. To survive, he is out there constantly preying upon others, probing for any human weakness like a ferret. The ghetto hustler is forever frustrated, restless, and anxious for some "action." Whatever he undertakes, he commits himself to it fully, absolutely.

THE AUTOBIOGRAPHY OF MALCOLM X

CHAPTER 15

———

A New Hustle

I never go back to an old hustle. It's like how in the natural world, each seed you plant is going to grow, eventually die, then cast off new seeds. If you don't constantly repeat that cycle, life itself stagnates and dies. The same is true of hustling. After covering my children's expenses and private school tuition for the year, I took the money I'd saved up from the paper game, over one hundred Gs, and bought me a brand-new burgundy Mercedes-Benz and just rode around Harlem, trying to figure out the next seed I was gonna plant.

For a year, I didn't do no hustling. I cruised the neighborhood in my Benz, hung out, danced at the Latin clubs, just relaxed and had fun. After reading an article in the newspaper about urban renewal coming to Harlem, and with Constance Baker Motley, the first black woman elected to the New York State Senate, telling us to own our own houses, June and I pooled our savings and bought a brownstone, which was one of the smartest decisions we ever made. We moved in with our daughter, Danique, and been living in that brownstone ever since. I had a new car, a new house, some savings, but I still didn't have a plan for the future. As my year off was coming to an end, I said to myself, *Okay, now it's time for me to figure things out.*

What about clothes? Fashion for me wasn't about expression. Fashion was about power. I would navigate the streets with a certain look until I could own the look. Being fly was a vehicle to getting around my situation in life. But guys liked the way I dressed, and I did know a lot about fashion. From my connection with the boosters, I'd sampled the market and built up a small customer base by selling pieces out of my trunk to the drug dealers I knew, getting a feel for what people on the streets wanted. Along with my dice skills, I was known for my clothes. And every now and then, in between my spiritual readings, I'd pick up an issue of *Vogue* or *GQ* from the newsstand and look at the new high-end fashions, trying to imagine my own variations on trendy designs. I didn't know what kind of clothes I'd sell or where I'd get the clothes from. All I knew was that there was a demand among the drug dealers in the community, and it made business sense to open a store of some kind to supply the demand. I was gonna open up a shop.

Before I do anything, I try to understand it from as many angles as possible. Is it dangerous? Is it risky? What are the consequences? Can I do it alone? Do I have to trust somebody? And if I have to trust somebody, whom can I trust to do this with me that's capable? From dice to credit cards, it was true of every successful venture I'd ever done: I needed a good team.

As usual, my first thought was Russell. He would be the perfect business partner for this clothing idea. He had the same kind of entrepreneurial spirit and intellectual curiosity as me. The drug game had flooded the streets with cash. We could provide the hustlers with a legit place to spend it. Just like we did with the gambling, together we could take the clothes game to unseen new levels. I also hoped opening a shop could be a way to keep my friends and family off the streets, which were getting more violent by the day.

Long after I threw away my credit card machine and told my friends to stop running that scam because the authorities were catching on, Russell was still in the paper game, using the proceeds for drugs and maintaining the lifestyle of his drug-dealer friends. One day, I drove over to where he hung out to try to sell some clothes out my trunk, but I also had another motive: to convince Russell to venture into the clothes business with me. I wanted him with me. We were best friends still, but we were pulling away from each other. We'd lost so many of our people, and I could see that he was in pain. The rule between us was always that we had to tell each other the truth. No matter how ugly or hurtful. That's how it's always been with my closest hustler friends. We hustle others, but we never hustle each other. Lies are what eat a friendship.

I'll never forget that day. We were standing in front of Lenox Terrace, which is where Russell was living at the time, near a bar called Doll's, where a lot of the big ballers from Russell's neighborhood used to hang out.

We had made a certain kind of steady, happy money with the paper game. But it wasn't anything compared to what these dealer guys was getting. The amount I'd been saving up to start my clothing shop was a good amount for me. But these dealers were sometimes getting shopping bags of cash every day. Russell was seduced by that. He wanted it for himself.

"Let me get fifty dollars," said Russell, as we stood there, leaning against my car.

We did everything together, but he had something more powerful pulling him in the other direction, towards the drugs.

"Russell," I said, "don't be with them, man. Come with me. We gotta get away from this life. You don't have to be in it. We'll sell clothes."

He shook his head and for a while, just stared off at the brick towers in front us, saying nothing. His eyes got wide and distant, like he was trying to imagine the future. If so, what did he see? "Man," he said at last. "Just let me get fifty dollars. I'll get you back."

Russell didn't need to hang out with those guys, and that's what I kept trying to tell him that day. He couldn't see how significant the decision he was making would be. It was one thing not to know what the future held. It was another thing entirely not to care. He couldn't fully understand the danger he was in. He was smarter than this. He was my best friend. I kept stalling him, promising I'd give him the fifty, but first he had to hear me out one last time. I was begging him to come with me, but he kept brushing me off. Finally, after I'd said all I could, I handed him the money and watched him disappear into the bar.

I'd had a few other gambling partners, but no one like Russell. It's like we were hustling twins. He's a Leo, I'm a Leo. We were both from the tenements. We was brothers, survivors. It was devastating that my attempts to pull him away from drugs didn't work. As I opened and built my boutique, Russell kept playing the paper game for another four years, in and out of court. Judges were still confused about what was going on, but they were slowly catching on. He was addicted to cocaine, but the fast money he got from the credit card game was just as addictive as the drugs.

When we reminisce on those days now, Russell tells me that he was dealing with a lot of turbulent emotions that he hadn't been able to control. That period was so turbulent for all of us, but especially for guys like Russell who grew up abandoned by everybody. His father hadn't been in the picture when he was a kid, nor was his mother, who lived in a nicer building with her numbers-runner boyfriend, leaving Russell alone as a child, in the care of a friend. After her boyfriend got killed, Russell's mother, who, like my mother, worked as a domestic in the homes of white people, was left behind with nothing, no money, and just like my mother, she started hanging out, drinking, and wasting away. Russell tells me now that he longed for the foundation that a family might have provided. In all other respects, we were so similar, but that was the big difference between us: I had a father I was close with, I had my brothers. Russell didn't have nobody.

In the black community, we often underestimate the importance of the childhood years. My brother Omar once explained it to me like this: "Man, the Catholic Church professes that if they get you the first five years of your life, then they got you for the rest of your life." That's when I started thinking about my own childhood. I wouldn't have had this analytical way of thinking were it not for my brothers, who clued me in early on. I had well-read siblings who were exposing me to the world, and I can't imagine what kind of mindset I woulda had without their influence. It took Russell a lot of years and a lot of reading before he realized that the source of his pain was connected to what he was missing from the early years of his life.

Russell was smart, observant, a real player. And that was part of the problem. The strongest game that a player ever plays is the game he plays on himself.

Everybody who stayed in the paper game went to jail, including Russell. He ended up serving a year at the federal prison in Allenwood, Pennsylvania, for the credit card scam, where he was in the bullpen with Mafia boss John Gotti. When Russell got home, the drugs started really tearing up his life, but by then, I was so busy with the shop, I hardly ever saw him.

On the main drag of 125th Street, near a used-furniture store and dive bar, there was a small storefront for rent. Like most of the buildings in Harlem, 43 East 125th Street was owned by a Jewish guy. His name was Abramowitz, and in addition to owning the building, he was a furrier. "You're going to sell clothes?" he said. "Perfect! You can sell my furs."

I played along, but the problem was Abramowitz's furs were

garbage. He made a killing off selling inferior furs at a markup, banking on the fact that his Harlem customers wouldn't know the difference. Abramowitz thought he could sell us anything. And he was mostly right. We didn't have all the knowledge about high-quality furs or places to buy them. See, after a furrier like Abramowitz made a regular fur coat, he'd take all the scraps from the floor and piece them together to make a second coat. Furriers wasted no part of the animal. They made mink jackets from mink heads, mink tails, mink bellies. When I looked at the pattern of Abramowitz's cheap furs, it looked all scrambled, not like the even pattern of a high-quality fur, but I'd walk around Harlem and see people wearing furs like the kind Abramowitz wanted me to sell. You know how chitlins are the cheapest scraps of pork? Well, he wanted me to keep selling people chitlin furs.

Abramowitz was offering a good deal on rent since my shop would be a good outlet for him to move his inferior furs. I negotiated a ten-year lease. He thought it was a win-win for him: he gets a tenant paying him rent plus additional income from the sale of his merchandise by the tenant. He even let me draw up the lease. We had a witness. Abramowitz signed it, then I signed. He didn't know what I had in mind. As soon as possible, I wanted to stop carrying his furs and sell my own quality merchandise.

When I opened my shop, my dream was to become a big-time furrier and cater to the underworld, where I knew the real money was in Harlem. The numbers runners, the grifters, the drug dealers. Harlem had a fashion history rich with fur coats. When you look at old photographs of Harlem, that's what you see people wearing. My mother and all her friends had furs; I remember her running around the house in her furs, chasing after my sister Dolores with a strap. Fur was an important status symbol, part of what folks would call "ghetto fabulous." At first, I sold my landlord's furs, but my approach to life has always been to find out what the best person in the game is doing and try to go beyond their level of expertise, beyond what anyone might have thought possible. First it was dice, then the paper game, and now it was gonna be furs. I bought books about furs to study the different types of skins. I still have all those books on a shelf in the spare room of my brownstone. From my reading, I learned that there were hardly any black-operated furriers in the United States. They had one black furrier in New York and two in Chicago. I said to myself, *Damn, there's only three black furriers in the country!* I visited all three of them, even took a road trip to Chicago, so I could study the game.

If I wanted to start becoming a player, I knew I needed to form partnerships with local suppliers in the city. I needed someone to show me the ropes. But the furriers that I dealt with didn't have experience with starting their own businesses. They were part of old family enterprises that had been founded long before them. It was also difficult to find acceptance into the old-school community of "real furriers." They didn't take me seriously. Finally, I got the contact information for a Jewish guy named Irving Jacobs, who I'd been told was a guru. I got introduced to him through a couple of guys who wanted me to fence stolen furs through my shop, but the coats they brought always had the monogram of the previous owner stitched into the lining, which made them worthless for re-sale. "I can't sell these with the linings," I said, handing back the furs.

"We got a guy who can fix that," said the fur thieves.

That's how I came to meet Jacobs.

Besides being an OG in the fur game, Jacobs had that hustler side like me. We hit it off. He began schooling me on the difference between fur types and how to really tell quality. He took me to the warehouses and showed me the process that the coats had to go through.

"The animal itself needs to be cut up into pieces, then made into long strips," Jacobs explained. "That's one guy. Then there's one guy who you need if the furs need to be dyed. Then there's another guy who does the cutting. No one person does everything involved in the production of a single fur coat. There's a whole supply chain you deal with."

Jacobs scienced me out on all that. He ended up being kinda like my mentor in the fur game. By the time I was ready to start buying furs for my store, I knew the difference between what was garbage and what was quality. Once I'd learned the ins and outs from Jacobs, I had to break the news to my landlord.

"I ain't takin your furs no more," I said to Abramowitz, who understandably got upset.

But it was too late for him to do anything about it. Dapper Dan's Boutique was already open for business.

Before I opened the boutique, some of my hustler friends offered to be investors. Big bosses like New York Freddie, before the DEA sentenced him to forty years in prison, wanted to be down with me when I opened up. These guys were eager to go aboveground into the business world and do something clean with their fortunes. "Man," New York Freddie said, "I wanna get you some money."

I knew he had it, too: the DEA found three million in cash when they raided his house. I ain't take his money, though. Even if these guys were my friends, I wouldn't take no drug money as a business investment. But the retail side was another story. I relied on them as customers.

Since I knew all the powerful guys in the neighborhood, all the bosses and kingpins and hustlers from all the different areas that me and Russell used to beat at dice, I had a ready-made clientele for my coats. When I finally opened up, that's why they came: it was Dapper Dan's place. They knew me from the streets. Advertising and marketing took care of itself.

"Where you get that fur, boss?" one of their workers might ask.

"Oh, I got this from Dap's new store, man!" they'd tell the crew. "Go over there and give him a play."

But because all my first customers were hustlers, upstanding members of the black community saw me as a blight on 125th Street. For many folks in Harlem, my shop was part of the problem, another undesirable side effect of the drug curse, and they wanted nothing to do with me. Almost as soon as we went into business, the rumor mill went into business. All the church folk would pass by sucking teeth and muttering.

"You know, he not really selling furs."

"Yeah, I heard he moving drugs in them coats."

"They definitely bringing dope out in them furs."

On top of that, the black press was ignoring me. I couldn't get any of them to do a write-up to help publicize the store. *Jet* ignored me, *Ebony* ignored me, *New York Amsterdam News* ignored me. Community leaders put out the word against me. Antidrug organizations in the community had deemed my shop off-limits. I was basically blacklisted by mainstream black society because of my clientele. In the early days, I'd see someone I knew from the neighborhood pass by the store, and I'd say, "Come on in. Let me show you what we got in here."

And they'd say, "Nah, I can't go in there."

Even though some in the community had a problem with my clientele, it didn't bother me one bit that my customers were hustlers and drug dealers. Just the opposite. Any success I had in the fashion game I owe to them. It made sense to cater to them, since they were the ones who had the cash and the desire to spend it. And they didn't care what anyone thought of them. They were bold and decisive. They were the perfect clients. And the love was mutual. They appreciated having a place where they could purchase high-quality clothes. They all wanted furs, but didn't know how to get them. They didn't wanna go downtown, feel embarrassed about whipping out a big bankroll at a department store. After I got the big-time hustlers, that was it. Every other street guy with money felt comfortable buying furs from Dapper Dan's, turning this way and that in the big mirror that took up a wall in front.

The fur business was beautiful. I found a wholesaler by the name of Fred the Furrier who would sell to me. He was the guy who had the contracts for all the Alexander's stores, the same stores I used to shoplift from when I was a teenager. Fred was one of the biggest players in the fur game. He was Jewish, and at the time I entered the game, the Jewish guys had it on lock. In later years, the Greeks would move in, then the Koreans. As someone who wanted to cater specifically to black people, I didn't threaten Fred the Furrier's market, so he had nothing to lose from a partnership. Black people were not anyone's market at the time, because furriers like Fred assumed black people wouldn't be able to afford high-quality furs. But they didn't know what I knew about the market up in Harlem.

At the time, there was no way I could make less than $1,000 on every coat I sold. That's how sweet it was. If I invested $700 at the factory for crystal fox or mink—$400 for the skin plus $300 for the labor—I could have a men's fur coat that retailed at $3,000. The prices were so inflated. Not unlike the dope game in the early days, the fur game was tightly controlled by a small group of businessmen that could do whatever they wanted with the price.

When I realized the kind of legit money I could make in furs, I began to see the real potential of a boutique like mine. Despite the negativity of some in the community, I decided to go full blast at the fashion game, which meant thinking beyond furs.

As sweet as it was, selling high-end furs to the hustlers couldn't sustain me through the year. It was a seasonal product and only really moved in winter. I needed something else to generate income during the other months, and that's what led me to the material that would become my claim to fame: leather.

Fred the Furrier's brother owned a wholesale fur factory out in New Jersey, and when I went out there to pick up an order one day, Fred's brother pulled me aside and started persuading me to branch out into leather wear.

"Look," he said, "my nephew and his friend started a company.

They're making beautiful leather coats, Dan. You're gonna love this coat. They're selling like you won't believe at A. J. Lester. Go talk to my nephew."

Leather had come into style in the late seventies, during the Black Power era, and had never really gone away. It was fashionable, but it was versatile, too. You could sell leather coats, vests, pants, shorts. You could wear it in every season. It felt like a good opportunity, so I went and met this nephew.

"My name is Andrew," he said, "and this is my friend and business partner, Marc."

Their new luxury-leather-goods company was called Andrew Marc. From that first meeting, I could tell these two white boys had vision and ambition. I wasn't at all surprised when their company went on, in later years, to become one of the biggest brands in the luxury-leather game, selling everywhere from Bloomingdale's to Neiman Marcus. At the time we met, though, they were like me: just starting their own company and making their first real play in the fashion game. I'd also done a little research on the two of them before our meeting and found out that they had a cool chick from Harlem working for them whom I knew from the neighborhood. When I'd asked for the 411 about Andrew and Marc, she'd told me that these guys were really on, so I went into that first meeting with a feeling that the three of us would gel together real smooth. And we did.

They showed me their new possum-lined leather jackets, the ones I'd heard they were selling at A. J. Lester. I was impressed by the quality; Andrew's uncle hadn't led me astray. The leather was premium, and the possum lining gave it an elegance. Andrew and Marc said they'd sell the jackets to me wholesale for $300 to $400 each. We shook hands, and just like that, I was in the leather game.

My next stop was A. J. Lester on 125th and Eighth Avenue, a stone's throw from my shop. A. J. Lester was where all the folks with money in Harlem went to buy their clothes. The dealers, the musicians, the athletes. A. J. Lester was one of the biggest names in

Harlem fashion, and like everyone else, I used to shop there, too, when I had disposable income from gambling. But A. J. Lester was my competition now. I wasn't there to shop. I was there to do research.

I went straight over to where they displayed the new leather jackets and found the same ones with the possum lining that Andrew and Marc had shown me in their warehouse. The price tag said $1,200, which was triple the wholesale price. I knew that the only reason they were charging so much was because they knew there wasn't no other competition in the area. So I reached back into the lessons my older brothers had given me when I was younger, and I saw what I had to do. To grow my customer base, I had to start undercutting the big dealer on the block. People mighta been ignoring me because of my hustler clientele, but I knew they couldn't ignore a bargain.

When the first order of leather jackets came in from Andrew and Marc, I set my price 33 percent lower than A. J. Lester. People would come into the store and ask:

"Is this the same jacket they got over at A. J. Lester's?"

"Same one," I'd say. "They selling it for twelve hundred."

"How much you selling it for?"

"Eight hundred."

Before you knew it, word got around in the neighborhood, and the Andrew Marc leather jackets with possum lining started flying off my racks. I was killin em with this jacket. But knowing my clientele and the high-end luxury game, I also knew that I couldn't rest on my success for too long. The key to staying relevant was to always come out with something different and new. I had to keep asking myself, *Why should anyone come to my boutique? Why spend their money on my clothes?* So I took a page out of my fur playbook and made the Andrew Marc jackets even more luxurious by lining them with fox. That was another hit, and the fox lining made them more expensive than the possum-lined jackets. Then my customers started coming with suggestions.

"Dap," they'd say, "why you hiding the fox?"

"Yeah, man, why you putting it on the inside like the white boys?"

They had a point, plus it was their money. I had Andrew and Marc start putting fox on the inside *and* the outside, so you could reverse it if you wanted to. It was my first attempt at customization and a learning experience in how to make clothes with the particular tastes of my customers in mind.

As my leather game started to pick up, A. J. Lester got wind that I was undercutting them with the prices on the Andrew Marc jackets. They weren't too happy to be losing all that local business to me, but I figured they couldn't do nothing but lower their prices to compete. Business is business.

Little did I know they had other ideas: they was coming for me.

I had two friends who worked at A. J. Lester who tipped me off. They called and said, "Dap, a guy from the store is coming over to check your jackets."

When I heard that, I immediately went out onto my little showroom floor and took all my Andrew Marc jackets off the rack. It didn't take long, since that first storefront wasn't no bigger than a closet. A few minutes later, a man I'd never seen and didn't know from the neighborhood came into the store.

"Can I help you with anything?"

"Just looking," he said.

I watched him as he browsed the racks of furs. This was a little odd because winter was drawing to a close, and it was already getting warmer out. I knew this must be the guy that A. J. Lester had sent to spy on me. I watched him sift through the coats, pinching the price tags and looking down at them with a poker face.

"Looking for anything in particular?" I said.

"I heard you got a good deal on some coats," said the man.

Oh, I said to myself. No question this was the spy.

I showed him some of the more expensive leather coats with the fox lining to throw him off the scent, since I knew that A. J. Lester wasn't selling coats like that. But as I watched him browse through those jackets, checking the tag on each one, I noticed that, mixed in among the fox-lined jackets, was one of the same possum-lined coats that A. J. Lester was selling. I had forgotten one. The spy pinched the price tag and looked at it with his poker face. I kicked myself at my mistake.

I didn't really know what the blowback would be for undercutting A. J. Lester. Whatever they could do to me, I didn't expect it to be that bad. I was new to the clothes-selling game, but I knew a thing or two about business. If I could move the product for less, it was on you to compete. That was part of the game. But when I went to get my next shipment of jackets from Andrew and Marc, I realized that I'd made a naïve miscalculation.

As soon as I walked into the room, I could feel that the energy of this meeting was very different than our first.

"Listen, Dan," they said. "We got a problem."

I was listening.

"A. J. Lester is complaining. We had a meeting with them the other day, and they're threatening not to do business with us anymore if we keep selling to you. We do business with them, you know."

Oh, I knew.

"And they're a big client of ours."

I knew that, too.

"They've got five stores, Dan. You only got one."

They wasn't telling me nothing I didn't know.

Finally, they just came out and broke the news. "We can't sell to you anymore," they said.

"Oh yeah?" I said.

"If you take our labor out," they said, "then we can keep the arrangement."

It was a slap in the face. In other words, they'd sell me the raw leather, but they wouldn't make me any more jackets. I knew that they knew I didn't have the skills or the equipment to make the jackets by myself. I'd had a lot of setbacks when I was setting up my shop. More than a few furriers slammed the door in my face before Irving Jacobs took me under his wing. One high-end shirt company refused to sell to me. I was used to rejection, but this broken partnership with Andrew and Marc, not a year into my new life aboveground, felt overwhelming. I'd basically been blacklisted, before I'd even gotten started. It was feeling more like my fashion career was going to be yet another dream deferred.

But I'm real defiant. It's that Malcolm X in me. As I'd come to find out, defiance can come with heavy costs, but it can also be a blessing. After I left that meeting at Andrew Marc, my spirit started spreading its wings. I walked outta there saying to myself, *Oh yeah? They think they gone stop me. They think I can't make these jackets. I'm gone find a way.*

But I couldn't get the same high-end merchandise as A. J. Lester or my other competitors. Nor was I a fashion designer who could turn raw materials into finished clothing products. I hadn't gone to fashion school. I didn't even know how to sew. These were enormous obstacles. They felt damn near impossible to overcome. I didn't know how or even where to begin.

———

CHAPTER 16

Boy Wonder

Not long after Andrew Marc stopped selling me their jackets, June and I spent an afternoon with good friends of ours, a married couple who lived downtown who would soon be godparents to our son, Jelani. I spent most of our time that day talking about my troubles in the fashion game. Since I'd opened, the boutique had been the center of my waking life. After pouring so much time and money into it, the question that my whole business now depended on was, *How could I make my own clothes?* Our community did not have access to the means of production or manufacturing necessary for high-end fashion. There weren't many black students in fashion schools, or black-owned luxury-goods factories where I could just take my furs and leather skins and ask them to create my designs.

When we left my friends' apartment, we happened to pass a man who was selling African arts and crafts on the sidewalk. He had a simple fold-up table covered with hand-carved wood statu-ettes, colorful handmade fabrics, and jewelry with intricate bead-work. While I stopped to admire, I experienced a powerful flashback to the time I'd spent in Africa, in particular my trip to Liberia. I recalled the shop of my Liberian tailor, Ahmed, who'd worked with me to build a whole wardrobe of suits and casual wear from scratch. Those were some of the flyest clothes I'd ever owned, and they were so well made, there wasn't a stitch out of place after all these years. His skills and knowledge rivaled those of any mas-ter tailor working in Paris.

A vague question formed in my head: *What if I could work with Ahmed again?* But then the thought suddenly took shape and hit me like a revelation: *Man, if I could find someone* like *Ahmed, then I could make my own jackets.*

I struck up a conversation with the vendor.

"You ain't from Liberia, are you?"

"Senegal," he said, his English accented with French and Wolof.

He seemed impressed when I told him that I'd been to Africa twice.

"Listen, man," I said. "I got a store up in Harlem where I sell jackets. I'm looking for some tailors." I handed him my business card. "You know any Africans that know how to sew and make jackets, tell them to come see me."

The vendor took my card, and within a week, a tailor showed up at my shop. He was tall and dark-skinned with thick sideburns and a short, sculpted Afro. This man came ready to work, just like the two dozen other Senegalese tailors I would hire in the coming years. He pulled a tape measure out of his bag and draped it around his neck. He took out a pair of big fabric shears. His name was Sekou, but soon everyone who came to the shop would know him as Big Sek. He'd become one of my best tailors, and when we needed more people, Big Sek helped staff my factory space with other skilled Senegalese tailors.

That's what started everything.

———

I can't sew at all. I'm not a tailor; I'm an observer and a people person. Big Sek would take a client's measurements as I made conversation, gathering information about who they were and what they wanted. I was fascinated with the process and machinery of making clothes, and I've always trusted my instincts and my eye.

I read trade magazines and went to trade shows and studied the different names for various cuts and styles and textiles. At the time, I had a basic idea of what made clothes high quality versus low quality, but I started studying all the details of the leather jackets we made. The stitching, the accents, the physics. So it was a lot of on-the-job learning. I had to develop a mode of communication with my clients and my tailors.

Me and Big Sek didn't have the luxury of spending a grace period experimenting with designs and using trial and error. We jumped right into putting together jackets.

Soon after I hired Big Sek, we began making custom leather jackets. I started to understand and enjoy the process of designing and came to love the collaboration with the clients and my tailors. The reputation of the store started traveling beyond Harlem and even beyond the five boroughs, and people began to wonder who this Dapper Dan was. People outside of the neighborhood didn't know what I looked like. They didn't know if Dapper Dan was just some made-up name or if I was a real person. Sometimes, people would walk up to Big Sek in the shop and slap him five, thinking he was me. He'd redirect them my way and say, "There is the couturier."

To keep up with the growing demand, I had to spend more and more time in the shop. I had to be there to help design the clothes with the clients as Big Sek took their measurements, and then I had to be there to translate the vision for the tailors and make sure they understood what needed to be done. I was coming to realize just how much time, skill, and effort it took to put together custom

clothing. You can't do anything on an assembly line. There's a reason it often takes those Savile Row tailors in London a month to
make a bespoke suit. But I didn't have the luxury of a month or
even a week. My clients sometimes wanted their pieces in twenty-
four hours, and to make that happen . . .

I was at the shop all the time.

I took naps, a couple hours here, a few hours there, but I couldn't
afford a full night's sleep. I had to be at the shop, ready to cater to
the hustlers when they came from the nightclubs, when the gambling spots let out, when a long day of hustling filled their pockets
with thousands of dollars of disposable income.

Each generation in Harlem has what I call a Boy Wonder. The Boy
Wonder is a street guy who captures the attention of the entire
neighborhood with his style. He's a hood celebrity—not an athlete
or entertainer, because those guys didn't really belong to us—but a
successful hustler from around the way who's so fly he triggers
style in Harlem. A Boy Wonder cops chicks, and his chicks are fly,
too.

Who's that nigga? the Neighborhood asks.

I'm that nigga, says the Boy Wonder.

Every day, the Boy Wonder stays consistently fly with that bulky
drug money. Every day, people be on the lookout for him. It takes
a lot of outfits to be Boy Wonder.

"Damn," they say. "You saw the shit he was wearing today?"

Consistent flyness is what separates the Boy Wonder from the
average well-dressed hustler. Back when I was younger, it was a guy
like Joe Jackson in his pinstriped suits and cocked hats who was
the Boy Wonder of his day, a trendsetting hustler all the young
guys looked up to as a fashion icon.

Around the time that I started making custom clothes, there
was no doubt who the Boy Wonder was: it was Jack.

James "Jack" Jackson (no relation to Joe) was a Harlem boss,

one of the biggest drug dealers in the neighborhood, with deep ties
to the Gambino family. He had a mean car that looked like a rocket
ship and that nobody else had. Later on, Jack would wind up getting convicted for narcotics racketeering by the feds and, to lighten
his sentence, snitch on Gene Gotti, the younger brother of John.
But before the feds arrested Jack, he was Harlem's Boy Wonder
and one of my earliest and best customers. And like I said, it takes
a lot of outfits to stay fly, so Jack was coming by the shop on the
regular.

Jack and his crew was making so much money off the drug
game that even his workers were coming to the shop and dropping
stacks on custom outfits to get fly like him.

One day, I was working in the store, sleep-deprived as usual,
when Little Man, one of Jack's best workers and someone who
gave him stiff competition for the Boy Wonder crown, walked in
with his girl. Everyone in the place started crowding around Little
Man's girl, admiring something she had in her hand. When I
walked over to see what all the commotion was about, the girl held
up a small brown leather clutch with a repeating pattern of gold
letters—an L overlapping a V—and symbols printed on the skin.

That was the first time I'd seen a Louis Vuitton up close. It was
a beautiful bag made with amazing craftsmanship. I could tell it
was expensive. As someone who knew all about leather, I marveled
at the stitching and the way the ink rested on the skin. Most of all,
I was fascinated by the excitement it was creating among my customers. Immediately, the gears began to turn.

"You excited about a little bag?" I said to Little Man and his
girl. "Imagine if you had a whole jacket."

There was silence.

"Yo," said Little Man, his eyes lighting up. "You can do that?"

"Hell yeah I can do that," I told him.

Really, though, I had no idea how I was gonna do that. I was too
tired to even realize the extent of what I'd offered.

———

To make good on my spontaneous promise to Little Man, I threw on my best suit, hopped in my Benz, and rode down to Fifth Avenue, watching the neighborhoods transform within minutes from crumbling buildings and vacant lots to immaculate townhouses and gleaming storefronts. My first stop was the Louis Vuitton store to do some research. New York fashion was going through a lavish era. Wall Street was booming, and the drug game was booming, ushering in a new period of conspicuous consumption all over the city. Luxury goods were becoming status symbols, and European heritage brands that nobody had ever heard of, like Louis, Fendi, and Gucci, were entering the mainstream.

The drive to the Louis Vuitton store was only a couple miles, but it was a world away from Dapper Dan's Boutique. I was the only black person in there, and I felt the place tense up when I walked in. The doorman's eyes never left me. No wonder none of my customers liked to spend their money down here.

I ignored the unwelcome reception to study the merchandise. Approaching the owners of a brand like this and asking them to partner with me was out of the realm of possibility, even though the clothes I sold in my shop were just as expensive and well made as the ones down here. I'd had a hard enough time getting far smaller white-owned companies to work with me. If I couldn't be trusted to walk around their store, how could I be trusted to sell their clothes? No doubt they assumed there wasn't a market for their brands uptown, and they probably wouldn't have believed me if I told them otherwise.

The research mission was turning out to be a bust. All I saw in the Louis Vuitton store was bags and luggage. I looked everywhere, hoping to find something, anything, that I could use for Little Man's outfit. But I didn't see nothing but expensive leather bags and trunks printed with that LV logo.

"Can I help you?" said a saleswoman.

"Yeah," I said. "Do you carry any clothing?"

She seemed confused.

"Leather jackets? Coats?" I said.

She shook her head. "We're a leather-goods company," she said. "You can try Gucci next door."

Back on Fifth Avenue, I started to worry about whether I'd made a promise that I couldn't keep. As soon as I walked into the Gucci store, my worry grew. Like Louis Vuitton, the Gucci store specialized in leather bags, luggage, wallets, and loafers. The store had a small section of clothing, but one look at what they had and I knew that my tamest customers wouldn't wear it, let alone someone as flashy as Little Man. The sizing and the cuts were all wrong. Most of all, none of the clothes had the beautiful Gucci logo: a subtle diamond pattern made of dots connecting a repeated crest of two mirrored Gs, one right side up, the other upside down. Crests and logos stayed on the inside of clothes those days, tucked away like a secret.

Just as I was about to leave the store, disappointed and mentally preparing my apology to Little Man for getting his hopes up, something beige hanging in the bag section caught my eye.

Gucci sold garment bags. Unlike the other pieces in the store, the garment bags were made from long lengths of fabric, enough uninterrupted cloth to play with and possibly use on a jacket. I took one of the garment bags off the rack. Ran my hand along the thin, pliable canvas. I could definitely work with this. Even though it probably wasn't enough for a whole jacket, I could get my tailors to cut it up and trim the sleeves or add accents with it. The garment bags weren't as expensive as the other bags. I could probably still turn a profit.

"Just the garment bag today, sir?" said the cashier when I went to check out.

"Yeah," I said. "That's it."

—

Little Man's jacket with the Gucci trim was my first effort at incorporating logos on a piece of clothing. Even though it wasn't Louis Vuitton, Little Man seemed happy enough with the final product. Not long after, he was at an event with Jack, his boss. The drug crews were always throwing lavish events where they tried to outfly each other. I don't know what Jack was wearing, and nobody else cared, either. Everybody was crowding around Little Man. The same excitement people had felt when they'd seen the Louis Vuitton pocketbook in my store was now radiating out among the hustlers in the neighborhood. Little Man's outfit was attracting more attention than his boss's, and as the night wore on, Jack got tired of hearing people say, "You see what Little Man wearing?"

There was a new challenger for the Boy Wonder crown, and Jack knew he couldn't let that stand.

"Dap make you that?" he finally asked Little Man.

Best believe Jack was in my store the very next day.

"Damn," said Jack. "How you gonna have my workers looking sharper than me?"

Jack wanted a Gucci jacket, too, but of course, he wanted it to be even more exciting and spectacular than what I'd made for Little Man. As Big Sek took Jack's measurements, I started to think about what I was getting myself into with this logo thing. I knew that as soon as people saw Jack walking around the neighborhood with his new outfit, I was gonna need a lot more fabric. He was the Boy Wonder, and every hustler in Harlem was gonna want a Gucci-trimmed jacket. So I went back down to the Gucci store and bought every single canvas print garment bag they had in stock. We was buying so many, they didn't know what was going on. I would spend thousands on garment bags. Week after week, I'd buy them all out.

That period of time was short-lived. I wasn't just selling clothes anymore. I was making them, and how I was thinking about business had to evolve to fit the new reality. As more and more clients started asking for monogrammed designs, I realized I couldn't keep up with the demand just by going to the Gucci store every week. The garment bags didn't provide enough material. I could only do accents with them, not a whole outfit, and people wanted whole outfits. With hustlers, flyness was competitive, and I had a chance to fan the flames of that competition with new designs that generated excitement.

How did Louis Vuitton print ink on leather? How could I do it with the same high-quality skins and techniques as them? How could I keep the ink from fading over time? And how could I do that on leather that was intended for clothes, not suitcases?

I didn't know the answers to any of these questions, so I did what I always do: I started reading and experimenting and sciencing it out.

CHAPTER 17

Closure

Silk-screening is a printing technique that traces back to China around the turn of the first millennium: it took about eight hundred years for silk-screening to reach Europe via the trade routes. The artist Andy Warhol popularized silk-screening in America in the 1960s, but most people didn't really wear silk-screened T-shirts with designs and images until the late twentieth century.

From my reading, I gathered that the silk-screening process was something I had to learn if I wanted to make my own monogrammed fabrics. So I bought screens and ink and a squeegee and we set up a silk-screening station in the shop. Our first run of logo-printed pieces produced a cotton sweatshirt with the Louis Vuitton pattern, which we sold for a hundred dollars, a lot of money back then for a sweater. The Louis sweatshirt only needed a small screen, but I wanted to explore how to make larger formats that I could use to print on longer rolls of fabric. My ultimate goal was to screen print

onto leather with the same crispness and consistency of a Louis
Vuitton pouch. But unlike printing on a cotton sweater, printing on
leather rolls big enough for a jacket posed a huge challenge.

Oh, man. Let me tell you something. I had to have three, four,
five of us working at the same time to silk-screen the Louis pattern
onto leather. For the stencil, I would cut out the original design
straight from the Louis Vuitton catalog from their store, take a little portion of it, and start taping a collage of all the parts of the
pattern. Tedious work. Once I'd taped it all together, making sure
it lined up perfectly the way it did on the Louis bags, I'd take that
to a special photo place that could shoot it big enough on the film-
positive paper needed to create the mesh-screen template. We had
to use huge, three-by-five-foot screens, triple the size of the ones
you'd use for a T-shirt or something, to print the pattern on big
slabs of leather.

I also had a challenging time trying to find an ink strong enough
to bond onto leather. Nobody knew this at the time, but the ink we
eventually found was so strong it would soon be outlawed in the
United States. Whenever it was time to print more fabric, we had
to have the place well ventilated. One of the guys whom I was
learning the technique from was a Jewish guy named Stephen
whose company was called Mystic Leather. He was an expert at
making high-quality knockoff bags, and I connected with him
through one of my tailors. Stephen had lost the use of one of his
lungs experimenting with these powerful inks. And having been
around them, I'm not surprised by that. But now go look at those
jackets I made. Three decades later, and the ink still hasn't faded.

In later years, as the reputation of the store grew and reporters
came knocking, I used to lie and say that I got all my fabric from
Korea. Whether it was dice, credit cards, or clothes, I understood
the importance of keeping techniques valuable to my trade a secret. But the truth about the fabric is that we made everything right
there in the shop.

Once I'd refined my silk-screening process, I didn't need to make trips to Fifth Avenue anymore to buy up all the garment bags at Gucci. I could make a whole jacket or jumpsuit out of leather that was covered in any logo or crest my customers wanted. Not just Gucci, but Louis Vuitton, Fendi, and Michael Cromer München, a new German brand known by its acronym, MCM.

As demand grew, I had to hire more workers, too. My tailor Big Sek introduced me to another Senegalese tailor, a friend of his, who then introduced me to another tailor, who brought another tailor, and so on. Soon, I had a team of skilled craftspeople, all of them from the growing Senegalese community in Harlem. In addition to hiring more tailors, I had to hire people to manage the store some late nights to keep from burning myself out. We were open at all hours of the day. I'd never once hung a "Closed" sign on the front door. That meant I needed people I could trust to run the place in my absence.

Consistent with the approach of my earlier El Dictator years, my sisters weren't allowed anywhere near the shop. I still didn't want them hanging out with street guys, didn't matter if they was grown. It didn't matter much anyway, since they were all living elsewhere. My youngest sister, Doris, had moved to Virginia for college in 1969, become a schoolteacher, got married, and never returned. Continuing her own spiritual quest for meaning, Deborah was living on an ashram in Jamaica with her Hare Krishna husband. And, not long after our mother passed, Dolores had moved to Brooklyn, chasing the Afrocentric spirit of the Black Arts Movement, taking part in free writing workshops led by Sonia Sanchez and John Oliver Killens while raising a child and working a full-time management job for the Jacob Javits Center.

Omar, meanwhile, who had gotten into trouble with a dangerous crew of mobsters who'd put a bounty on him, had hopped a bus and left Harlem for good, settling into a quieter life in the suburbs, spending his days making oil paintings in his studio. He'd make trips back to Harlem every now and then, but mostly he was gone.

But James was around, still running the streets and doing drugs, so I hired him to help manage the floor. I was happy to have him close.

My charismatic brother, whom they called Cesar because he wanted to take over Harlem with his drug operation, had been brought low by addiction, and we'd fallen out of touch as a result. Back when I was still gambling for a living, I'd sometimes run into him on the block, and often he'd be strung out. I'd fight him for being high. I mean, I'd literally fistfight him for getting high because it broke my heart to see my once powerful older brother like that. In those years, James had a number of close brushes with death, some of which he jokes about today. For example, he would be up in his apartment for two to three days straight, shooting dope. The drugs made him paranoid about going outside. He'd be sitting up there, alone, disgusted with himself, nobody coming to see him. One day, he said to himself, *Lord, I can't take this pain no more. I'm gonna kill myself.*

So he put his head in the oven and turned on the gas.

As he was waiting for the gas to knock him out, probably wondering if he'd go to hell or not, waiting and mourning and weeping for the end to come, he started to realize that too much time had passed already, and he wasn't feeling nothing. Which was when it dawned on him that there wasn't no gas coming outta that stove, because he hadn't paid the gas bill in a month and they'd cut service. It's a funny story now, but am I ever glad he didn't pay that bill. James would eventually turn his life around. He'd go back to school, get his degree, and work as a counselor for people with substance-abuse issues, which made us all proud.

My father would also come by the shop to visit me from time to time. He was getting old, in his eighties by then, and showing signs of dementia. I held on to that memory of him almost getting hustled by the department store for his Easter suit, and as soon as I started making clothes, he was the person I most wanted to make look fly. I made sure he always left my store dressed better than anyone else in Harlem. I'd show him a few jackets, a couple suits, and I'd say, "Dad, what you wanna wear?"

And he'd say, "I like what you wear."

So I'd dress him in the same clothes that I wore myself, and we would walk around Harlem dressed up like twins. The first suit and tie he ever owned he bought from my shop. I was real proud of that.

Because it was my place, the store was becoming a center of all kinds of knowledge and learning: street wisdom, black consciousness, and spiritual inquiries. In our downtime at the shop, I tried to get James interested in metaphysics so that he could start changing his lifestyle. I turned him on to the teachings of Hilton Hotema and others I'd picked up in the intervening years. But he wouldn't listen. He would sometimes come to work high, laughing for no reason. "Why you laughing?" I'd ask him. "You ain't got time for laughing. Nothing in your life should be funny to you now." But he'd just shrug.

Like the clothes I was making, my spiritual understanding was custom-designed to my view of the world, informed by my reading, experience, and particular understanding of history. I'll take an idea from one book then tie that in with another based on my own analysis. I had never really bought into organized religion, but I was fascinated by the historical need for it. Whether it was religion or science, I always wanted to get to the root of an idea. I couldn't call myself Christian, Muslim, or anything else, but I'm a true believer in the interconnectedness of human history, science, and metaphysics.

While I was sciencing out the printing process, I started getting really into the symbolism of fashion-house crests. These brand logos have a power over people that I wanted to understand better. I was already heavily into symbolism and numerology from my spiritual reading, so when I started printing Louis Vuitton patterns on leather, one of the first things I did was look up the symbol. I went down to the main branch of the New York Public Library in midtown, where there was this huge room dedicated to the history of European family crests, and tried to find all the fashion-house crests: Gucci, Burberry, Fendi, you name it. I wanted to see how these symbols had evolved. When I found out that the Bally family didn't have a crest, I created one for my line of Bally jackets. I wanted my whole line to look rich with history—not just European and Judeo-Christian history, but also African, Muslim, Eastern, and others.

While I sat in that library reading room, delving into this history of symbols, I was beginning to see the light about the timeless, mythic power of logos, like the symbol of the tree, which shows up in the Old Testament and in Buddhist scripture, or the symbol of the star, or the symbol of the circle. Words and numbers, after all, are just symbols representing a certain shared understanding. You got a billion Christians, a billion Muslims, a billion Hindus, a billion Buddhists, and a billion who believe something else, and they all believe that theirs is the true pathway to God. I came to all the religions with an open mind, even dead religions like Greek mythology and the gods of ancient Egypt, giving each the benefit of the doubt that there must be something in these myths—Jesus, Buddha, Vishnu, Muhammad—that resonates with people and connects with a higher cosmic power. One of the things I learned from all my spiritual readings and delving into other religions is that there are many pathways to God, but that, across religions, there are visual and narrative symbols which often seem to be in conversation with each other: snakes, eyes, wheels, stars. Symbols are doorways to myth and information.

Now that I'd figured out how to silk-screen onto leather and schooled myself about the meanings behind all the heritage-brand symbolism, I still had to convince guys like Jack, who were looking for more than just trims and accents in Gucci canvas, that my self-made monogrammed leather was worthy of being worn. I knew none of them would be caught dead in a knockoff, so I had to convince them that, while it had the high-end materials and craftsmanship of a luxury item, it was something new and different. They had to see that I had taken these brands and pushed them into new territory.

I knocked them up, I didn't knock them off.

I blackenized them.

Jack took a second, looked at his new Louis print leather jacket in the mirror. Even though we'd collaborated and gone back and forth over the design, you never knew what a client was going to think when he finally tried on a piece. Especially Jack, who had a great eye.

He turned left, right, left again. He ran his hand over the screen-printed monograms on the leather. At last, he said, "That motherfucker *mean!*"

I slapped my hands together. If the Boy Wonder approved, I knew the rest of Harlem would be at my door in no time. And I was right.

That was it. That was the turning point.

It was a regular day at the shop when I got the call I'd been dreading for a while. My sister Doris was on the other end. She had recently moved my father to live with her in Virginia after it became clear he could no longer care for himself. I could hear the tears in her voice.

I always tell people that I stayed open all day every day for nine years straight. But that's not entirely true. In the nine years that we were open, there was only one day that I ever closed Dapper Dan's Boutique to the public, and that was on the day they sent Robert Day's body back to New York to be buried. Though he was in his mid-eighties, it was a deep loss for me. He was my hero. I was happy that both my parents lived long enough to see me come back from addiction, from prison, from the street. To me, that was my greatest accomplishment. That they lived long enough to see me change my life, and Daddy lived long enough to see me open the shop.

After the funeral, all my brothers, sisters, nieces, nephews, and children went and gathered at my store for the repast. Though it had rained all morning during the burial, the day turned warm, sunny. We took pictures out front with my Polaroid camera, fur coats hanging in the window. Then we went inside, sat, ate, and told stories. It was the first and last time that I ever let my sisters inside the shop.

We sat there with most of the lights off, just remembering and thinking. I thought about what it musta been like for Daddy the year he first set foot in New York. Everyone going around on horses. Street trollies clanging everywhere. And in the middle of all that, a little black boy from a small town in Virginia walking alone on the streets. Twelve years old. An orphan. Not a penny to his name. You have to be a strong person to survive in the city at any age, let alone as a child. I thought about the strength it took to be a black man in America and to survive with your heart and soul intact the way he had. If he was anything, Robert Day was strong, and with all his strength, he loved us.

It's hard to describe how much that love meant to me, to all of us Day children. I looked around my shop, the clothes I'd designed hanging around me, and I thought about the young people who'd soon be wearing them. In the years to come, so many of my customers would have their lives cut short or traumatically affected by the drug game. And I wondered how many of those guys had ever felt love like that, or would ever be able to give love like that.

I shed tears. I shed tears for my father. I shed tears for what we had lost and what we would lose. I shed tears for all of us, but I also shed tears for the beauty of his love and the strength that it had given me. Despite all the trauma, the light my father had left inside me was still burning and would keep lighting my way.

My father was a survivor, a fighter. Those hardworking, re-sourceful people like Robert Day, who had made the Great Migra-tion from the South and had come to places like Harlem, intent on succeeding, inspired me to be bold, to take risks, to see openings that I might have taken for granted. And despite the pain of losing him, I knew that same resilient spirit lived in me as well. Lord knows how much I would come to rely on that survival spirit in the years ahead.

In the midst of our family moment, a customer came knocking at the front door of the shop. "Y'all closed?" he said.

My brothers and sisters turned to me.

I got to my feet. "We never close," I said, rolling up the grate and switching all the lights in the store back on. "Come on in."

CHAPTER 18

—

Crack

My first storefront at 43 East 125th Street was no bigger than a small grocery store, with an area for my merchandise out front, and space in back for a sewing machine where Big Sek and one or two others would be tailoring. Within a few years of opening, we outgrew the first shop and expanded into a larger space next door. We turned the original space into an arcade—Pac-Man, Centipede, Mario Bros.—to generate additional income and also to keep my nieces and nephews busy and off the streets.

As we expanded physically, I was also pushing myself creatively as a designer. I enjoy the energy you can generate and the powerful statements you can make through fashion. I love getting people excited about what I can create. But similar to my gambling days, I had a somewhat scientific approach to fashion. My ego was never invested in popularity. I was always observing my customers and their desires. Even though I wasn't on the streets no more, I was plugged into what was going on through them. I knew they were making tons of money off the drug game, but I also knew the danger was growing. Prison sentences were getting longer, which meant more people were in chains. Families were getting torn apart. Poverty was getting worse. Beefs were getting deadlier. My designs grew out of an understanding of my customers' lives. I was reflecting their feelings, their risks, their ambitions, and their dreams in the clothes.

Now that I was able to print any symbols I wanted on large rolls of leather, I expanded my scope beyond clothes and set aside room in the new space for upholstering car interiors. Before I ever heard of anyone else doing it, I merged high-fashion brands with cars. Luxury cars had always been a part of the hustler repertoire, expensive status symbols of wealth and power. I wanted to upholster the interiors of these status symbols with even more symbolism. As always, I used myself as a test subject as well as a billboard, upholstering my burgundy Benz with beige-on-beige and burgundy-on-burgundy Gucci print. Later, I bought myself a cherry-red Jeep Wrangler and upholstered it in white leather with cherry-red MCM print. LL Cool J was so crazy about my Jeep, he made me loan it to him for the music video of "Big Ole Butt."

Those two cars might be the designs I'm proudest of, maybe even more than the clothes. I parked them right outside the shop, almost like bait: they created a certain atmosphere. I drew on my gambling experience to practice organized deception: everything I did to generate excitement was intentional.

On weekend nights, the scene outside the shop along the sidewalks of 125th was amazing. You had all these luxury cars—Bentleys, Benzes, Rolls-Royces—parked up and down the block. My hustler friends would come into the shop and hang out. Jack or someone would be wearing something I made, taunting their workers. "Man," they'd say, popping a collar, "you can't make nothing like this fly." That energy was special; it reminded me of nights as a little kid, when Curtis and I would sit and watch the glamorous gangsters leaning on their Cadillacs outside the Woodside Hotel, wanting to be part of that magical world. I'd come a long way from the days when I had to steal food before school cause I was so hungry, wearing shoes with cardboard patches on the soles. Unlike so many of my friends and customers, I'd figured out a way to be successful without relying on drugs or theft. I'd risen out of the underworld. But I wasn't naïve about why I had so many customers who could easily drop thousands of dollars on my clothes.

Drug trends change just like fashions. Certain drugs are fashionable in a certain era, and then for the next generation, a new drug becomes the substance of the moment. Crack cocaine didn't hit New York until 1984, when my shop had been open for a couple years already, but it changed everything. Even though cocaine had been around for a long time, it hadn't been everywhere on the streets like heroin. When I was coming up, coke was the party drug for hustlers who had the money to afford it, and heroin was the street drug for the junkies. Now they'd figured out how to make powder cocaine cheaper by diluting it and cooking it on a stovetop with baking soda to make it harden into rocks. Hustlers could take a small amount of powder and transform it into a large amount of product, which meant greater profits. A drug that had once been seen as a rich man's luxury was now cheaper and more addictive than booze.

Crack arrived into an already chaotic environment and made everything worse. What made crack different was the mainstream attention it got. Magazines like *Newsweek* were now drumming up fear, calling crack a national crisis. Fifteen years after President Richard Nixon declared a war on drugs, President Ronald Reagan went on TV in the summer of '86 to declare an even bigger war on crack. When they passed the Anti–Drug Abuse Act later that year, almost all of the $1.7 billion went to law enforcement, which helped fuel police brutality and mass incarceration. From the time I opened my store to the time I was forced to close it, the US prison population in America quadrupled. Despite the fact that heroin and cocaine were bought and sold in white communities just as much as ours, the prisons were filling with mostly blacks and Hispanics. The new drug war turned an already cursed game into a racist nightmare of unprecedented proportions.

My friend Hasan was one of the first people I knew who personally established a connect with some Colombian suppliers. When we was locked up together in Aruba, there was this Colombian dude that led Hasan to a new direct supply channel for his Harlem-based crew of dealers. You had guys going back and forth to Colombia, doing what those white boys with the Black Tuna Gang used to do with reefer.

Crack was transforming the whole nation, and once again I was bearing witness to the curse of another epidemic on our community, destroying lives all around me with violence, addiction, and incarceration. A whole generation in Harlem was traumatized by this period. At the same time, it was making a whole lot of my customers rich. Boy was there money. In terms of supply and demand, I couldn't have picked a better time to open up. The drug money was there, and these dealers needed to spend it. My shop was quickly becoming a hub for powerful guys in the drug game. Everyone knew I knew all the bosses in Harlem and that I was cool with them, so people thought that maybe, if they went to Dapper Dan's at the right time, in addition to getting fly, they could also make a connect and meet someone who might be beneficial to their business. Despite my feelings about the curse of the drug game, I didn't wanna make my main customers feel like they couldn't be themselves. I stayed out of it. What they talked about was none of my business. It was important that they trusted that my shop was not just a safe and welcoming place, but also a place of healthy competition and excitement. As crack spread through drug networks, so did the reputation of my clothes. Wherever the kingpins from Harlem mingled with kingpins from places like Chicago, Philly, DC, or

Baltimore, someone was bound to be wearing a Dapper Dan outfit, maybe at a nightclub, a basketball game, a boxing match, or Freaknik, the Atlanta festival for black spring breakers.

"Damn, where that nigga get that at?"

"He said he got it in Harlem at Dapper Dan's."

"Dapper who?"

The number of out-of-state plates on the sedans outside my shop began to grow as word spread beyond the city and into other parts of the country.

Our operation was growing, which meant overhead was growing. I could only do so many custom pieces in a given week. To ensure a steady stream of work, I continued to stay open all day. I had to wait until the clubs closed so that I could be there when the boutique became an after-hours spot. Every weekend, the hustlers would come with their crews, and they'd turn the shop and the sidewalks outside into a fashion show for underworld royalty. By four or five A.M., once people had left, I'd pull the grate halfway down to let any latecomers know I was still inside. I'd lock the door, and as long as no one came lifting up the grate, I'd be able to take a little catnap before sunrise.

When you see me in pictures from that time period, I always look wiped out. My grandkids tell me now, "Damn, you looked older back then." I'd work eighteen straight hours at the store, then go home for six or seven hours, from morning to early afternoon, then I'd go back and put in another eighteen hours. Even though I wasn't sleeping much, I tried to take care of myself, running six miles a day and keeping to a vegetarian diet. Keeping healthy wasn't just good for me, it was good for business.

While the brand was growing in the outside world, I was also finetuning my retail strategy. I noticed that, while I liked having my brother working the retail side of the store, it didn't always help to generate sales. When there were men in the store, the hustlers would always be trying to get a deal, thinking they were being over-charged (which was, in fact, often true if James was helping them). Soon, I realized that I needed to start playing with egos more. Money was not an issue with my customers. It was all about respect and the way they felt. So, I hired attractive young women to work the floor, figuring that the presence of the girls would force egos out. Sure enough, that got rid of the haggling. Now the hustlers wanted to flaunt how wealthy they were. They'd pull out a big roll of hundreds and peel off a stack of bills like it was nothing.

As much as I could, I also tried to share my retail space with other local vendors who were on the come-up. I would let jewelry makers and T-shirt designers sell their merchandise in the shop. They had to be making things that went with my clothes but that I didn't make. Leather belts, Gucci-shaped earrings, Afrocentric medallions.

Some of those vendors would go on to make a name for themselves beyond my shop. I gave space to a talented T-shirt designer named Darold Ferguson. Only a teenager at the time, Darold had a charisma and creativity that reminded me of myself when I was younger. Everyone in the neighborhood called him D Ferg, and he would go on to open his own shop in Harlem, creating a huge movement with his Ferg 54 fashion line. He would make an even bigger mark on hip-hop culture through his graphic design, creating the original logos for Andre Harrell's Uptown Records and Diddy's Bad Boy Records. Although D Ferg passed away from health complications in 2005, his influence and legacy continue through his son, Darold Ferguson, Jr., who went on to flourish as an artist, designer, and rapper. He calls me Unc, I call him Neph, and the rest of the world calls him A$AP Ferg.

New creativity was coming from outside of Harlem, too. I heard about a group of guys doing airbrushed designs on shirts and sweaters out in Queens who called themselves the Shirt Kings. Like a lot of young people at the time, they were into the whole graffiti thing, which I didn't know much about; their innovation was taking that graffiti style and applying it to fashion. I partnered with Edwin Sacasa, a.k.a. Shirt King PHADE, and had a wall full of his designs hanging in my store. PHADE and I been working together ever since. He's one of the loyal ones. Some of PHADE's designs started playing around with name-brand logos and symbols, too, so you could come into the shop and get a Gucci jacket by me with a matching Gucci-flavored graffiti shirt by PHADE.

For high-end accessories, I had a friend of mine named Ishmael Muhammad selling expensive Italian jewelry in the shop. Ishmael was a real radical, righteous Muslim. He kept halal, never smoked, never drank, didn't eat pork, and prayed east on a little rug five times a day right there in the store. He was usually accompanied by his son, Little Ishmael, who couldn't have been more than five or six years old. They didn't cut the most intimidating figures, sitting there with the prayer rug and the sparkly jewelry, but Ishmael was tough as nails and grew up on the streets. Man, I'll never forget the day that a customer came into the shop and made the mistake of pissing him off. Ishmael had been trying to sell him some jewelry, and rather than be polite about it, this young hustler turned to Ishmael and said, "Man, get that shit out my face."

When I heard that, I said to myself, *Uh-oh*.

What this guy failed to realize was that Ishmael was an OG. He'd been a successful coke dealer, capitalizing on the Colombian connection brokered by our mutual friend Hasan, and had taken that money and opened a restaurant in Chicago, which didn't work because the menu didn't have pork or alcohol on it. After Ishmael sold the restaurant, he took the money and bought $100,000 worth of jewelry in Italy, moved back to Harlem, and started selling it to customers in my shop. He used to be heavy in the streets but didn't want no part in it anymore.

"What you say?" said Ishmael.

"Nigga, you heard me."

Oh, God.

Ishmael calmly took his jewelry display and moved it into the back of the shop behind the counter, out of harm's way. Then he came back onto the floor and snatched the guy up off his feet—Ishmael worked out every day—slammed him into the circular racks, threw him onto the floor, tucked his knees into him, and started choking him out.

"Don't you know I'll kill you, nigga!" Ishmael howled.

Meanwhile Little Ishmael, all three feet of him, was standing over his father yelling, "Tell that nigga, Daddy! Tell that nigga!"

Despite the rare altercation with a rude customer, which in that case made for a story we still laugh about today, the energy in the shop was always positive. And that's the way I wanted it. A haven, a center, a hub. Later, when we expanded again, I made sure to set aside space where my children and my nephews and nieces and other kids from the neighborhood could play and watch kung fu movies. In the summer, the store was like a playground: one for kids in the day, another for ballers at night.

Customers flocked to the store knowing full well that Louis Vuitton didn't make clothes, and Gucci didn't make jackets, with logos all over them. I was doing something else. I was doing Dapper Dan's. I deconstructed the brands down to the essence of their power, which was the logo crest, and reconstructed that power in a new context. The names and the crests signified wealth, respect, and prestige. My customers wanted to buy into that power, and that was what I was offering. They didn't have to go downtown, didn't have to wear something done in colors they didn't like, with sizes that didn't fit them right, made by someone who hadn't taken the time to know them and understand the specificity of their lives and experiences. At Dapper Dan's, they didn't have to compromise. Not only did the clothes make them look good on the outside, it actually made them feel good when they wore it.

My reputation on the streets was evolving into something bigger than I'd envisioned. In the span of a few years, the boutique had turned into a name brand. The clothes were starting to stand for something bigger than me. I didn't even think about the impact it might be having beyond New York, or in the culture at large. My focus was the same as it had always been: providing for my family, serving the people in my community, developing my spiritual education, and not being broke. I would have been satisfied doing that for the rest of my days.

But then along came this rap thing.

CHAPTER 19

—

Paid in Full

Like a lot of American cities, New York used to be a place where people made stuff. When I was growing up, there were factories everywhere. I even worked in a Styrofoam factory one summer when I was a teenager, a job I got thanks to Killa, my old hustling buddy. But when companies started outsourcing jobs to cheaper places outside the US, a lot of the factories in the city closed down. The death of American industry hit New York same as in other parts of the country and only added to the hardships of working people in our community.

But it also meant there were all these factories closing down right as I was building my own little factory, so there was a lot of equipment on the market that I could get for cheap, if I knew where to look. I read the auctions section of *The New York Times* every week, and whenever I saw something interesting, preferably a clothing factory closing down and selling off its machinery, I went to check it out. Sometimes, I'd take a friend, who usually had no idea what I was up to, and we'd go down to the Navy Yard or wherever it was and be the only black people at the auctions, except for the truckers who were hauling the equipment. At first, I was just going for research to see what people were buying and how they did it. But soon, I'd go with a shopping list; I started snatching up all the machines we needed for the shop.

We also needed more room for our operation: a big ventilated area for our fabric printing, a larger space for the workers to do their cutting and sewing, and a bigger showroom for the retail experience. We'd outgrown the first storefront and expanded into the one next door, and when that still wasn't enough, we moved into a three-story building down the block, 38 East 125th Street. The first floor was big enough for me to build a small apartment in the back, something I'd always wanted for those nights when I couldn't get home. There was a mezzanine level where I could comfortably put my tailors with tables and all the machines I was buying at auction. There was a top floor that had good ventilation for the ink fumes. There was even a subbasement where I could store furs in the off-season. I had a dream of building out the basement and turning it into a nightclub, which I was gonna call Dap's Den, but that idea never panned out.

As the boutique grew in size and popularity, we started attracting new kinds of customers. I was making clothes for neighborhood basketball stars like Walter Berry and Mark Jackson, including the suit Mark wore for his Rookie of the Year ceremony. I was making clothes for track stars like Diane Dixon after she won a gold medal at the Olympics. I was making clothes for so many people, I don't even remember who the first rapper was to walk into my store, but whoever it was, they came referenced or accompanied by a gangsta. Without question. In the early days, no rapper would walk straight up in there; they assumed the shop belonged to real hustlers.

At the time, crack had way more to do with my success than rap.

My clothes were expensive, and in the early days of hip-hop, rap-pers didn't have money like the hustlers and athletes. Later, when hip-hop conquered the world, artists would figure out how to capi-talize on the movement, but back then all the biggest names in rap were just starting out and getting hustled by the music industry. Some thought it was a passing fad and questioned whether it was even music. There was no money in rap, so I wasn't focused on the rappers. I didn't care if they stayed outside or worked up the nerve to come in. I had a business to run.

Not everyone had street connections, so a lot of the rappers didn't feel comfortable coming in by themselves without an intro-duction from someone who was already my client. Some rappers, like Jam Master Jay of Run-DMC and Eric B. & Rakim, had gang-ster friends, so they were among the first rappers I met and started designing for.

The day Eric B. and Rakim walked into the shop, I didn't know much about them or their music. That was true for the majority of the rappers who started coming to me. Most of my hustler clients liked rap, so I usually had it playing in the shop for them, but I preferred the stuff that I grew up on—jazz, R & B, and Latin music. Rakim was barely outta high school, but he had an old soul, a spiritual side to him that I connected with immediately. He'd con-verted to Islam at the age of sixteen and would go on to be one of the most influential rappers of his generation, using his lyrics to explore the teachings of Five-Percenter spirituality, a Harlem-born movement that grew out of the Nation of Islam. When Rakim re-ferred to himself in his music as the God MC, it wasn't just a boast. It was a coded reference to Five-Percenter metaphysics. Once a rap-per like Rakim had crossed the gangsta barrier of the shop, then he would invite another rapper, and that rapper would bring in their rapper friends, and so on and so on, until before I knew it, a lot of my customers were starting to come from the music world.

No matter who you were—hustler, athlete, rapper, or singer— I had a straightforward process for working with you. When the customer came in, I would say, "What do you like?" They could create from their head, and I would tell them what might look good and what I could do for them. But Eric B. and Rakim would always leave it up to me. That was true for a lot of my customers. People would often want the clothes I had on, because that sanctioned it. They'd say to me, "Come on, Dap. You know what you do, just go on and do it."

So I would go on and do it.

I would keep it consistent. Black people, we tend to be very matchy-matchy. One of the harshest critiques you can get is "You ain't matchin." I always made sure to create cohesive color schemes. I wouldn't go out of the range of the aesthetic I was feeling at a given time, unless a customer asked for something specific. But clients can be really creative. Like, someone might come in with an Armani suit and say, "Yo, man. Look at how they made this suit. They ain't make it to fit me." Maybe they didn't like the cut or the lapels or something. So I'd make a whole new Armani-inspired suit with a bolder color scheme and a monogrammed logo pattern. My creative vision bloomed from helping my customers express their own identity.

That's how the outfits Eric B. and Rakim wore on the cover of their debut album came about. They'd just signed a record deal with Russell Simmons at Island Def Jam and wanted to make a powerful statement. They wanted to rock something special for the album cover, something that would express the personas of two young black men from the streets who had dared to call their debut album *Paid in Full*. They needed something iconic.

They said, "Go at em, boy!"

I knew I wanted to do something for them that interpreted Gucci. Even though Louis was popular, they just had the basic print pattern. Gucci had a greater impact on me as a designer because there was so much more I could do with it. I would rarely design a Gucci look that didn't have the Gucci colors. I tried to remain true to the spirit of the label, almost like I'd been commissioned by them. Even with my clientele, you had people that didn't want the letters all over the outfit. Some just wanted the red and green piping on a jacket, and that's the signal right there. But for the *Paid in Full* cover, I went against my normal instincts with the color scheme and I made two matching leather jackets with black-on-black Gucci print leather. For accents around the collar, cuffs, pockets, I did Gucci print in white leather. On the front of both jackets, I layered the black and white leathers to do a remix on the Gucci logo, with two prominent mirrored Gs. I knew there was a B-boy look of colorful tracksuits with fat lace sneakers that was being popularized at the time, but I wanted to push that look into the next evolutionary phase.

I wanted to turn these B-boys into B-men.

Paid in Full came out in the summer of 1987 and became a huge hit, eventually going platinum. Now you had people inside the hip-hop world asking themselves the same question hustlers had been asking each other for the past few years: "That's slick! Where they get that?" Thanks to artists like Eric B. & Rakim, rappers started to realize that they could have a certain kind of cachet in the mainstream if they wore my clothes. But even then, I didn't see them as doing me no favors. Long before he made the *Forbes* list, Russell Simmons would come into the shop stoned on angel dust and just be ogling my female employees. "What's his problem?" my brother James would whisper to me. "Let me kick his ass out."

If anything, I was the one doing these rappers a favor, making them look like the powerful street bosses who had popularized my clothes. I was a generation older than the musicians who were part of the golden age of hip-hop, and we didn't see these rappers the way the rest of the world was beginning to see them. Fat Joe was working at a sandwich shop a couple blocks away from me and would come into my boutique from time to time talking about rap, but I didn't even know he himself was a rapper. Andre Harrell, the founder of Uptown Records and Diddy's first boss, was building a legendary roster of artists like Mary J. Blige, Heavy D, and Jodeci, but in the early days of his company, he couldn't afford to buy my clothes for his artists to wear in their videos, so I had to loan him whatever I had available.

Everyone from the streets knew what the deal was when they walked into my shop. We didn't talk money or haggle over prices. Bosses like Jack probably only wore the stuff I made them once or twice. Wearing one of my designs any more than that was looked down upon. But when rappers started spreading my reputation into the mainstream, I had to work with people who weren't getting money like the hustlers. The exposure was good, but it affected the way I did business, bringing in a whole bunch of young artists and their fans who didn't have money to afford what the dealers could. The cheapest two-piece set we had was $375, but most pieces were in the four-figure range.

Remembering what my father had almost gone through to buy a department-store suit, I instituted an interest-free layaway program for folks who couldn't pay everything up front. They'd put a down payment, then I'd hang their finished outfits in the window for display. Sometimes, customers just wanted the same thing that they'd seen a rapper wearing in a video, so they'd get the exact outfit. The rappers didn't care about people copying them after they wore a piece. It was a form of flattery. All they cared about was not copying other rappers. They might pull me aside and whisper, "Dap, don't let anyone see my thing before I wear it." Or, if they had something on layaway, they'd ask me not to hang it up in the window, both to keep the design secret and to hide the fact that they didn't have the money to pay it all up front.

And to Teddy Riley, LL Cool J, and the Boogie Down Productions crew: technically y'all still owe me money.

The rappers aspired to the hustling lifestyle, but most of them still kept their distance from the hustlers. When the music people came to my store, they often had to wait outside until after the drug crews were done shopping. Everyone feared the hustlers. I saw hustlers literally tell celebrities what to do, like the time I watched Eddie Murphy get clowned at a party for denying an autograph to a hustler's girl. She walked back over to her boyfriend and told him what happened, and this gangster went right up to Eddie and said, "Did you tell my woman no about that autograph?" I think Eddie mighta defecated on himself. He was glad to get outta the party that night.

As I got to know some of the rappers, I began to genuinely enjoy their company. They were creative, well-read, and could get deep with me, which was something I'd been missing. Although I mostly catered to the drug crews, that didn't mean I always enjoyed spending time with them. All they wanted to talk about was three topics: sports, sex, and hustling. I was constantly being bombarded by that kind of conversation at the shop, consistently beaten down by it. It might have been exciting to people who never experienced it, but not to someone who grew up in an environment where sex and materialism could become mental prisons.

On a personal level, I really connected with a lot of the rappers. I had all these ideas in me that I'd been harboring. About religion and leadership and the power of myths to shape human minds. When you look back at history, you see that what's true isn't as important as the kind of truth a people need at a given point in time. I wanted to understand the nature of those who laid down the structures of thought that shaped civilizations, like Galileo or Gandhi, so that I could try to figure out the truth that our people needed to survive the dark times we were experiencing in America. I was trying to tie a string of continuities between different time periods and histories and philosophies and religions and teachings. I didn't want to leave no stone unturned in my search. When I started conversing with like-minded creative people, it triggered all of these latent ideas that I'd been reading and processing my whole life about the power of art and culture to change the world.

One of my favorite guys to talk with was Biz Markie. He'd come to the store after the clubs let out and stay until the next day broke. I'd get a call from him and he'd say, "I'm comin over there, man. We gone break day. C'mon, Dap. You know how we do, man." And sure enough, I'd be taking a nap and hear the grate come up at three or four A.M. and hear his voice. "You know, Dap, I'm out here!" Me and Biz used to just sit out front of the store and kick it until dawn, cracking each other up with stories. Nobody could tell stories like Biz, always so full of funny lies and exaggerations. I love Biz Markie. The other one who always used to hang out was Jam Master Jay from Run-DMC. He would be in the store for hours and became a good friend; my first visit to a recording studio was with him.

I had a practice of taking Polaroids of everyone I made clothes for and posting them on a corkboard near the front of the shop. Now the board was filling with rappers who were getting national attention: Big Daddy Kane, Nice & Smooth, the Fat Boys, Roxanne Shanté, LL Cool J, Run-DMC, the Jungle Brothers, and KRS-One's Boogie Down Productions. During the day, kids leaving school would come by and snatch the Polaroids of their favorite rappers, so I had to move the photo board behind the counter to deter that.

Once the music people started coming and wearing my clothes, celebrities from all over who were friends with them also started coming. I was close with Public Enemy's Chuck D and Flavor Flav and even met with them at one point when they were thinking about starting their own clothing line. They were the ones who first brought Mike Tyson to the shop. Mike was in his early twenties, and he liked Public Enemy. He embraced the hip-hop culture, and hip-hop artists embraced him, making references to the young champ in their verses. I don't remember my very first meeting with Mike, because he soon became a regular. He was on the verge of superstardom, making a name for himself—not only for his skill and strength in the ring, but also for his personality and style out-side of it. On one of his early visits to my shop, Mike brought along his girlfriend at the time, a nineteen-year-old British model named Naomi Campbell, herself on the verge of superstardom.

From looking up to Sugar Ray Robinson as a kid, to traveling to Africa to watch Ali fight in the Rumble in the Jungle, I have always had a unique place in my imagination for boxers. Mike held the same fascination for a new disillusioned generation: he was the first champ for the hip-hop era. He had a gold tooth and a fade. Like the gangsta rappers of that time, he embodied the frustration of an entire generation who'd been villainized by society. We enjoyed the discomfort Mike created. He told reporters to "fuck off" on live TV, and in turn they called him a thug because they couldn't call him the other word. Mike was scary because Mike wanted others to feel the fear that guys like him had felt all their lives, growing up poor in neglected racial ghettos all across the nation. Mike was hip-hop.

Most nights at the shop, around one or two A.M., it was like there was a party going on. The cars would be piled on the block, people everywhere. The shop was gaining attention beyond the streets, and the attention brought in more business. To fill the constant stream of orders, I needed even more space than the three-story building we'd just moved into. I took out a lease on a 2,000-square-foot mini-factory on 120th Street between Second and Third avenues, where I had my nephew supervising a night crew of eleven tailors. That was strictly a warehouse and production site, with sewing machines running dusk to dawn, fabric shears squeaking and snipping, all the Senegalese guys eating together out of a big-ass drum and talking to each other in Wolof. I had them on call round the clock. If someone came in Friday night and wanted something by Saturday morning, we'd get it done.

Guys on the street who knew me from back in the day started spreading rumors about me gambling with my celebrity clients, but the only gambling I was doing was playing a game I came up with that I called Punk Out. I played it with gangsters who needed clothes on a turnaround of less than twenty-four hours. They might call in the morning needing an outfit later that night, so I'd say, "I tell you what. If I have it ready, you pay double. If it ain't ready, you get it for free." That was Punk Out. I only lost one time, when one of my workers messed up on a $1,200 jacket that I had to straight-out give the customer for free. That was as far as my gambling went anymore. But that didn't stop the gossip mill. Ridiculous rumors started flying around that I was making money off my customers by luring them into dice games. "That nigga trimming Tyson," they'd say behind my back. If they had stopped to think about it for a second, they woulda realized it didn't make no sense. Why would I have to steal from Mike when he was paying $7,000 for a jacket? As a matter of fact, Mike racked up a $25,000 bill at the shop, and it took me five years to collect that money. I worked as hard as I did because I never wanted to go back to trimming people at dice games ever again. All I wanted to trim was fabric.

As we created new looks for rappers, the hip-hop movement kept growing. One of the biggest signs of that growth came in the summer of '88 when a new Saturday-morning show devoted to hip-hop debuted on MTV. The show was called *Yo! MTV Raps,* and it was a turning point in the relationship between street culture and the mainstream. Hosted by the journalist, artist, and hip-hop pioneer Fab Five Freddy, *Yo! MTV Raps* aired for two hours every week and featured interviews with rappers, live performances, and music videos. They had guests like Run-DMC, Biz Markie, LL Cool J, Bobby Brown, and Salt-N-Pepa, and the first video that MTV ever aired on *Yo! MTV Raps* was "Follow the Leader" by Eric B. & Rakim. Everybody on the show was already a regular Dapper Dan customer.

Yo! MTV Raps became an important outlet for hip-hop music, but it was just as important for hip-hop fashion. For the first time, people were not only getting to hear this street music, but they were also getting a chance to see how the artists dressed and what kind of clothes they wore. Since people across the country were already getting a weekly dose of my clothes without realizing it, MTV eventually sent Fab Five Freddy to my shop with Eric B. to tape a segment. They had us out front next to my MCM-upholstered Jeep, then we did an interview inside, surrounded by all my designs. The publicity of being on MTV was a big deal. It was the first time anything mainstream like that had ever happened to me.

Though the show focused on black artists, it wasn't created by black producers. *Yo! MTV Raps* was the brainchild of a white-boy hip-hop fanatic named Ted Demme. Ted would later become well-known as a filmmaker, directing Johnny Depp as a drug smuggler in *Blow*. Back when I met him, Ted was just a young guy, a couple years outta college, who was down with hip-hop. I had a great relationship with Ted, God rest him. He was really one of my earliest supporters and wanted to help break me out into the larger pop-culture world.

"Yo, Dapper," he'd say. "Any time you want me, I'll come here and film."

The landlord for my storefront was a guy named Jay Weiss. Jay was watching *Monday Night Football* with some friends of his, when they mentioned me on the air in connection with a notorious fight that took place outside my shop (more on that later). Jay nearly choked on his pretzels. "That's my tenant!" he shouted to everyone around the TV. "Dapper Dan, he's my tenant." Shortly after that, he called to tell me the story. "They didn't believe me that you were a tenant of mine." I think Jay could hardly believe it himself that I'd made it to national TV. But as hip-hop moved into the popular culture, so, too, did my store. Now that I'd made it to *Monday Night Football,* Jay took an interest in the boutique. He happened to be married at the time to Kathleen Turner, the actress, and when she found out about the kind of clothes I was making, she sent Jay to the store with a request. "She wants you to make her an MCM bustier," Jay told me. "She'll wear it to the Academy Awards." Unfortunately, the timing didn't work out, so I never got around to making that bustier for her. All that mainstream attention wasn't something I expected for myself when I started in the fashion game, but it didn't bother me. As long as people were happy to spend money at Dapper Dan's, I was happy to make them fly.

But I was also getting attention that wasn't so welcome. At the same time that I had MTV coming to the shop, I was still catering to gangsters and drug dealers, and some of those guys were being hunted by the authorities newly empowered by Reagan's escalation of the drug war. Subpoenas would come in the mail for me, requesting receipts and documentation for what some of my drug-dealer customers had spent. When they couldn't catch the bosses red-handed, they tried to build a tax case against them instead, which was why they started bothering me. Car dealers, clothes stores, anyplace these guys possibly spent money got a subpoena. The feds would keep calling, and I'd always say, "Man, I don't know what they spent. I'm an outta pocket place."

I had already seen the consequences of getting even peripherally involved in the drug game. I coulda made more money connecting people than selling clothes, but I refused. I fired anyone on staff who even attempted to profit off of introductions in the store. I ain't play that at all.

But what was going on in the streets was even more disturbing. After the economic crash in the late eighties, life in the city kept deteriorating, as old bosses got put away for long sentences and new drug crews started popping up. Getting a supply of drugs was easier than ever. When the Italians had the game, you had to know somebody to get drugs. They could designate certain areas to certain people, and there was an unspoken *Yo, don't hit him, he's admired* policy. Now all you needed was a little start-up cash. Two or three guys on the same block could have a connection and then you'd have them beefing over the block. That's when it started getting real murderous. The guys I grew up with who were involved in the drug game started to turn against each other.

The murder rate in the city spiked to an all-time high during this period. The flood of new drug suppliers caused mayhem in the streets, not just through the turf wars but also through a rash of kidnappings. Any new dealer who was making money became prey. There were crews who began to specialize in ransom kidnappings. That period was such a trauma. It really feels like we lived through a war.

Drugs and racism were destroying black communities all over the country. And Harlem was the worst of the worst. There was a crack house four or five buildings down from my store. The people I saw going in there, man, I could not believe it. I'd see decent-looking people go in there before work and, in the blink of an eye, get their whole lives destroyed. The drug situation in Harlem was like what you see in Brazil in the favelas. Often, the police didn't even bother. You know an epidemic has hit when you see the community turning on itself. Back when I was younger, if someone robbed a soda truck, everybody in the neighborhood would be drinking soda for the rest of the day, and if you didn't share the stolen soda, then you'd get a beatdown for being greedy. There was no longer that sense of collective benefit. No one was connected to each other anymore, so that left everyone vulnerable. The new frontier wasn't just about looking fly anymore. It was about surviving the war going on outside.

CHAPTER 20

—

Beef

I knew a guy who ran a security agency downtown in Hell's Kitchen. He would do protection for people, bodyguard stuff. He had a side hustle selling state-of-the-art bulletproof fabric, which he eventually got busted for. The material he sold was made of super-hard nylon. It was flexible but very strong. As a bullet penetrates the levels of the demi-armor, the nylon layers lock it in. That's not to say it ain't gonna knock you out if you get shot point-blank. But it was the best material you could buy, the very same stuff manufactured for the NYPD. The technology behind it came from the Israelis.

I started experimenting with some of the bulletproof material to see if I could incorporate it into clothes. It was a little bulky for a regular leather jacket. You could tell it was there underneath, the same way you could tell when police was wearing a vest under their clothes. The material also wasn't as soft as leather, which made it heavier and more uncomfortable. Today it would be very hard to get away with bulletproofing because everything is so fitted. But back then, it was a loose-fit era. Eventually, I figured out a way to hide the material by fitting it into a bomber jacket and adding quilting inside the leather so it had that puffy effect, which was what everybody liked anyway. I got it to where you couldn't tell the jacket was anything but a jacket. I made one for my damn self.

I had a friend with a business selling fire alarms, and every time there was a fire in the neighborhood, him and his partner would blanket the neighborhood hand-selling their wares—that's what bulletproofing was like for the boutique. Whenever there was a beef, I would always get guys coming to me.

Every funeral these young guys went to, it was like a revelation. "Man," they'd say to themselves, "I don't want to be lying here next." They'd be in the shop later that night.

For anyone who was skeptical about the bulletproof material, I had them read the manufacturer's booklet that I got from my connect downtown, but I wasn't leaving it at that. I allowed the customer to test it out. They could go up on the roof of our three-story building and shoot the jacket themselves. Being from the street, I know they didn't wanna hear no shit about some bullets going through after they got shot. I said, "Listen, you shoot it. If you happy with it, then I'll put it in the jacket."

If you had a real beef, you didn't just wear the bulletproof coat when it was cold out. You wore that joint all summer. Bulletproofing became a big business for me. Guys would ask me for bulletproof hats, too. I'd always have to give a disclaimer. "I'll make you a hat, man," I'd say. "But it ain't gonna save your life. If the bullet graze you, it'll help, but if it hits you straight on, you gonna have a concussion that'll kill you anyway from the impact."

I'd sold a bomber with a bulletproof vest to this one guy with a lot of murders in Brooklyn. One day, he returned to the shop.

"Damn, Dap!" he said, wincing. "Look what happened to me." He held up a shirt and showed me a big bloodstain on it. "They shot me under the fucking jacket."

I said, "Damn."

"Dap," he said. "I need you to make me a *long* one."

I was gonna have to buy quadruple the amount of demi-armor to cover the whole coat, and the material wasn't cheap. It would end up costing him a lot of money. But that's how I started making the snorkels.

A snorkel is a three-quarter-length parka with a deep hood. You can zip it all the way up in cold weather, leaving a little opening for your face. The first time DEA agents set foot in my shop hunting receipts, one of them held up a snorkel and said to me, "So you're the fucking wise guy making the bulletproof jackets that we gotta deal with when we come for these guys." A snorkel is made with big pockets in the front, big enough to store whatever you might need. Some hustlers I knew used to stash rolls of money in those pockets, and the night Nicky Barnes and them reopened the Apollo, they walked onstage to make it rain on the audience. They would be snatchin bills out their snorkel and throwing them into the audience. It was a double pocket, so you had two separate spaces. Some money on this side, drugs on that side, and maybe room for a weapon. You don't want to have to fumble, either. You can just go in there and get rid of something in a hurry if you needed to.

Once I started making them, everybody wanted a snorkel. We did it in Gucci, Fendi, Polo, MCM, everything. But the most popular snorkel I ever made was the one I designed for Alberto "Alpo" Martinez, which came to be known as the Alpo coat. Alpo was a stylish young hustler from East Harlem and a rising contender for the title of Harlem's Boy Wonder. He was one of the cats who used to always be in the store asking, "Hey, what Jack get?"

After Jack got arrested, there was an opening for the title of flyest hustler in the neighborhood, and Alpo filled it immediately. He was a handsome young guy. He pulled chicks. He was tight with all the gangsters from Frank Lucas's crew. He also had a wild side, making a name for himself popping wheelies and doing tricks on motorcycles. He had all the elements to make him a memorable Boy Wonder. Unfortunately, Alpo followed in Jack's footsteps in more ways than fashion, getting arrested for drug dealing and facing the death penalty for murder; like Jack, he cooperated to shorten his sentence. I made Alpo's snorkel with the leather Louis pattern for the front panels and pockets, while the sleeves had a lighter shade of brown. The Alpo coat remains the most requested piece I've ever made.

The attention I give my customers when they come into the shop isn't just a way to make people feel appreciated so they can keep coming back. Listening closely is the key to my creativity. My designs are a response to the energy a client gives me. I thrive off that one-on-one exchange. I don't think of myself as an artist or even as a couturier; I'm just using fashion to tell their stories.

Or just trying to keep them on this side of life.

At certain points in the year, usually around the holidays, it wasn't unheard-of for the shop to make ten, twenty, once even thirty-two thousand dollars in a single day. My production and sales staff had ballooned to almost thirty people, and I was paying close to forty grand a month on payroll. Any profit I had after rent and materials went back to supporting my children and their educations, and anything left from that went right back into growing the business. But as business boomed, it was getting harder to manage everything on my own. There was always drama coming at me from all sides. If it wasn't the authorities investigating my clients, it was my own workers turning on me.

One night, I had a big project that required me to spend the night at my warehouse over on 120th Street. I hadn't been to the warehouse in some time, so I was looking forward to seeing how the operation had been going under my nephew's supervision. As soon as I walked in, I smelled trouble, literally smelled it. I was hit by the unmistakable stench of reefer and the sight of my nephew casually smoking it at his desk. When he saw me, his glazed and bloodshot eyes got wide as he hurried to put away the joint.

I said, "I be got damned."

I hadn't even finished dressing down my nephew when I heard someone come knocking. I had no idea who could be coming to the factory at this hour. I opened the front door, and there were three women dressed in short skirts and high heels standing there. I knew immediately what line of work they were in, and they were asking for some of my tailors by name.

"Who is *you*? Where Amidou at?"

I said, "I be got damned."

I couldn't believe it. I was furious. Not only was my nephew smoking reefer during operating hours, but my tailors were soliciting prostitutes on the job. And that was just what I'd discovered in the first few minutes that I was there. Who knew what else they'd been doing on company time? Their behavior was jeopardizing our whole operation. I gave everyone a tongue-lashing that night and decided to move my nephew over to the main store, so that I could personally keep an eye on the factory for a while. I hoped that would be the end of it.

For the most part, I had good chemistry with my workers. As a boss, I tried to strike a balance between firm and fun. The hand that molds you must console you. Even though I had to put my foot down sometimes, I like to think we had a good time. Like when I brought a live python down into the mezzanine where my day shift was working. I didn't know that a lot of the Africans were afraid of snakes. The ones they knew from Africa could kill you. As soon as they saw me walk in with that python, they all jumped up. There was a tiny window in the back of the workroom. Have you ever seen thirteen Africans jumping out of a window? Them niggas was gone.

But the drama kept piling on and it wasn't no laughing matter. Whenever somebody messed up a garment or got an order wrong, they wouldn't tell me the truth about it. "Who did it?" I'd ask, but they'd keep quiet. They were protecting each other. Not long after I found out that the night crew had been inviting prostitutes to the factory, I also discovered that they'd been stealing from me. They were using my fabric and equipment to knock my stuff off, making inferior items to sell behind my back. One month, I went to pay the landlord our rent for the factory space, and he joked, "You don't have to pay me rent this month. Just give me what your workers have been stealing from you."

Man, I was under so much stress. I felt alone at the center of everything I'd created, without support or people I could trust. My brothers and sisters had lives of their own: James was spending more time with Omar in the suburbs to get away from the chaos of the streets. I'd more or less fallen outta touch with my old friends like Russell and Curtis. They were still out on the streets hustling, using, and struggling with their own demons.

When all my warehouse workers confronted me one day demanding more pay, my stress got the best of me, and I snapped and fired everyone. I said, "I'll start over without you." Over the course of a few days, they all started trickling back, coming to me one by one. Eventually, I hired everybody back except for one tailor whose workstation was always a mess cause he felt that cleaning it was women's work. I didn't play that. I told him, "You see me sweeping, and I'm the boss."

It was one headache after another. When my phone rang before dawn one morning and I picked up to hear my nephew's voice, I said, "What is it this time?"

"Sorry to wake you up, Uncle Danny," he said. "Mike Tyson just beat the shit outta Mitch Green right outside the shop."

"Say what now?" I didn't like the sound of that one bit. I threw on some clothes and drove over to the shop. There was a crowd still gathered outside in the summer night and everybody was buzzing about the unscheduled heavyweight bout they'd gotten to witness up close for free. Luckily, the police hadn't gotten involved just yet. I went straight to my nephew to get the story about what had happened.

According to my nephew, the infamous street fight outside the shop between Mike Tyson and Mitch "Blood" Green started because of kids. Specifically, there was a group of neighborhood kids that I always had hanging out at my shop. These were problem kids. The only kids I wanted around me was problem kids, because what wisdom I had was for problem kids. Many of these kids came from bad situations—neglect, AIDS, addiction. If I could steer them away from the drug game by giving them a place to be, getting them to go on jogs with me, and giving them little errands to run, maybe they'd think twice about being out on the streets all the time like I had been when I was a kid. I tried to get them before they were twelve, before puberty struck. Once they get those raging hormones, it's over. On the second floor of the store, I'd set up a bunch of cots for them to sleep on at night. Sometimes, their whole families might need a place, and I'd have mothers and grandmothers sleeping upstairs with them. It was my way of sharing the wealth and creating the kind of community that I remembered growing up in, where everybody was like family and people took care of each other. Those kids needed something like that, especially with the neighborhood more broken and dangerous than ever.

Two years before I picked up that call in the middle of the night, we had all watched Mike go the distance against Mitch Green in front of a sold-out Madison Square Garden. Then, Mike was nineteen years old and the world was just starting to understand his powers. He was 20-0, with all but one of those victories coming by way of knockout. He was knocking guys out within minutes. Nobody had seen anything like him.

But Mitch was his first real challenge in the ring, another tough street guy from the Bronx, a brawler, a little older and a few inches taller than Mike. Even though Mitch was higher up in the rankings going into the fight, Mike was positioned to take home a quarter million dollars, while Mitch was only guaranteed thirty thousand, thanks to the promoter of the fight, Don King. When Mitch objected to King's unfair payout, the chairman of the New York State Athletic Commission strong-armed him into fighting anyway. Mitch had no choice, but maintained that Don King had conned him out of a fair payday.

Mike won the fight by unanimous decision, but it wasn't a clear victory like his other bouts. In the eighth round, Mitch came back with a barrage of blows that stunned Mike, bringing the crowd to its feet. Mike looked vulnerable for the first time in his young career. And it was a testy fight. There were a couple rounds where you could see them swinging at each other long after the bell had rung. There was bad blood.

I have a lot of sympathy for Mitch Green. He was a good boxer, and like many before him, he fell into financial ruin after his dealings with Don King. After his loss to Tyson, I'd see Mitch hanging around Harlem all the time, usually high on angel dust. The kids who stayed upstairs at the shop used to tease him: "Mike Tyson kick yo ass!"

"He ain't beat me," Mitch would say. "He ain't beat me."

On that particular night, the kids were out front, trying to escape the summer heat, when all of a sudden, they saw Mike Tyson pull up in his Rolls-Royce and walk into the store with his friend Walter Berry, the basketball player. The kids knew exactly how to get their entertainment for the night. They ran straight to the area where they knew Mitch Green always be at. Sure enough, they found him there and told him, "Mike Tyson kick yo ass and he around at Dapper Dan's right now."

Mike was there to pick up a jacket I'd made him with the words "Don't Believe the Hype" stitched on the back in black block letters, a reference to the popular Public Enemy song of the same title. Later, Mike would hold up the jacket at the press conference to discuss what had happened that night, a cast around his right hand as further proof.

But it was because of those kids that Mitch knew Mike was in the shop in the first place. Mitch made his way over to the store with his woman in tow. "So Mitch walks in, right," my nephew told me afterward. "Didn't say a word at first. Just staring at Mike."

"You know you ain't beat me," said Mitch. Then he said it again. "You know you ain't beat me."

At this point, the tension inside was thick. It was obvious Mike didn't want no trouble. Mike held out his hand and said, "Come on, man, let's be all right, man. Shake my hand."

Mitch just kept staring at him.

My nephew redeemed himself from his earlier reefer smoking incident when he thought to grab the store's Polaroid camera and keep it on him while the two professional heavyweights stared each other down across the store.

"Come on, man," Mike repeated. "Shake my hand."

When Mitch finally shook Mike's hand, everybody let out a sigh of relief. But we all knew Mitch was a head case. He followed Mike outside to his car, repeating, "You know you ain't beat me. You know you ain't beat me."

"Come on, man," said Mike, getting irritated.

Just as Mike was about to get into his Rolls, Mitch broke the side mirror clean off of it.

"Yo, why you playing me like that?" said Mike, getting in his face. "Why you playing me like that, man?"

Mitch made a move at Mike, grabbing for his shirt and then his pockets, like he was trying to mug him. Mike's wallet fell to the ground, and that's when Mike snapped, throwing a punch to Mitch's chest that immediately put him on his back. But it was Mike's next punches, when Mitch was lying on the concrete, that did all the damage.

My nephew said he never saw the punch land, but he and everyone else heard it. "Oooo!" said the kids. While Mike was standing
over Mitch, fists cocked, my nephew was snapping pictures of it all
with the store camera. With Mitch on the ground, Mike landed one
right hand after another that closed up Mitch's left eye and broke
his nose, but also left Mike with a hairline fracture. All this information came out in later reports of the fight, but what people don't
know is that after Mike knocked him down, he got on top of Mitch
and started choking him out. That's when people jumped in and
finally got Mike off of him. "I'll kill you and your bitch, too," Mike
said before driving away in his car and leaving Mitch bloody in the
street.

Like I said, I have a lot of sympathy for Mitch Green. He had
three titles, but his struggles with drugs and money sent his life on
a downward spiral. He took Tyson to court over the assault, and
nine years later, the court ruled in his favor, awarding him $45,000,
which wasn't even enough to cover his legal fees.

The street fight between Mike Tyson and Mitch "Blood" Green
brought me the most national attention I ever had, including the
mention on *Monday Night Football* that my landlord saw, but once
again, it wasn't the kind of attention I wanted. The next day, the
story broke in *The New York Times* with the headline "Tyson Hurts
Right Hand in Scuffle with a Boxer." They wrote that my shop was
"a business called Dapper Dan, which Tyson described as an all-
night clothing store that caters to performers," where he had gone
"to pick up an $850 garment." For a lot of people who had no idea
who I was or what I was doing, the story must have left more questions than answers. What the hell was Tyson doing shopping for
clothes at four in the morning? What was an all-night clothing
store anyway? Who spends $850 for a garment in Harlem?

Because of the fascination Mike held for people all over the world, news about the street fight with Mitch Green traveled far and wide along with the name Dapper Dan. You have to understand, Mike Tyson was a cultural phenomenon. Only twenty-two years old, he was already a boxing legend of mythic strength and speed. There was a Nintendo videogame based on him—not as the hero, but as the villain you had to defeat. Mike was undefeated, with half of his opponents never making it out of the first round. In a fight earlier that summer against undefeated champion Michael Spinks, the richest match in boxing history, Tyson didn't just knock Spinks out—he ended the man's career in ninety-one seconds. And now, the injury to his hand meant that Mike had to postpone an upcoming match. Reporters were calling from South America, Europe, everywhere, and when they learned that I had photos of it all, I became very popular with a few publications.

Reporters from the *New York Post* and the New York *Daily News* gave me $750 each just to see with their own eyes that the pictures I claimed to have actually existed, the quickest $1,500 I ever made. After I showed them the pictures, the bidding war started. *Star* and the *National Enquirer* joined in the auction. The offer went up to $150,000 for the photos, but in the end, I refused to sell them. It was a street thing. I didn't want to get Mike in any more trouble. One of the tabloids figured that I wouldn't give them up because I wouldn't hand them over to a white guy. So they flew up some black guy on staff for them in Florida to ask me. That didn't work.

Around the same time, Don King set up a meeting with me. He wanted to make sure that I wasn't going to use the photographs to profit off of his valuable young commodity, but mostly it was clear that he was only there to perform for Mike. "Ain't gone be no extortion," he said to me, playing up the façade of a tough guy protecting his client. I wanted to say, *You bushy-headed nigga, you the only one that's stealin from Mike.* But it wasn't my business, so I just let it go.

Even a year later, when *New York* magazine did a short profile on the shop, one of the first things they mentioned was the Tyson fight. Along with the regular daily dramas, it was the thing that kept following me, shining a bright new spotlight on me and the shop. And then the spotlight turned into a searchlight.

CHAPTER 21

———

The Vise

Early on, the fashion industry wasn't concerned with me at all. I was an outsider who worked on the periphery. Besides the occasional visit from a model like Naomi Campbell, no one from that world ever visited me, with good intentions or bad.

Did I think I might catch hell from the brands for co-opting their logos? Yeah, the thought crossed my mind. I was aware of the risks, but you gotta understand, I'm a gambler at heart. The whole time I was in business, I was rolling the dice.

At the same time that my operation was growing, the counterfeit game was starting to blow up in New York. Knockoffs were a big industry, especially in places like Manhattan's Chinatown, where fake Gucci and Louis bags were flooding the streets. There was big money in the sale of counterfeit goods, and those who were in the knockoff game knew they were doing something illegal. They were often connected to criminal networks that sold other illegal products. There's no question they were thieves. As a matter of fact, in the years to come, my own designs would get knocked off by the same crooks that made bootleg versions of Louis, MCM, and all the other brands.

Intellectual property is still a gray area when it comes to fashion appropriation. Designers are constantly borrowing and sampling and getting inspiration from different cultures and from each other. It's even more blurry in the art world. Andy Warhol's career was one knockoff after the next. Campbell's soup probably coulda shut down Warhol for stealing its logo and selling it for profit, but instead of getting lawyers to seize his paintings and end his career, the company sent him an appreciative letter for the homage and a shipment of soup.

That's how we saw it. Everyone I made clothes for knew I was making something original. My customers knew what they were paying for, and it wasn't Louis, Gucci, or MCM. The Louis print ensemble and matching kufi that the Real Roxanne wore on the cover of her album couldn't have been made by anyone else for anyone else. I moved the heritage brand aesthetic away from that Madison Avenue look and gave it that distinct uptown flavor. I was taking those logos to places the brands never would and making it look good on us. What the jazz musicians did with covers I was doing with fashion. You couldn't get what I was making anywhere. I wasn't no bootlegger.

But the brands didn't see it that way. Because of all the knock-offs going on at the time, intellectual-property law was starting to be a big field. Not long after the whole Tyson thing, I popped up on Madison Avenue's radar. Someone found out that there was a place in Harlem putting logos all over clothes without permission, and to them, I musta seemed like another crooked New York counter-feiter.

Louis Vuitton was the first company to raid my shop. One day, a bunch of armed investigators just walked right in and started taking clothes off the racks like they belonged to them. A lawyer handed me their documentation, explaining that this was a seizure due to infringement of the Louis Vuitton trademark. I read the paperwork. It was a court order from a judge that allowed them to confiscate any materials related to the production and distribution of what they perceived to be counterfeit goods. They started putting everything I made that had Louis on it into trash bags and carrying them outside.

Fur-lined snorkels, cotton sweaters, leather jumpsuits, bucket hats. All that good material, gone. All that time I'd spent working with the customers to design them, gone. All the man-hours my tailors had spent meticulously crafting them, gone. They treated my stuff like it was garbage. I watched them fill their black trash bags with my designs, shoving in one piece after another. It was like they were dragging a part of me to the landfill.

I had already done some homework on Louis. When the founder, Louis Vuitton, started making canvas trunks in Paris back in the 1850s, other European trunk makers copied him relentlessly. His designs were copied so much he had to start putting his name and trademark on the luggage until finally his son took out a patent. The family soon became the biggest name in European luggage, continuing to profit during World War II through collaboration with the Nazis. Even though, at that point, the company had never produced a single jacket or sweater, they were handing me papers saying that my merchandise was illegal. My brother James, who was in town at the time, stood beside me watching, and he could see me getting upset. He just leaned over and said, "Don't say nothing."

The raids from the fashion industry quickly became a regular occurrence. I kept on making clothes and doing business the way I always had, and they kept coming in unannounced, handing me court orders, and taking what I'd made. The militant side of me said, *Oh yeah? You think you gone stop me?* I decided I wasn't gonna change nothing, court orders be damned. The next time Louis came to seize property, I made sure to move all the Louis stuff to the basement. I had a friend of mine bring a couple of his dogs over, so when they opened the basement door to search it, they heard the pit bulls. All of a sudden, the lawyer from Louis Vuitton didn't need to check downstairs anymore.

But that trick couldn't work forever. Whenever I thought the raids were finally letting up, they'd start back up again, this time at the request of Gucci, next time at the request of MCM. They just kept raiding me and raiding me. They were raiding me broke. There was an empty storefront next to mine where I started hiding clothes, but they even found them there. They were relentless. One afternoon, maybe a half hour after MCM had gotten through raiding me, confiscating eight or nine large bags full of clothes, I got in the car to run an errand and spotted the agents who'd just been in my shop hanging out at a gas station. What I saw made my blood boil. They were taking the clothes they'd seized and splitting them up between themselves.

Oh, I had a fit. I drove back to the shop and told James what I'd just seen. I was ready to get street on em and do something about it. But James, in his forties now and getting sober, just said, "Let sleeping dogs lie."

So I left it alone, but the next time MCM agents arrived, I called all the people from around the neighborhood to come to the store and said, "Y'all can have everything!" We were snatching the stuff back from the agents and giving it to the people. Everybody was taking off in all directions with brand-new MCM outfits, running wild at their good fortune, playing tug-of-war and keep-away with the agents.

Even though we were losing business because of them, the raids just became another part of the everyday drama that we had to live with. Whether it was fashion-industry lawyers or DEA stakeouts or LL Cool J having a tumultuous affair with my shopgirl, I still had a business to keep alive.

One way I did that was staying on top of the latest manufacturing equipment. I loved going to the trade shows and talking to people, getting a feel for where the technology was heading. That always excited me and helped take my mind off all the stress. The raids were compromising my ability to get my clothes made in a timely manner. They were seizing custom pieces made for specific clients that I had to make again from scratch. It was having a chilling effect on business. People weren't ordering like they used to. I needed a new thing that I could hit them with that would get them excited about my pieces again. While I was at one of the trade shows, I found it.

It was beautiful and big as a Cadillac: a six-headed, seven-color, state-of-the-art computerized embroidery machine made by the Japanese company Barudan. A salesman explained to me that it was the top embroidery machine on the market, and it cost almost sixty thousand dollars. "I always tell people," he said, "don't think of the cost. Think of it as an investment. A few years from now, it'll pay itself off ten times over." I'd been studying embroidery before it blew up in the fashion world a decade later, and aside from Ralph Lauren's little Polo horse, nobody was doing full-logo embroidery. Computerized embroidery looked to me like the future. I could add a new dimension of sophistication to what I was doing. I was sold.

I bought the Barudan, paying for it in cash. It was one of the most expensive purchases I ever made in my life and almost emptied me out, but I knew that once I had it up and running, I'd be back in the game stronger than ever. Like the salesman said, it was an investment in the future of my company and the future of street fashion. It was going to help me weather this storm. Watching them deliver and set up the huge machine in our factory, I was more excited and hopeful about the business than I had been in months. I had big plans for how I was gonna use it. There was nothing more exciting to me than experimenting with new technology in a way that no one had before. As a test run to christen the machine, I embroidered the name of my late father—Robert

Day—on a large piece of fabric. That was the first time I got to use the machine, and thanks to Fendi, it was also the last.

The lawyers who represented the Fendi family were from a private Madison Avenue law firm called Pavia & Harcourt. Most of the firm's business was in the financial sector, but they were also trail-blazers in the intellectual-property field. One of their up-and-coming stars was a Puerto Rican lawyer from the Bronx named Sonia Sotomayor. She would go on to be appointed the first woman of color on the Supreme Court, by President Obama, but at the time that I was running my boutique, she was working private practice, and Fendi was her first big fashion case. She helped them raid counterfeiters in Queens, and since someone musta heard that I used Fendi logos, and was already getting raided by the other labels, Fendi and Sotomayor decided to raid me, too.

Even if she hadn't gone on to her historic career, I'd still say this about her: Sonia Sotomayor was the person in all the raids on my store whom I respected the most. I'll tell you why. The day she supervised the Fendi raid on me, there were also some agents representing MCM there. I was still mad about how I'd seen MCM agents splitting up my clothes for themselves at the gas station, and they were probably still mad about how I got all the people in the neighborhood to steal the clothes back last time they raided.

When the MCM people started seizing things and putting them in trash bags, Sotomayor stopped them and said that they needed to show me the court order first. It was required by law. So we stood there waiting.

But they didn't have one.

"No," said Sotomayor. "Then you can't do that."

And that's when future Supreme Court justice of the United States of America Sonia Sotomayor made these motherfuckers replace all the merchandise they'd stolen off my racks.

I asked myself how many of the previous raids had been done without the right documents. That's when I started waking up to the fact that the fashion industry had gotten slick on me. It turned out that MCM had sometimes been raiding me under false pretenses. I knew something was off about the way they did things, but wasn't exactly hip to it until Sotomayor spoke up and kicked the MCM people outta my shop.

But she still had to raid me, and though she was very cordial about it, she did her job, documenting the evidence and watching the investigators carry away more bags full of my designs. I normally don't remember the lawyers who raided me, but on top of sending away the MCM people, she said something else that stuck with me. I had a piece I'd just finished for Big Daddy Kane hanging there in the store. It was a full-length black-on-black plongé leather Fendi coat with a shawl—full black glamour classic style.

As she admired the coat, I overheard her say to one of the investigators, "Wow, this guy really belongs downtown." See, I knew before anyone else that she'd make a good judge.

Then they tossed the coat into a trash bag.

I started taking road trips to sell my clothes in other cities, setting up drops with my outta-town clients. That way, I could generate sales while decreasing the amount of vulnerable merchandise I had in the store at a given time. But that meant Dapper Dan's Boutique had turned into a shadow of itself, with barely anything on the shelves.

I got hired to do the wardrobe for the "I'm Large" music video by DJ Chuck Chillout and Kool Chip, which was directed by Ted Demme, my friend from *Yo! MTV Raps*. Kool Chip and Chillout were always coming up with these crazy concepts for videos, and for this one, they imagined a secret war on hip-hop being carried out by a villain named Dr. Ill. The good guys in the video were members of the Hip-Hop Society, and Dr. Ill wanted to destroy them. Part of Dr. Ill's plan involved kidnapping Dapper Dan, which coulda been a metaphor for what the fashion industry was doing to me. They had me do a cameo in the video. In my two seconds of screen time, you can see me struggling while Dr. Ill's henchmen throw me into a waiting van in broad daylight.

That was entertainment, but kidnapping had become a real threat in the city. It was almost an industry in itself, with crews all over who specialized in kidnapping big people in the drug game. Kidnapping crews would target an individual in a successful drug crew, and once they'd kidnapped him, they'd ask a ransom from the guy's drug crew to ensure safe release. Not only did these guys have to worry about getting caught by the DEA, they now had to be on the lookout for kidnappers. Since it was happening to young men of color who were seen by society as criminals, it got little attention in the mainstream.

The kidnappings were another terrible side effect of a cursed game. Many kidnapping crews were motivated as much by ideological hatred as they were by greed. The drug game was shattering all the connections the community had to itself. The whole thing felt completely outta control. Anyone who was making money became prey. There was no telling who would be next.

I was gangsta-affiliated, so up until then, I never had to worry about security at my store. In nine years, twenty-four hours a day, the only people who ever took anything from me were the fashion companies walking it out the front door and my tailors sneaking it out the back. We were never robbed, never held up. Not once. Being from the streets and connected to the folks in the community had been protection enough. But after I saw that big-time dealer from the Bronx get pistol-whipped bloody and dragged into a car outside the shop, I started to wonder if anyone was safe anymore.

One afternoon, when I drove down to pick up my youngest son, Jelani, from preschool, one of the teachers came up to me. I could tell by the look on her face something was off. There was a woman, she said, who had come by earlier in the day claiming she was there to pick up Jelani. "We never saw her before," said the teacher, who knew me and June well. "And when we asked for her name, she just left."

It was a disturbing story, but I didn't know what to make of it. Later that night, when I told June about it, we both sat there, confused more than anything. It would only make sense later.

I had a GMC Safari van that I kept parked outside the shop. Whenever I was in it, I'd have the engine running, which is typical when you hustling. Some days, I'd be in there with one of my kids. A couple times, I took Jelani with me across the bridge to New Jersey to sell clothes after his preschool let out.

But on this particular night, I'm by myself. Who knows what I'm thinking about. Probably business and what I was gonna do next with all these raids emptying out my inventory. The stereo in the car is on, playing Tito Puente, and since 125th Street is one of the busiest in Manhattan, I don't pay any mind to the sound of a car pulling up beside me and one of its doors opening and closing.

Half a minute passes, and the other car is still parked beside me, idling. My street antennas start to go up. I look back over at the guy behind the wheel. He's by himself in the car, and every once in a while, our eyes meet. I start to sense something off about his body language. I check my rearview mirror and turn my head around to check out my blind spots.

"Why you keep looking around?" says the man in the car beside me.

Something don't feel right. My antennas are up, but the reception isn't as keen as it should be.

All of a sudden, I hear the sound of footsteps and a bent, hooded figure rapidly approaching the driver's-side door. It is too late now. There is someone I haven't seen. He snatches open my door.

"Get in the back of the van!" he says, as I feel the cold nozzle of the gun press into the side of my head. "Get in the back of the van!"

I just freeze. I don't do nothing. While he keeps shouting at me to get in the back of my own van, I look at the gearshift on the side of the steering wheel. The van is running, but it's in park. My street knowledge is kicking in. I remember what I have to do in a situation like this, what my brothers and I learned through experience. These kidnappers know me as the guy who sells expensive clothes to the drug dealers, but they don't know I'm from the street originally. The last thing they want is resistance. "Get in the back!" he shouts.

The gun is still pointed at me, but I have to fight. I need to lean forward. Wrestle the gun away. Pull the gearshift into drive quick and step on the gas. Something. Anything.

You ain't letting them take you.

Still in the driver's seat, I make my move: I use the door to push him.

The gun goes off. He takes off running.

I'll never know if he shot me on purpose or if the gun just went off by accident, but I felt a fire on my back, and the force of the impact knocked me out of my seat and onto the ground. At first, no one from the shop came out to see what had happened. They were down in the mezzanine unaware of the activity out front. The only one who eventually ran outside was Beverly, one of my shopgirls. She'd heard the gunshot and came over to where I was slumped on the side of the van.

She helped me to my feet. But at that point, I was not in my rational mind. I was in shock. A sudden wave of paranoia crashed over me as she picked me up. I started saying to myself, *Maybe she was in on it. I don't know if she's down.*

Because I had lost feeling in my arm, Beverly put me back inside the van on the passenger side and sat behind the wheel to drive me to the hospital. But having just fought off a kidnapping, I wasn't about to let anyone drive me anywhere.

"My arm dropped," I said, climbing back into the driver's seat. "But I ain't drop."

I shifted down into drive and put the pedal to the metal. I made a sharp U-turn in the middle of the street and went the wrong way down a one-way. At last, a couple minutes later, I pulled into the hospital, and as soon as I walked through the doors, I collapsed.

For the next thirteen days, I was laid up in the hospital recovering from the bullet, which had entered through my back, just missing my heart. A centimeter the other way and it woulda ruptured my aorta, killing me. The bullet then ricocheted off my rib and traveled up my chest, until it lodged in the base of my neck, landing so close to my jugular vein that the doctors couldn't even go in and remove it. They had to run a catheter through my leg all the way up to my neck to see how close the bullet had come to my jugular, because if it was even touching the vein, it could have put me at risk of an aneurysm. In the end, the doctors didn't have to do nothing to me. The location of the bullet meant surgery was outta the question. The bullet is still lodged at the base of my neck.

While I was in the hospital, my brothers took turns watching the shop and keeping guard over me. I thought back to the kidnapping I'd witnessed just the week prior and how I'd done nothing to intervene. And I shuddered at the thought of whoever had sent that woman to try to take my youngest son from preschool. The pain I was feeling wasn't just physical, it was spiritual and psychological, too.

During those two weeks I was in the hospital, I got word from my brothers that the mothers of my children had been making calls about my condition. In my traumatized state, those calls didn't seem like they were made outta concern for me and my health, but rather like they wanted to know if they could finally collect on the life insurance policy that I'd taken out for them and our children. Those thoughts only reminded me how isolated I'd become from my family. That paranoia didn't do nothing but deepen the sorrow and make me feel more alone.

The trauma of the botched kidnapping and attempt on my life lingered long after I had healed from my gunshot wound. To this day, when I see someone in a hood, with a certain kind of posture, my palms start to sweat and my adrenaline starts to rush and I get hyperalert. If I see a couple cars lingering at the corner, I'll note it in the back of my mind. I'm fighting those flashbacks all the time.

A kinda grief came over me after my botched kidnapping. I wanted to be in a different existence. I wished I'd led a different life where I could be completely innocent of all the terrible things that I'd witnessed and been a part of. I was tired of that fear, that desperation, which constantly kicks in when you've been raised on the streets. I wanted to be away from all of that, and because I couldn't go nowhere, I started to withdraw into myself. All along, I'd just wanted to make people look good. I'd just wanted to sell clothes and read my spiritual books and watch my children grow up. I didn't want the streets to dictate my life anymore. Getting shot was an epiphany, as near-death experiences can be. One question kept running through my mind: *How can you be in the streets but not of it?*

CHAPTER 22

Game Over

I've never loved being in the public eye. I've always been reluctant about putting myself front and center. But after the failed kidnapping, I really didn't like dealing with people no more. I stayed in the back of the store most days or stayed home and let my brothers handle the business. It felt like there was this vise that was tightening around me. The everyday drama had soured into something worse. The shop felt cursed.

When I finally got back into a regular work schedule, my head wasn't where it needed to be anymore, and that left the business in a vulnerable state. With all the raids, we were already a shadow of our former operation. All my bets were on the embroidery machine. It was the only thing in my life that brought me any kind of hope for the future.

During this time, as part of the case brought against me by Fendi, I had to go downtown and make an appearance in court.

When it came to my business, I always put time, effort, and passion into research, from printing techniques to salesmanship to machinery. But I didn't know much about lawsuits and courtrooms. I hadn't done my homework in that area. After all the raids and getting shot at, I wasn't in no kinda mental or physical shape to motivate myself to do that research. And I was about to pay for it dearly.

My court appearance that morning wasn't nearly as serious as my other experiences as a criminal defendant, but it was about to be the straw that broke the back of Dapper Dan's Boutique. I went representing myself; I didn't even think I needed a lawyer. The judge read out the case and gave me the option to admit to liability and pay damages.

I'd never dealt much with people outside my community. Part of that was my mother's influence, not trusting white people. The justice system was part of that white world that I didn't have faith in. So I chose to fight it. I knew I wasn't guilty and hadn't done anything wrong. I argued what I'd always believed: that my creations were not counterfeit goods but interpretative homages. Fendi didn't make snorkels or sweatsuits; they didn't even have a menswear line yet. Once I'd finished pleading my case, the judge said, "Okay, y'all go to the lawyer's office for a deposition."

Off we went to the offices of Pavia & Harcourt. I had my guard all the way up. Before we even started, I slapped down my tape recorder and told them, "I'm recording everything." I was sitting there all militant, had my jaw clenched, my chin in the air. But the thing about being militant is, if you don't know how to handle the sword, you slice yourself.

Being the first person in my community who'd ever been in a meeting like that, I had nobody to come before me to say, *Yo, this is how this go. You pay the damages, take the hit, and keep it moving.*

Instead, the lawyers got an injunction, and the injunction allowed them to take away all my Fendi furs and all the means to produce what they deemed counterfeit goods. This meant that they could confiscate all my machines, and they did, including my brand-new Barudan embroidery machine that I had placed the hopes of my entire business on.

All told, they took a quarter million dollars' worth of merchandise and equipment. My Jewish friends in the clothing business would ask me later, "Why didn't you tell them the machine was mine? That way, maybe you could've kept it."

I hadn't thought of that, either. The machine coulda been the basis of an entire new business. I coulda started a new lease somewhere else and moved into a whole new area. But it was too late.

I was devastated.

Then I was furious. I was angry that they got me like that. I lost a quarter of a million dollars all because I didn't know how to talk to white people.

The road was dead-ending, and I was bitter from all the time I lost trying to keep Dapper Dan's Boutique alive. All those hours, and what did I have to show for it? Without my spiritual reading to keep me sane, I don't know where I would have ended up. It was the reason I kept waking up in the morning, staying sober, exercising, eating healthy, even while I saw the business crumbling before my eyes.

But in all those nine years of work, I couldn't remember no one ever asking me for book recommendations. None of the street guys I made clothes for ever asked what I was reading. No one ever said, "Dap, what does it mean to live a good life?" Or, "Dap, what you think is our design and purpose here on this earth as human beings?"

For nine years, I'd given every waking hour to the shop without so much as a vacation or a holiday. I'd been fighting since the beginning, since A. J. Lester had me blacklisted for undercutting their prices. And what did I have to show for it? A bullet lodged in my neck. An empty storefront.

There is always some kinda war goin on outside, but the real war is inside. And I was fighting a war with myself about what I had achieved with the boutique. I knew I had made an impact, but was I any closer to whatever it was I was truly searching for? Like it says in the Kenny Rogers song I used to play for my hustling buddies before we went on a job, *You gotta know when to hold em, know when to fold em*. It was time for me to fold em and walk away from the boutique and all that came with it.

I was tired of fighting. I didn't want to own a shop no more. I didn't want to manage a factory. The vise grip that I'd been in my whole life, which was always squeezing me between the streets from below and a racist system from above, had finally squeezed the fight outta me. And, in the process, it squeezed the doors of Dapper Dan's Boutique shut.

Yet another casualty of a cursed game.

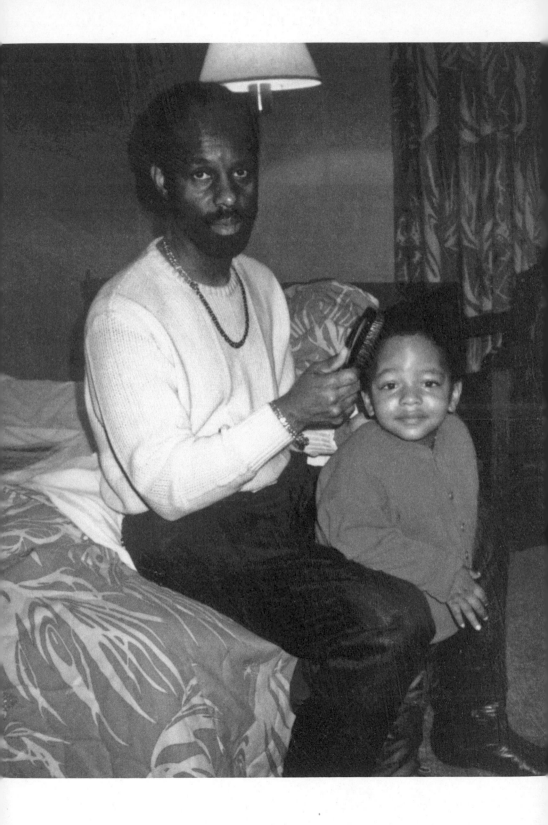

PART IV

—

UNDERGROUND RUNWAY

If I strive, then maybe I'll stay alive.

RAKIM

CHAPTER 23

Flatfoot Hustling

After the shop closed, I disappeared from public view for a while. No one knew where I went. For three months, I just laid up in bed. Physically and mentally, I was drained. I wasn't returning my friends' calls, not because I didn't wanna talk to them, but because sometimes I need to shut down to protect my thoughts and myself. I needed to isolate and figure out a way forward.

My family was starting to really worry about me, though. I wasn't eating; I was shedding weight like never before in my life. It was a dark period. I only left bed to drive June to work, take Jelani to nursery school, then pick them back up at the end of the day. Fendi didn't need to put me in jail, because I was doing it to myself.

June had a steady job in the billing department of a hospital, so while I laid up in bed doing nothing, we were living off her salary, which wasn't enough for all the expenses. The bills were piling up.

We were behind on our electric. We were behind on our mortgage. She and I would sit around the table putting pennies into rolls so we could scrounge up enough money for groceries. That's how broke we were. More than once, my sister Deborah would come by with a box of groceries to help us restock the fridge and the cabinets and say, "Damn, it's cold in here." That was because winter was approaching and we couldn't afford oil to heat the house.

It was a painful time. Around then, June's mother passed, and because we were so backed up on the phone bills, they cut our line, which meant her family couldn't even get in touch with her for emotional support. And though I didn't know it then, we almost lost the brownstone. June's a very private person, so she kept this a secret from me for years, but when we lapsed on our mortgage payments, the man we bought the house from set up a meeting with her to try to buy the brownstone back. He had her sitting in a room with his lawyer, and he wanted June to give him back the deed, so that we could rent instead of own the house from there on out. We would have lost the house then, if it weren't for June's cousin and sister who bailed us out.

Outside my room, I would sometimes hear the voice of my daughter Danique, home on college break. "Dang, what's wrong with Daddy?"

Daddy was weary.

Sometimes, during my years hustling dealers out of their money, when I felt the mood turn against me, I'd place a bet and say, "Watch my money while I take a leak." Then I'd just leave the bet and never come back. This thing with the shop felt different. This wasn't cutting losses. This was defeat. It was me who felt like a sucker.

I'd worked harder at making my boutique a success than I'd worked at anything before. It had been the culmination of my life, my energy, and my money, and there was nothing left. Having built the business from a place of pride and defiance and watched it take off, I saw now that I had miscalculated, overplayed my hand. I blamed myself, but I also blamed the public nature of what I'd done. Even though I went in on my own terms, once I broke out into the mainstream, I was operating in a world where the house always won. I had exposed myself to forces that I could not protect myself against, a mistake I vowed never to repeat.

I figured people was whispering rumors about me soon as the raids started. The boutique had my name on it. My identity was connected to the store. I can only imagine how creative they got at the barbershops when I lost everything and closed down.

"I heard he had to sell his brownstone."

"How he make all that money offa clothes?"

"It don't add up. He had to be doing something else."

"And he got shot, too."

"He ain't so dapper now."

I laid up in my room thinking about what to do next and how to do it. Slowly, I got my appetite back. Regardless of what the perception was, I knew I was gonna stay in the fashion game. It felt like what I was meant to do, and I believed the market for what I was doing was only gonna grow. I told myself that I'd keep things more manageable next time. I didn't have the energy for all that drama no more. No way was I ever gonna keep a public storefront like that again. It was too visible, too much of a target. I'd change my business approach, but I wouldn't change my attitude about making clothes. My brand stood for defiance, not fear. I was gonna keep making us look good using the best materials and techniques no matter what the fashion people tried to tell me. If I was gonna succeed on my own terms, I needed to stay underground.

But first I needed to get outta bed.

June is so special. She'd stayed out of my fashion business up until then, only visiting the shop a handful of times over the years. But now we was broke, and I didn't have money for the bills like before. And I was stuck. "We have to do something, Danny," she said.

"You can't lay here all day not doing anything. We're not getting anywhere."

"What I'm gone do, June?" I said.

"You know how they have those tour buses coming uptown now," she said.

"Yeah."

"We can go out there with the vendors. Sell something to the tourists."

It wasn't a bad idea. We had all noticed the tour buses that were starting to make their way up into Harlem, mostly Europeans looking for a taste of the black neighborhood they'd read about in books, the home of the Cotton Club and the Renaissance and soul food.

So I made a bunch of simple iron-on Chanel T-shirts, because that was the cheapest material I could afford at the time. June and I took one of those metal fold-up tables and set up shop right on 125th Street alongside the other vendors. The street was packed with tables. There were as many as a thousand vendors lining 125th Street on a good weekend day. Some had been there for years, but many were new, a sign of a struggling city that had lost hundreds of thousands of jobs over the past few years. Harlem had been abandoned. My family was a prime example of that. I was the only member of my immediate family still living here. Everyone else was gone. But how could you blame them? The mecca was a wasteland. Boarded-up brownstones. Overgrown lots. Now, Mayor Giuliani's "broken windows" policy, which associated poverty with crime, gave the police license to punish poor neighborhoods like Harlem, where brutality was the norm.

Nevertheless, walking along 125th Street in the early nineties was an overwhelming sensory experience. You'd smell sandalwood as you passed the incense vendor's table, you'd see the face of Booker T. Washington or Ida B. Wells on the bookseller's table, you'd hear soul music blasting from a stereo at the cassette and CD seller's table. The sidewalks overflowed with the richness of African American culture, history, and style.

That first day, a bus stopped nearby and a German tour group stepped out. They walked from table to table, taking photographs with their 35 mm cameras. Some of them stopped by our table, smiling at the T-shirts I'd made and speaking to each other in German.

I held one of them up against my own chest, trying to get back in the salesman mode. "How about two for ten?" I said. They smiled and nodded politely. One of them snapped a picture of me. After a while, they climbed back into the tour bus and drove away. As soon as they left, another tour bus passed by, and then another. I started counting them. One hundred and forty-four tour buses came and went along 125th Street. We ain't sell one T-shirt.

That was all the motivation I needed.

The humiliation I felt as June and I folded up our table at the end of the day was powerful. But rather than being left defeated, I dug in my heels. It got me out the house more, which I needed. I kept on going back to my spot on 125th Street with my fold-up table and my T-shirts. People from the neighborhood would recognize me from time to time, but they didn't wanna buy nothing, just wanted to talk. I couldn't sell those T-shirts for the life of me. It was one big embarrassing step backwards from having a three-story building with the biggest celebrities in the world lining up outside. But like all my oldest friends, June knew I always did my best work when I had my back against the wall, and every day that passed that I wasn't making money, I was feeling pressed deeper and deeper into a corner.

One day, I came home from selling T-shirts to a cold, darkened house. They'd cut the power on us weeks ago. During those long, chilly nights without heat, as June and I and our young son, Jelani, shivered beside each other in the same bed to keep warm, I thought, *We can't live like this.*

I had to do something.

The next morning, I dug up an old pair of dice, and as we sat around the breakfast table in our coats, clouds coming out of our mouths, June noticed me moving the dice around in my hand, practicing.

I said, "I don't like breaking people."

She was silent for a moment. Then, "Well, can you just do it one more time?"

"Yeah," I said. "One more time."

I make sure I always prepare for the reality that I might have to start all over. Guys like my uncle Fish Man Eddie had instilled that "flatfoot hustling" work ethic in me from childhood. I coulda asked my friends in the entertainment business for some start-up money, but there's this pride and dignity thing about hustlers in Harlem. We don't accept no handouts. Back in my early gambling days, I remember breaking guys down, taking them for all they had, and whenever I'd show pity and try to slide them some money, they'd always say, "Don't give me nothing, man. I get mine. I don't need nothing from you, man. Give that to your bitch, man. I get mine."

That pride I grew up around was so powerful, and that's why I never went to anybody for help. Right or wrong, my attitude was, if you see me fighting a bear, help the bear. I don't need nothing from nobody. I had gotten us into this situation, and I was determined to get us out.

I started gambling again. Much as I didn't want to do it, dice was the fastest, surest way for me to make money. There is nothing I know better than gambling. Not metaphysics, not fashion, not spirituality, nothing. I know how to win money at gambling better than I know how to do anything. But I hated it.

I took twenty-five dollars to a gambling spot run by a young hustler named Gino, whom I used to school about dice before I went into clothes. From the moment I started playing, I could tell by the way him and all his friends were betting that they wanted to see me broke. Hustlers secretly love seeing another hustler go down. I'd hear about guys saying, "You know Dap fucked up, right?" They thought I was all washed-up. But the street didn't know all the sides of me. They didn't know about my reading, my thinking, my spiritual life. If you told them that I used to be a journalist and poet, a lot of those guys would have called you a liar. I never revealed what I was made of to anyone aside from my best hustling friends like Russell, because I knew that there was no place out there in the streets for that part of myself. But that meant most guys didn't know me.

Gino wanted to prove that he was better than me, so him and his guys were treating me like an old relic. They in there playing two-dice, but they didn't know the first thing about the mathematics of it the way I did. I stayed focused on probability and parlayed twenty-five dollars into five hundred. They switched to playing cee-lo, but I didn't take the bait, because the probability wasn't high enough. If I don't like the spread you give me, I'm not betting. Patience, you know. Soon, this rich guy in the spot starts losing his money to Gino at cee-lo. When Gino was done banging him, I asked the guy if he wanted to play two-dice with me, flashing my five hundred dollars like, *What's up?*

I placed the exact same bets I had with Gino, playing the odds just like Vegas. It didn't take long before I'd made enough to pay down the heating bill. A few minutes later, I was ready to purchase some new sewing machines. A couple more throws after that, I could buy some rolls of fabric downtown and hire back one or two of my Senegalese tailors.

Before I knew it, I was back in the fashion game.

———

Now that I had the money, starting up again shoulda been easy. I knew how to do this. My first stop was the Garment District in midtown to buy fabric. But getting there was a whole other issue. I didn't have the cash for car insurance or gas no more. If I wanted to go down to get some fabric, I had to use the subway, and that was a big psychological hurdle for me.

In my hustling days, we used to have an expression for a guy who used the subway. We'd say, "I know you ain't come outta that hole." If you a hustler, you didn't go down in the subway. I hadn't been on the New York City subway in over twenty years. I didn't even know how to anymore. I still had a reputation to uphold in the streets, and using the subway was like an admission of defeat. When I mentioned this to my older brother Omar, he shook his head in frustration. "Go down and take the train, man," he said. "Ain't nobody gonna see you."

So I swallowed my pride and took the subway downtown. I had to stop caring about how people perceived me. I didn't need no-body's validation. I knew what I was capable of, and regardless of how you look at me it don't make no difference to me. I'm going to do this and I'm going to get this. I would never give up on myself.

But when it came to the subway, I had no idea where I was going that day trying to get to the Garment District. I was so confused, I accidentally took the PATH train and wound up in New Jersey.

CHAPTER 24

───

Highways, Not Runways

I took the gambling money I'd won and built out a home studio on the ground floor of our brownstone. For the next twenty years, I ran the majority of my fashion business from there, making trips to the Garment District to haul big rolls of fabric on the subway. The experience of having my intellectual property copied by my workers had pushed me into a space of secrecy. People had stolen my designs, my techniques, even copied the kind of ink I used. So I was all about automation and being able to cut down the number of people I relied on for manufacturing. I wanted to personally control as much of the process as I could.

One of the first additions to my new studio was a computer and some software. It was 1992. I heard about the release of a new version of the graphic-design and illustration program CorelDRAW, which ran on Microsoft Windows. With CorelDRAW 3.0's state-of-the-art technology, I could create and manipulate images on my

PC. But I didn't know the first thing about computing, so my oldest son, Danny, Jr., taught me how to use it. I was looking to push the means of production into the future. That's a big part of what creativity is to me, using new technology in a way that no one would think of using it.

I was excited by the beauty and power of personal computing. It felt like a historic invention. I used to go up to my room and work with CorelDRAW, and the time would just fly by as I explored all the capabilities and variations of what I could do with the software. I could play with the functions endlessly, creating new ideas with the press of a button. I was still going to the trade shows every year, walking from booth to booth thinking about how I could take the newest machines and modify them for my own use with the computer. Once in a while, I'd take my grandkids to trade shows. "Listen, if you go and see how things are born," I'd tell them, "then you can grow them yourself."

Once I figured the computer stuff out, I started getting interested in other forms of new technology that could help streamline and secure my process, so I began reading up on sublimation printing, a form of digital textile printing which uses heat to transfer dye onto paper or fabric. With a sublimation printer, I didn't need people to help me with the silk screens. I bought one of the first, entry-level sublimation printers. It was so rudimentary and early in the technology that you'd have to replace cartridges one at a time after each pass to print in full color. But with just a computer, printer, and heat press, I could cut out all the middlemen involved in my fabric-making process before bringing it to my tailors. Whereas before I needed four people holding these big screens over the fabric, now I didn't need nobody.

Because of my desire to keep the team small and trusted, most of my business was gonna have to rely on mass-producing, not customization. Five people working to mass-produce specific items in a few different sizes can match the output of twenty-five workers doing customized clothing. Although I did some custom work from time to time, for the next twenty years mass production was the process that kept me alive.

Now that I had the home studio rolling, I was eager to start making clothes again and already had some ideas about what to try next. From the time I'd spent on 125th with the other vendors, I'd gotten a feel for what clothes were in style in the community. I saw that the Guess brand was gaining popularity, especially among young women, so I decided that I'd make Guess outfits for girls. I'd design a Guess symbol in CorelDRAW and print it on a top in un-Guess-like colors, then repeat the color and fabric on a matching skirt. Once I made a batch of those and brought them out to the table, they started moving like crack. I was selling like sixty a day. Then I took the profits and flipped it to make a line of Timberland jackets, playing with the logos and colors as I did with the Guess line, and those sold even better. Often, I'd bring my son Jelani's friends or other kids from the neighborhood to do their homework and help me sell the clothes, giving them a cut for their help. I always liked to have young kids around me, especially those who I thought were most vulnerable to ending up on the corners.

I knew what them kids was going to go through before they went through it, so I tried to make them understand their own mindset. "The value you place on how you create fun for yourself determines who you are," I'd tell them, receiving blank stares in response. "Do you understand what I'm saying?" They could not see the beauty of their own innocence: the desire for materialism and pleasure had already been created in them, but they couldn't spot it developing. I was fighting back against the mentality of guys on the corner that was inside them and trying to keep the innocence alive in them. I paid them to jog with me in the morning before setting up my table. Then at night, I would buy them pizzas and sit them on our stoop and talk.

My time as a vendor on 125th Street was short-lived thanks to Mayor Giuliani, who added more inspectors to the police department's anti-vendor task force and started really cracking down, rounding us up and placing us in designated open-air markets far from heavy-foot-traffic areas. If a vendor resisted, even if he'd been there for years, he got arrested. The mayor and his police did this out of what they called "quality of life" concerns. Since most of the vendors were black, it was obvious whose quality of life they were concerned about, and it wasn't ours. The exodus of black people fleeing the chaos of Harlem in the seventies and eighties paved the way for a new era. For the first time since the early 1900s, you had white people moving into the neighborhood and buying up property. The gentrification of Harlem had begun, and I had to find another way to reach customers.

I thought of my gangster clientele spread out all over the country. Now you had younger guys who maybe grew up hearing about me from their hustler uncles and fathers. Gangsters, rappers, and MTV: those were the three main ways my name had traveled. It also moved through the jails. The gangsters didn't care if I'd been shut down or called a bootlegger. My stuff is rebellious in nature, which means it's really for people who are least controlled by rules or laws or public opinion. The gangsters were the first to appreciate that. The people who are controlled by those things would be unlikely to gravitate to my clothes. I still had a network of customers from Miami to Los Angeles, Baltimore to Detroit. Because the store didn't exist, they couldn't come to me no more, but what if I went out to them?

During the period when the raids were happening, I started making short trips across the river to sell clothes at the drug spots in Newark, New Jersey. It was just a matter of expanding my range to other cities and getting on the highway for longer trips. I hired Omar's son, Sayid, to come with me. With a trunk full of merchandise and both of us dressed in the clothes I'd made, we hopped in my Jeep and took the Dapper Dan show on the road. We went from Harlem all the way down to Orlando, hitting all the towns along the way where I knew the gangsters and dope dealers and hustlers were at, then drove back to New York, hitting all the places we'd missed.

Over the next several years, I saw firsthand the devastation that the drug game had caused in black communities all across the country. I learned a lot about America, some things I already knew and others that surprised me. I learned hustlers in Florida and Los Angeles really like big coats, even though they didn't have no need for them. I saw the growing disparity in black and white communities everywhere, the segregation that seemed to be starting back over again, aided by the drug war. Getting into the minds of drug dealers from other places was interesting—the Detroit mob, the Connecticut mob, and especially the Philly mob. I learned that the young guys in Philly were so buck-wild because they were starting to get into Lick, a street name for codeine, while the young hustlers in New Jersey were getting into pills. I learned that the most effective mobs, like the Junior Black Mafia in Philly, was all Muslims who didn't smoke or drink. At the time, the crew was led by Aaron Jones, who's now on death row. With them, it was all business, and that's what made them so powerful.

We sold clothes to big bosses like Aaron, and we sold clothes to backwater hustlers in rural communities. I'll never forget me and my nephew Sayid, who was studying at Hampton University in Virginia at the time, was up in a little city nearby, and we heard that this local dude named Goldy wanted to see us. He was some kind of hustler, and he owned a club. We didn't know much about him, other than that he wanna buy some clothes, so we went over to his club to do some business. It was a real country atmosphere in there. Everybody was sitting down, ain't nobody dancing. Then the song switched over on the jukebox, and all of a sudden, everyone sitting around jumped up like a gun had been drawn. I looked over at my nephew and could see the terror in his face as he started getting to his feet. Now I'm freaking out. We didn't know what was happening. My nephew muttered, "Oh, shit." We was both on our feet about to run out the club, but we didn't hear no gunshots yet, so we just froze. That's when we start to notice that everybody, including Goldy himself, had gotten in line on the dance floor. They had all simultaneously jumped up not because somebody had a weapon but because the song had changed and it was time to do the "Electric Slide." That was some real country shit.

I still had a handful of clients in the hip-hop world who stayed loyal after I got shut down, but most had moved on. They started their own fashion labels, like Russell Simmons with Phat Farm. They started wearing clothes made by the new streetwear labels that were emerging in the early nineties, like Cross Colours and FUBU. They started to gravitate towards a preppier look with brands like Ralph Lauren and Tommy Hilfiger. People were always into Ralph Lauren and Polo, because of that aspirational lifestyle he created, but in the late eighties and early nineties, Polo actively reached out to its black customers with Polo Sport, featuring African American model Tyson Beckford prominently in their ad campaigns.

Hilfiger was getting props from the rappers and reaching back out to them, too. Grand Puba appeared on Mary J. Blige's debut album, *What's the 411?*, rapping on the title track:

> *Well I be Puba on this here*
> *The nigga from last year*
> *Girbauds hanging baggy*
> *Tommy Hilfiger top gear.*

And after that, Tommy gave him a bunch of free clothes. He did the same thing with Snoop Dogg before his memorable *Saturday Night Live* appearance, performing on national TV with a big "Tommy" logo on his shirt. Hilfiger was one of the first mainstream designers to see the advantage of marketing to that hip-hop generation, using artists as billboards for his brand. Rappers like Snoop, Puba, and Raekwon were giving these brands millions of dollars in free advertising in exchange for free clothes.

Once I saw the impact that those brands were having in the

streets, I started doing my own versions of Polo and Tommy. I made an original Ralph Lauren pullover with a half-zipper and filled it with foam rubber to give it some body. Some of my friends in the local fashion game told me not to do it. "No one's going to buy this," they said. But at the time, the oversized look was in. Ralph was using nylon that would just droop, but I used material that had body to it. People liked the way it felt.

Working with three of my African tailors, I made sixty of those pullovers a day, every day, seven days a week, for seven months, and sold every last one of them. I was selling jackets wholesale for thirty-five dollars apiece to retailers. I would go to Jersey to the vendors over there, and they'd be literally chasing me down the street for the chance to sell them at a markup. These jackets penetrated the culture so much that, one day, a sports-section article showed in full color a man sleeping in line for Yankees tickets wearing my Polo pullover. Soon, bootleggers started copying me. Every time one of my designs blew up in popularity, they'd take it to China, copy it, and bring it back, which was frustrating.

More and more, hip-hop culture stood for all youth culture in America. Though I wasn't there, everyone in Harlem has heard the story about when reps from Hilfiger pulled up to 125th Street, popped the trunk, and just started giving away free clothes to people lucky enough to be passing by.

The brand's desire to corner the hip-hop fashion market eventually led him to me. I made a custom Tommy jacket for a popular guy in Harlem named Dard. It was a bubble jacket made of satin. It was fire, it was sensational, if I do say so myself. Everybody was eyeing it, drooling over it. Dard wore it out to the club one night while he was hanging with Tyson Beckford, who was one of his good friends. Also at the club with Tyson that night was Andy Hilfiger, Tommy's younger brother. At the time, Andy was working at a division of his brother's fashion label focusing on musicians. I guess he was something of a musician himself, so he was going to all the places rappers went to buy clothes, looking for fashion inspiration. When he saw Dard's Tommy jacket, he flipped.

"Who made that jacket?" Andy asked. When Dard told him, Andy replied, "Tell him I want to see him."

When Andy Hilfiger sent for me, I didn't see it as something I needed or even wanted. The only people I cared about were my customers. I was doing fine by myself. I had just clocked $100,000 in seven months from the Polo pullover. I never took the meeting. I wasn't into white people. I didn't hate them, but I didn't trust them, especially after my recent experiences with the European brands. If I worked with Hilfiger, I never thought that I'd get a fair shake.

I could understand why Hilfiger wanted me to design for them, though. My designs had deeply saturated the culture. They had been everywhere, on album covers, music videos, and red carpets, and I would be able to capture the imagination of people on the street in the way that the brand wanted.

Nobody was gonna own me, though. Since my militant days with *40 Acres and a Mule,* that liberation spirit never left me. We can be partners maybe. But no more plantation stuff. Not for me. That's never gonna happen. So I told Hilfiger no.

That wan't the last time I got approached by a major brand. When I said no to working for this other company who shall remain nameless, they told MTV that they would no longer spend advertising dollars at the network unless my clothes were blurred out. If an old video had my clothes in it, or a rapper came on *Yo! MTV Raps* featuring outfits that I had made, they'd blur out the whole look, so you couldn't see it. They censored all my designs, not for graphic imagery or foul language, but in retaliation for my refusal to work for them. I had a great relationship with MTV, especially with Ted Demme. But after MTV started blurring me out, Ted broke everything in the TV game down to me, and I began to see how it worked. A network like MTV relied on keeping their advertisers happy, and one of their big fish wasn't happy with me. I understood why they suppressed me. They did the right thing for themselves. But they didn't do the *right* thing.

It was particularly gangsta when you understand that, at the same time this brand was seeking to profit from the streetwear trends that originated in my shop, they also seemed to be using their power and privilege to suppress my designs in the media. Either they wanted me as their slave or they wanted me gone.

Rather than get upset about it, I took it as motivation. Those were just the kind of *Oh yeah?* moments throughout my life when I fought back the hardest. *Oh yeah, you think you gone stop me?*

We'll see about that.

CHAPTER 25

———

Harlem River Blues

I love driving. I like driving across bridges especially. Something about crossing a bridge makes you feel like you're going away from all the things you don't want to be bothered with. It's freeing. I was back on the road, going from state to state selling merchandise and trying to stay on top of the trends and styles along the way.

People knew me everywhere, so I'd go right to those pockets of action where I knew the drug dealers hung out. I'd take weekend trips down to Baltimore and hit the drug spots. If you've ever seen HBO's *The Wire*, I was going to those same drug spots they were talking about in that show. I'd be there while they were bragging about "shootin niggas from New York." They only felt threatened by guys who went down there to sell drugs or to mess with their girls, so I had a strict policy for anybody who'd go on those trips with me. One: you don't talk to nobody about drugs. Two: you don't talk to none of the girls.

It was in Baltimore that I made one of my most important discoveries. It wasn't about fashion. I drove over to this church one night on a tip that there were some guys getting out of some kind of meeting who were looking to buy clothes from me. When they finally came out the church and I asked them what they was meeting about in there, they told me they was part of a drug-treatment program called Narcotics Anonymous. I'd never heard of it before. They said they'd been dope fiends before, but now were clean and had a community of other people to share their stories with and feel less alone in the world, thanks to NA.

My time as a heroin addict was only a short period, but there wasn't no NA back then, so when I would try to get people like Curtis or my brother James to quit using the way I had, they'd always just tell me, "Man, everybody can't be like you." That always frustrated me, but I would never give up trying to get them clean. I would never accept that, because I learned from Hilton Hotema that what's good for one is good for everybody. But besides me, I didn't have no examples of successful recovery to show them.

Now I had all kinds of stories from these guys coming out of the NA meeting in Baltimore to tell James, Curtis, and especially Russell. After Russell finally got out of federal prison for the credit card hustle, the drugs destroyed his life, and during the years that I ran the shop, I'd lost touch with him almost completely. I'd wanted him to be my partner when I started the boutique, and I wanted him beside me now on the road. But he needed to get healthy first. Those guys at the NA meeting were worse off than him, and they were coming out of that program fully transformed.

I got hold of Russell when I got back in town. I'll never forget, we were sitting on my stoop. "Russell, I seen it," I told him. "People is coming back."

For the next year, I helped Russell get clean. Mostly, I wanted him to know there was a place for him in this world. That he would not be alone as long as I was around. I paid him $350 a week to stay off drugs, to stay connected. While he started attending NA meetings, my house became a refuge for him. He stayed with us, getting healthy in mind, body, and spirit. He started reading his way out of his pain.

Russell's been sober for over twenty years now, and Curtis and my brother James, who both wound up going back to school to become drug counselors, have been sober for almost as long, using their firsthand experiences to help others.

When you're getting high, you get locked into a way of being. You get comfortable, and you don't think there's anything else out there beyond that. But then, when you get clean, you realize there are higher forms of pleasure—spending time with friends, exercising, learning a new idea. And these pleasures are on a different level of intoxication than anything a person can experience on drugs. You realize that self-control is a ladder not just away from addiction, but towards a higher spiritual plane.

I've seen it so many times, and obviously, I experienced it myself when I was recovering from heroin. Guys get born-again, become Muslim, or craft their own spiritual truths, like me. Whatever the specifics, the underlying principle is the same: our actions have consequences in life, and the actions that matter most are the ones that abide by some higher law. Because you won't find truth in the streets. You won't find it in the courts or in mainstream American life, either. You'll only find it in the realm of the spirit, the soul, the part of ourselves that connects us to the past, to each other, to the universe itself. I can't tell you how many street guys I've seen fill up with emotion during a stretch in jail as they remember too late that those rare moments of peace and connection we experience in life are the ones that matter more than the pursuit of material gain.

After Russell got healthy, we started making trips together, the dynamic duo, hustling just like we did back in the day. Visiting these black communities in other cities across the country, I started realizing how special Harlem is. We're one of the only communities in the world with such a diversity of poor people in the same pot. People rightfully think of Harlem as a black neighborhood, but they often overlook the fact that guys like Russell and me grew up with Italians, West Indians, Irish, and Puerto Ricans, and our cultures and styles and flavors intermingled freely. Growing up, we had all kinds of Italian and Jewish and Greek friends. I never realized how powerful that was until I got on the road and started observing how isolated so many of the black communities were in other places. You find black guys in Harlem who grew up dancing to salsa and merengue. I thought black people did that everywhere. The West Indian Day Parade and the Puerto Rican Day Parade started in Harlem. Little Italy in Harlem was the first Little Italy in New York. When you have all that cultural chemistry stirred up in the same pot, the brew is amazing. That brew is Harlem, and from it, we got the whole country and the whole world high.

Sometimes a thing happens, and you think that it happened to knock you down, but it turns out the experience really knocked you up. That's what those years after I closed the shop were. On those long road trips across the country, I got to learn so much about our people. I was taking in so much of black style and its amazing regional varieties. As an observer, it was a big education for me to see that diversity, the differences between Baltimore and DC, Detroit and Chicago. To see the many ways black people dressed, the different music we liked, the different brands and colors and looks that we gravitated towards.

As the years passed, I watched my neighborhood go through

the new upheaval of gentrification. While my parents and their generation had turned Harlem into the black mecca we remember it as, my generation was traumatized by the drug war and economic neglect. Of all my siblings, I was the only one who remained in Harlem. Our generation fled these state-sponsored traumas, turning our neighborhood into a ghost town that developers were eager to swoop down on and start profiting from. Now white people were moving into Harlem in record numbers. By the late nineties, black people were no longer the majority in Harlem. A Starbucks opened on 125th Street, ushering in a new era of corporate takeover and rising rents. The richness of Harlem's history was still attracting young black professionals and creatives, and you also had white people who wanted a piece of that history, too. But a growing number of new Harlemites just wanted cheap real estate to flip and didn't care about the people or the past; they were the kind of neighbors who called the police to shut down a sidewalk dice game.

I continued to work in the shadows, where it was safe, making my road trips and serving my gangsta clients. Sometime in the late nineties, I heard a knock and opened the door of my brownstone to find a young woman who said she'd been looking all over for me. She was a stylist sent at the request of the rapper Ghostface Killah. She'd driven uptown without any address besides "Harlem," and started asking random people on the street if they knew where Dapper Dan was at. And they'd tell her, "He been ain't had that store." But she got lucky and ran into someone who knew where I lived.

I ended up making something for Ghostface, a black-on-beige sweatsuit and matching safari hat with the traditional Gucci pattern, which he wore in the video for "Cherchez LaGhost." When the video came out, people was going crazy for that sweatsuit, and I started doing more stuff for Ghostface and the rest of Wu-Tang. This was back when the fashion budgets for rap videos was outrageous: six figures just for clothes. More stylists with big budgets came literally knocking at my door. I was the best-kept secret in the game. I even made the stylists learn a secret knock for when they came by the house at night. They could see my African tailors working on machines at street level, but unless they got the knock right, my guys wouldn't move to open the door.

I made stuff for Aaliyah, Cam'ron, Nelly, and Busta Rhymes, and I even managed to sneak some custom Fendi past MTV's censors in G. Dep's "Let's Get It" music video. The one celebrity I always wanted to dress but could never connect with was Michael Jackson. Back in the shop days, I used to keep a picture of him up behind the counter; our nickname for him was the Elusive One.

I was also meeting new superstars, like in 1999, when I got a visit from a young up-and-coming boxer named Floyd Mayweather. He was being managed by Eric B. at the time and wanted me to design some boxing trunks for him. He'd grown up hearing that Mike Tyson used to shop at my store. Floyd was really creative with his fashion input, always with a vision of what he wanted. He never settled for the first idea, always took it and developed it. As his star started to rise and other big brands kept reaching out to him for endorsement, he made the forward-thinking decision to stay independent and start his own label. Pretty Boy Floyd was a young guy, but his soul connected more to my era. He liked the furs, the leathers, the exotic skins—ostrich, gator, lizards. Floyd was from Michigan, and from my road trips, I knew that they were still heavy on that pimp style in the Midwest, so I started making his trunks and even collaborated with him on his jewelry collection. I've been working with him ever since.

As my designs worked their way back into the mainstream, people started mistaking them for Fendi and Gucci. Through the stylists, I'd hear stories about customers showing up at the Gucci store downtown asking for sweatsuits like the one Raekwon wore in

"Protect Ya Neck (The Jump Off)," and the Gucci salespeople would just look at them, confused, because Gucci wasn't making no sweatsuits back then.

Around that time, *Vibe* magazine published a tribute to me, even though I had refused to be interviewed for it. I was still nervous about the public eye. The article got a couple parts wrong, calling me the son of a furrier and saying I had tailoring skills. But it was nice to read people saying nice things about me.

Hip-hop kept my name alive in other ways, most memorably when I got in the middle of a beef between Fat Joe and Jay-Z, both of whom were my customers. Shirt King PHADE has pictures of Jay-Z when he was real young coming to the boutique with Big Daddy Kane, but I don't remember ever meeting him during the years when my shop was open. When I got caught up in his beef with Fat Joe, who name-dropped me on his song "My Lifestyle," Jay-Z reintroduced me to a whole new generation with the line "Wear a G on my chest, I don't need Dapper Dan." But because my brand was already strong in the community, it didn't do to me what his "I don't wear jerseys I'm thirty plus" lyric did to destroy the nationwide throwback craze.

In the early days, the rappers were like all of us in the neighborhood, looking up to the hustlers on the corner. They wanted to dress like the hustlers. Now I was watching the rappers reach a level of power, wealth, and influence in the culture and community that was surpassing the hustlers'. Soon everybody in the community was looking at the rappers and wanting to dress like them. They replaced the strength of the corners by bringing the corners mainstream. A kid came up to me the other day with his father, and the father said to him, "You don't know who this is? This Dapper Dan." The kid said, "Yeah, I heard that name on a lot of records, but I ain't know that was a real person."

Another evening, my sister Deborah called me up after she'd gotten home from work with something she was desperate to share. Deborah and her children had just returned to New York from an isolated life on a Hare Krishna ashram in Jamaica. She didn't know anything about hip-hop; her kids didn't even know who Michael Jackson was.

"Danny," she said. "You won't believe what happened to me at work today."

Ironically enough, Deborah worked as an assistant manager for a Louis Vuitton store in Great Neck, New York. An email had posted to the company's intranet about me, about how people were accusing the company of stealing design ideas from Dapper Dan. "One of my coworkers showed me the email," said Deborah. "I told her, 'That's my brother!'"

Her coworker couldn't believe it.

"She said, 'Wait, Dapper Dan is your brother? And you work for Louis Vuitton while they're stealing from him?'" Deborah had to pull her coworker into the break room and tell her to keep her voice down.

I wasn't too upset when I saw the new Louis Vuitton collection. European brands like Louis and Gucci were clearly building off ideas I'd been developing in my boutique years ago, the very same boutique they raided over and over again.

I don't put too much energy into thinking about appropriation. If you wanna talk appropriation, slavery is the greatest appropriation ever. I don't know where people get this idea of racial equality from. I didn't expect nothing but appropriation and exploitation from the fashion industry. From being around gangstas my whole life, I was always dealing with people who defined the laws for themselves. So how am I gonna cry about these white people doing me dirty? At least they were doing variations of what I already did and keeping the integrity of the meaning.

I was more upset with how the early hip-hop fashion brands interpreted what I did than I was with the Europeans who interpreted my designs. The Europeans allowed my work to be appreciated on a higher level, whereas the black brands who interpreted my fashion took it to a lower level. All those early streetwear brands that had sprung up in the years after my shop closed would soon become relics. Phat Farm, Cross Colours, FUBU, Karl Kani, Mecca, all these guys who jumped into the hip-hop fashion game after me didn't do their homework. I always wished they woulda built something atop my foundations. Instead, they came, copied, profited, then disappeared without an impact, leaving no legacy behind, no business to pass down, no new knowledge to share. They ain't control the manufacturing and distribution chain the way the European houses did. To me, that ignorance was most upsetting. We had hip-hop music and fashion on the same trajectory when I was running the boutique, but while hip-hop music kept ascending to greater heights, the hip-hop fashion brands took it downstairs, and that positioned the European brands— Gucci, Versace, Louis—to capitalize on the high end of the hip-hop market.

Whenever I would ask my clients about those fly-by-night streetwear brands during my underground years, they'd say to me, "I ain't dealing with that black shit, man." The reason was simple: those other early hip-hop fashion labels wasn't protecting the quality and integrity of their brand. Eventually, hip-hop fashion would enter a new, more sophisticated era focused on quality, with people like Diddy starting his Sean John label, which was taken seriously because he took fashion seriously. In due time, the heritage brands started to wrap their arms around hip-hop, this black street culture it once scorned, and they had no choice, because hip-hop had already wrapped its arms around the world.

I don't believe in destiny. It always upsets me to hear people say *Everything happens because it was meant to happen.* That is a dangerous way of thinking. I don't wake up thinking the world is gonna be fair to me. If it is, thank you. But my mother, my father, and all the guys in the neighborhood I knew growing up never walked around assuming people were gonna be fair to them. If you ask me my way of living, I think right makes right. But for me to interact with people and assume that they believe the same thing I do, when they could very well believe the opposite, that *might* makes right, I'd be a damn fool. I'd be a damn fool to think anyone's gonna open a door or build me a staircase in the name of equality. You gotta kick the door down yourself.

I was just creating what we liked. I never thought of myself as an artist, or in any fashion-industry terms. I was just getting it on like we get it on. Interpreting how we wanted to feel. I was playing jazz with fashion. When we find a way to interpret our feelings into fashion, we are responding to something chemical in us, as black people, that we are able to tap into.

When you look at styles past, they recycle themselves. If it was right, how did it fall out of style? If it's wrong, how's it back in style? I don't personally think there is right and wrong in fashion. But there is a weak and a strong. Because whoever the dominant personality is, whether it's the hustler on the corner or the artist on a stage, whoever has that dominant influence, other people gravitate towards that strength. They buy into that person, and by following their fashion, it's almost like they're purchasing a part of that person's power and personality. I always understood that need, so I give my customers the space to fulfill it.

I see each customer as an actor auditioning to be in this big, generational movie I'm making. We are already working within the shared frame of reference of my designs, and they want to be in the shot. It's my job to find a comfortable role for them. I never wanna be in that traditional fashion-runway zone, telling people how to feel. I want them to tell me how they feel, and then I want to extract those feelings and build fashion outta that. I want them to feel important and connected to that good energy my clothes give. I want them to wear them knowing they played an active part in their own look. I'm not trying to change nobody. I'm trying to bring out what's already inside of people. I want to give people what they want before they know they want it. It's not about the runway, it's about your way.

Who are you really? How do you really feel? What makes you feel strong? What brings you joy?

Some mornings, when I would take the neighborhood kids for a run before starting my day among the vendors on 125th Street, we'd catch our breath near the waterfront on the Harlem River, and I'd tell them about the old days when we used to swim there.

When we was their age, problem kids just like them, we'd come down here on a hot summer day and strip down to our underwear, but before we dove in, we had a trick to figure out which way the current was flowing and how hard. It could be too strong if you weren't careful. What we'd do is take a Popsicle stick and toss it into the river. We'd watch to see how it moved and which direction it went and how fast. After watching the stick float, we'd figure out the best place to leap.

Those neighborhood kids would be looking at me like I'm crazy. They'd say, "Ain't nobody tryna swim in that nasty-ass water."

They were right. The rivers around New York are too polluted now for swimming, filled with toxins, industrial waste, and who knows what else. It probably wasn't safe to swim in back then, either. I didn't tell them that I contributed some litter myself the day I threw my credit card machine in the river, quitting the streets for good to start a new career making clothes.

But I've always liked that Popsicle-stick trick. I like the ingenuity of taking something meant for one purpose and reusing it for something new. There's nothing fancy about it, just a small thing that most of us take for granted. It might not look like much to others, but it had value to us. I like the lesson it teaches about resourcefulness, and how being observant can save you from trouble.

You could say that my life has been similar to that Popsicle stick floating in the Harlem River, seen as trash by some but offering something valuable to those paying attention, knocked around by the same tides that carried ships from Africa with my ancestors, riding out ahead so others can figure out the best way to follow, eventually drifting out into the big sea, going where the current takes it. But never going under.

THANK YOU!

I was born with nothing. When you go to church and get the Holy Ghost, you leave feeling complete. You go through the week and come back looking for it again. Somewhere along the way, I lost that feeling of completeness. I began to look for it in every belief that I could find to study, but in the end, I found it again in everyone dear to me, and for this I am grateful.

Mikael, thank you so much for transforming my voice and soul into written word. I was amazed observing you become me as you transcribed my story. Even now, I wonder how you were able to transition so well from who I am back to who you are.

Allison Devereux, you are the first person from the outside to come inside my cultural bubble whom I have been able to have real conversations with, both inside and outside that bubble. You have become so dear to me that you have earned a nickname for when you are inside the bubble—*but I won't share that with everybody right now.*

To the entire MacKenzie Wolf team: You have no idea how comfortable you made it to enter a world that was completely alien to me. I thought I would crash-land, but you all turned me into Rocket Man! Kirsten Wolf, thank you for believing in my story. Rach Crawford, thank you for helping to take this story to the next frontier. Many thanks to Kate Johnson, Renée Jarvis, Gillian MacKenzie, and Jason Richman at UTA for believing in this project and dedicating your considerable time and effort to ensure its success.

Caitlin McKenna, you are so incredibly human. Thank you for insisting that this book should not be just a fashion story. You heard all facets of it and knew they needed to be shared. I never thought that someone would take *my* story and demand that not one emotional episode be excluded. In fact, you demanded I expand them and develop this into a human odyssey.

To the entire Random House team: You guys make me think I'm Obama! Thank you for making me feel so presidential. Greg Kubie and Maria Braeckel, thank you for your willingness to step outside the box with an outside-the-box guy like myself! Emma Caruso, you have been enthusiastic and supportive of this project right from the start. Thank you to Andy Ward, Tom Perry, Kelly Chian, Robbin Schiff, Jess Bonet, Katie Tull, Dana Blanchette, and Matthew Martin for your care and integrity.

To my Gucci family, I must thank you for showing me the human side of a corporate empire that I did not know existed. Susan, Alessandro, and Marco, thank you for your partnership, grace, trust, and honesty.

I am humbled by the love and support from fans near and far. Thank you to my beloved Harlem community for having my back from the very beginning of this journey; Black Twitter, I am in awe of and forever grateful for the power and magic you possess.

Many thanks to my friends. Curtis, Smiley, Russell, and Moon, our friendship has stood the test of time. Omari, your friendship has been an unexpected blessing; thank you for recording the audio version of my story.

Reading is the key to all knowledge, and I am thankful for what I have learned from the writings of Dr. John Henrik Clarke, Malcolm X, and Krishnamurti, whose inspiration has been my guidepost as a man.

Family is everything to me. I would like to thank my father for the incredible work ethic he passed on to me. In 15 years, he never missed a day of work, and, as a result of the Great Snowstorm of 1947, he was late only once. I am profoundly thankful to my mother for introducing me and my siblings to the Holy Ghost. I can think of nothing else that has kept us so strong for our entire lives. Dolores, Deborah, Doris, Carl, Cary, and James, I continue to be uplifted by your love and support.

It is my hope that my children, Chuckie, Danny, Jr., Danique, Ayeisha, Daniella, Tiffany, Malik, and Jelani, will continue to pass down my stories and that all of my beautiful grandchildren and great-grandchildren will stand tall on the foundation that has been set for them.

To June, my wife of fifty years, you are the source of my strength and my greatest friend. I love you.

About the Author

DANIEL "DAPPER DAN" DAY is a Harlem-based streetwear pioneer who operated an eponymous boutique in the 1980s catering to gangsters, athletes, and musicians. Known for their defiant appropriation of European heritage brand logos, his designs have been featured in exhibitions at the Museum of Modern Art, the Smithsonian Institution, The Museum at FIT, the Metropolitan Museum of Art, the Museum of the City of New York, and London's Design Museum. His boutique reopened in 2017 in a major partnership with Gucci.

dapperdanofharlem.com
Facebook.com/DapperDanHarlem
Twitter: @DapperDanHarlem
Instagram: @DapperDanHarlem

About the Type

This book was set in Baskerville, a typeface designed by John Baskerville (1706–75), an amateur printer and typefounder, and cut for him by John Handy in 1750. The type became popular again when the Lanston Monotype Corporation of London revived the classic roman face in 1923. The Mergenthaler Linotype Company in England and the United States cut a version of Baskerville in 1931, making it one of the most widely used typefaces today.